ADVERSE and PROTECTIVE
CHILDHOOD
EXPERIENCES

ADVERSE and PROTECTIVE CHILDHOOD EXPERIENCES

A Developmental Perspective

Jennifer Hays-Grudo and Amanda Sheffield Morris

AMERICAN PSYCHOLOGICAL ASSOCIATION
Washington, DC

Published by
American Psychological Association
750 First Street, NE
Washington, DC 20002
https://www.apa.org

Order Department
https://www.apa.org/pubs/books
order@apa.org

In the U.K., Europe, Africa, and the Middle East, copies may be ordered from Eurospan
https://www.eurospanbookstore.com/apa
info@eurospangroup.com

Typeset in Meridien and Ortodoxa by Circle Graphics, Inc., Reisterstown, MD

Printer: Sheridan Books, Chelsea, MI
Cover Designer: Nicci Falcone, Potomac, MD

Library of Congress Cataloging-in-Publication Data

Names: Hays-Grudo, Jennifer, author. | Morris, Amanda Sheffield, author. |
    American Psychological Association
Title: Adverse and protective childhood experiences : a developmental
    perspective / by Jennifer Hays-Grudo and Amanda Sheffield Morris.
Description: Washington, DC : American Psychological Association, [2020] |
    Includes bibliographical references and index.
Identifiers: LCCN 2019043795 (print) | LCCN 2019043796 (ebook) |
    ISBN 9781433832116 (paperback) | ISBN 9781433832758 (ebook)
Subjects: LCSH: Child development. | Life change events. | Developmental
    psychology.
Classification: LCC HQ772 .H39 2020 (print) | LCC HQ772 (ebook) |
    DDC 155.4/189—dc23
LC record available at https://lccn.loc.gov/2019043795
LC ebook record available at https://lccn.loc.gov/2019043796

http://dx.doi.org/10.1037/0000177-000

Printed in the United States of America

10 9 8 7 6 5 4 3 2 1

To Doron and Mike
for holding the nest.

CONTENTS

PREFACE: THE HOLE IN THE BRIDGE

Picture a large group of friends having a spring picnic beside a river that flows through their town. Suddenly, they hear a cry from the river and see a child being swept downstream. One of them kicks off his shoes, jumps in, and brings the child to the riverbank where the others gather around to make sure she is okay. While taking care of her, they hear another child, and then another, followed by another, and another. Soon everyone is either rescuing children from the river or helping those pulled to shore recover from nearly drowning. Then they notice that one of the friends has left them and is running upstream. They call to her, saying, "Where are you going? We need you here!" to which she replies, "I'm going to find the hole in the bridge."

When we first learned about the Adverse Childhood Experiences Study and saw the data linking childhood adversity with later risky health behaviors, chronic illnesses, poor developmental outcomes, and the links between early adversity and neurobiological adaptations to stress, we realized we had found the hole in the bridge. This is not to argue against pulling struggling children (and adults) out of the river—we can and should do all we can to keep them from being swept out to sea and help them recover once they are safely ashore. Our efforts must begin to focus, however, on finding and repairing the treacherous bridge that sent them into the river in the first place.

During the past 2 decades, multiple studies with thousands of people from diverse populations have established a strong and consistent connection between adverse childhood experiences (ACEs) and later health and chronic conditions. Many health professionals recognize this connection, but it is only now reaching a wider audience. Similarly, research by developmental psychologists on how to protect and compensate for childhood adversity has yet to be disseminated to those committed to understanding and treating the effects of ACEs. This book combines existing knowledge about ACEs with developmental research on preventing, buffering, and treating the effects of adversity, stress, and trauma on child development and subsequent health and functioning.

Adversity can literally "get under the skin," changing cells, the brain, and even DNA. The human body is programmed to respond to danger in ways that promote survival, enabling us to *fight*, *flee*, or *freeze*. This was adaptive for our ancestors, who literally encountered tigers and bears, but these responses in the face of modern-day stress are a leading cause of heart disease, cancer, obesity, substance abuse, and a host of mental health and relationship problems.

Just as the effects of ACEs influence development, so do nurturing experiences. The lifelong effects of positive childhood experiences can mitigate the detrimental effects of ACEs. As developmental psychologists, we have identified the most important of these protective and compensatory experiences (PACEs). PACEs include experiences such as unconditional love from a parent or other adult, having family routines, developing talents and skills through hobbies and sports, and volunteering in the community.

In this book, we consolidate the most recent and scientifically sound research on childhood adversity and what developmental scientists know about preventing and treating the long-term consequences of ACEs. We describe relevant discoveries from psychology, neuroscience, biology, and integrative medicine. We begin with an overview of ACEs and PACEs (Chapters 1–2), then describe the neurobiological and intergenerational effects of ACEs and PACEs (Chapters 3–4), and end with research and ideas for helping adults, children, and communities develop plans for minimizing the negative effects of ACEs and promoting PACEs (Chapters 5–8). Many chapters have activities that aim to help readers apply the science to everyday life, and there is a list of resources and suggested readings, as well as questions for reflection, at the end of the book.

We wrote this book because we are looking for answers. Are ACEs real? If so, how do they change our bodies, our brains, and our behavior? What can we do about it? How can we apply decades of developmental research on resilience to the new science of ACEs? We found answers not only from our own discipline of developmental science but also from fields as diverse as epidemiology, epigenetics, immunology, neuroscience, and infant mental health. The answers are still coming. Like any vibrant scientific endeavor, new studies are raising new questions as quickly as they answer old ones. What we know now is that ACEs are real, but they can also be defeated by making future ACEs less common, ameliorating currently occurring ACEs, making PACEs more common, and acknowledging and treating the effects of past ACEs in our own lives and in our communities.

Most people reading this book will have had at least one ACE. We know this because every epidemiological study in large populations in the world has shown this to be true. Many of us in the helping professions have more than one (Esaki & Larkin, 2013); thus, we assume that many readers will have a personal interest in this topic. That is why, unlike many academic books, we use figures, graphs, diagrams, and stories to engage the whole mind and body as much as possible. We also include activities and conclusions at the end of each chapter to organize and bring focus to the application of ACEs and PACEs science in our own lives and those around us. We have tried to make findings from multiple disciplines accessible to the "nonmajors" in those fields while ensuring that enough detail is included to be informative. Although we have used the terms *adverse childhood experiences, early life adversity, stress, toxic stress,* and *trauma* almost interchangeably throughout the text, we are certainly mindful of their different meanings and have tried to use the most appropriate word or term in describing various studies and situations in which they apply. Similarly, terms such as *resilience* and *protective factors* may not always be distinct. As research explicating the effects of ACEs and approaches to preventing and treating those effects progresses and is applied in ever widening contexts (Leitch, 2017), we expect that our language and terminology will also advance.

The audience for this book is students, researchers, clinicians, and health care providers who want to gain knowledge regarding the interdisciplinary science of early life adversity, lifelong resilience, and related intervention and prevention programming. This book can be used to reflect on one's own history of adversity and resilience and to help others who are dealing with the lifelong effects of ACEs.

Finally, this book is intended to launch new investigations into ACEs and PACEs, to provide an interdisciplinary lens through which to view the multiple types of effects of enduring childhood experiences, and to recommend evidence-based approaches for protecting and buffering children and repairing the negative consequences of ACEs as adults. We take a "whole body" approach in this book and present interventions that integrate physiological, cognitive, emotional, and relational practices for healing from ACEs and promoting resilience. This book is not intended to be an alternative to psychotherapy or other clinical interventions in cases where trauma and stress have seriously impaired health and functioning. ACEs have cumulative effects on health and developmental outcomes, and serious physical and mental health consequences have been observed with increasing ACEs. We encourage readers to go beyond our book to access the resources and websites presented throughout the book and in the concluding section.

ACKNOWLEDGMENTS

We are grateful to many people for their help and support as we wrote this book. Our editor, Ted Baroody, made invaluable suggestions, helping us craft a book that we believe will help move this field forward. We thank Christopher Kelaher at APA Books, who convinced us to write this book rather than the one we thought we wanted to write. Chris, you were right. We are especially appreciative for the two anonymous reviewers for their thoughtful insights and recommendations. Harriet Spain's reviews were enormously helpful and constructive. We are also grateful to our friend and colleague Joli Jensen, whose book (*Write No Matter What*) was published just exactly when we needed it.

We have many friends and colleagues who have guided our journey as we set out to learn about topics that were new to us. For Amanda, this involved gaining more neuroscience knowledge, and she is grateful to Kyle Simmons, Kara Kerr, Florence Breslin, Jerzy Bodurka, and Martin Paulus. For Jennifer, this involved learning about epigenetics, and she is especially grateful to Kent Teague and Ariel Grudo for their patient explanations. Thanks to Jason Beaman and others in our departments and colleges for supporting us. Jordan Love has assisted both of us in organizing our obligations so that everything got done and has been a great editor. Erin Ratliff assisted us in multiple read-throughs and final edits. We are grateful for the research support we have received from the National Institutes of Health (Grant P20GM109097) and the George Kaiser Family Foundation, which has allowed us to pursue our interest in adversity and resilience.

Most important, we are grateful to our families who made sacrifices so that we could write and rewrite for the past several years. Our husbands, who are great supporters of this effort, were also some of our best editors and sounding boards. They share our aspirations for a safe and nurturing world for all children.

THE EFFECTS OF ADVERSE AND PROTECTIVE CHILDHOOD EXPERIENCES

You are the sum total of everything you've ever seen, heard, eaten, smelled, been told, forgot—it's all there.

—MAYA ANGELOU

INTRODUCTION

In this section, we begin Chapter 1 with a description of the landmark Adverse Childhood Experiences (ACE) Study conducted in California in the 1990s. We then discuss the research on ACEs and related types of adversity published during the past 2 decades in populations that differ in important ways from the original study. We provide evidence of the cumulative and co-occurring effects of ACEs and their prevalence throughout the world. We also discuss different approaches to defining adversity as new questions emerge from research with more diverse populations.

In Chapter 2, we present the antidote to ACEs: the protective and compensatory experiences (PACEs) that buffer the effects of adversity on development. When we began studying the effects of ACEs on development and health, we were surprised that little of the substantial literature on resilience had been incorporated into adversity science. In response, we developed PACEs based on the theoretical and empirical research on child development and resilience conducted during the past 50 years. PACEs focus on nurturing and supportive relationships and resources that provide children opportunities to develop and grow.

We end the chapters with surveys of childhood experiences, providing suggestions for ways to incorporate the surveys into clinical practice, research protocols, and self-reflection. As you read the first two chapters, we invite you to keep in mind the hole in the bridge story from the Preface, reflecting on the power of adversity and resilience to explain the enduring effects of childhood (ages 0–18) experiences on lifelong health and success.

1

Adverse Childhood Experiences

The largest, most important public health study you never heard of.

—JANE ELLEN STEVENS

In 1998, Dr. Vincent Felitti, a physician with Kaiser Permanente Health Plan, and Dr. Robert Anda, a cardiovascular epidemiologist at the Centers for Disease Control and Prevention (CDC), published an article in the *American Journal of Preventive Medicine* that transformed the way we think about childhood adversity and resilience. The "Relationship of Childhood Abuse and Household Dysfunction to Many of the Leading Causes of Death in Adults: The Adverse Childhood Experiences (ACE) Study" (Felitti et al., 1998) was the first large-scale study showing that adverse childhood experiences (ACEs) are (a) common, (b) highly interrelated, (c) have cumulative impact, and (d) account for a large portion of our health and societal problems. Since that original publication, scores of studies have confirmed the scope of ACE effects, the neurobiological plausibility of a causal relationship between ACEs and later health, and potential protective factors to prevent or mitigate these effects. In this chapter, we describe the findings from the original sample of patients whose ACEs, health, and well-being have been thoroughly studied, the results of other epidemiological studies that expand these findings, and the questions kindled by this new frame of reference for understanding the enduring effects of early life experiences on development and health, touching briefly on the underlying mechanisms and processes linking childhood

http://dx.doi.org/10.1037/0000177-001
Adverse and Protective Childhood Experiences: A Developmental Perspective, by J. Hays-Grudo and A. S. Morris

adversity with later health and well-being before turning our attention to protective and resilience-promoting experiences in Chapter 2 of this volume.

THE ADVERSE CHILDHOOD EXPERIENCES STUDY

The origins of the ACEs study can be traced to the 1980s and the Kaiser Permanente Health Appraisal Center in San Diego, which has routinely provided comprehensive health evaluations for more than 1.3 million adult members of the Kaiser Foundation Health Plan in the San Diego area during the past 30 years (Felitti, 2019). As director of Preventive Medicine, Vincent Felitti created one of the largest and most effective health appraisal systems in the world as well as effective intervention programs to improve patient outcomes. The Kaiser Permanente obesity clinic was designed for patients needing to lose significant amounts of weight for health reasons, and their progress was closely monitored by Dr. Felitti and his colleagues. When they began to see a pattern, with a large proportion dropping out of the program after losing all or most of their goal weight rather than earlier in the process, they began asking questions. Interviews with more than 200 of the patients revealed that a majority had a history of childhood sexual abuse. Patients recounted story after story of using food and eating to cope with feelings of shame and worthlessness resulting from childhood abuse. Initially, Dr. Felitti was in disbelief. He thought, "This can't be true. People would know if that were true. Someone would have told me in medical school" (Felitti, 2018). He began to realize that, from the patient's perspective, obesity was not a problem but a solution: Eating made people feel better, and being overweight formed a type of protection from further abuse.

When Felitti (2018) presented these findings at a national obesity conference, he was soundly criticized by an obesity expert for believing "fabrications spun by patients seeking excuses for their failures." Several researchers in the audience from the CDC, however, thought Felitti's data and ideas were intriguing. They suggested he contact their colleague Dr. Robert Anda, who was studying the effects of depression and hopelessness on heart disease outcomes. Felitti and Anda saw the potential connection between the Kaiser Permanente patient experiences and the depression and heart disease in the CDC samples, and they developed plans to survey the entire Kaiser Permanente San Diego patient population. After more than a year of combing through the literature on the multiple forms of adversity described by Felitti's obesity clinic patients, they created a scientifically sound, self-administered questionnaire. Approval to question patients about their childhood abuse histories was not easily obtained from the institution's Review Board for the Protection of Human Subjects. In the film *Resilience* (Pritzker & Redford, 2016), Felitti shakes his head, remembering his colleagues' resistance to asking these questions of their patients, as if repression was the established standard of treatment for trauma. After nearly a year, the study was approved, and the questionnaire was mailed to more than 26,000 patients. More than 17,000 responded. The results were stunning. Dr. Anda recalls sitting in his study when he opened his laptop and clicked the link to the results from the CDC analytic team. He looked at the results and wept. Like Dr. Felitti, he never imagined there was so much trauma, so much pain, all around us. This middle-class, mostly college-educated, well-insured sample of adults repeatedly reported childhood histories of abuse, neglect, and family conditions that more powerfully predicted poor health than any risk factor ever before seen.

ACE Study Methods

Members of the Kaiser Permanente Health Plan who came to the Health Appraisal Center for routine evaluations between August 1995 and March 1996 (survey Wave 1; response rate 70%) and between June and October 1997 (survey Wave 2; response rate 65%) were included in the study. At this appointment, patients also completed a standardized questionnaire that included health histories, health-related behaviors, and psychosocial evaluations, all of which were included in the ACEs Study database. They were mailed the ACEs Study Questionnaire 2 weeks after their appointment. The combined study cohort was 18,175 (68% average response rate); the average age was 56 years. More detailed descriptions of the study methodology are available (Anda et al., 2006; Dube, Anda, Felitti, Edwards, & Croft, 2002; Felitti et al., 1998).

All survey items referred to respondents' first 18 years of life. Items used in this questionnaire were adapted from a collection of existing measures and involved more complicated scoring than the 10-item questionnaire now typically used in clinical and research contexts, which has response choices of *yes* or *no*. For example, response options adapted from the Conflict Tactics Scale (Straus & Gelles, 1990) categories were *never*, *once or twice*, *sometimes*, *often*, or *very often*. The two categories of *physical neglect* and *emotional neglect* were added when the second wave of data was collected, along with other items shown to be of interest in Wave 1 (Dube et al., 2002). Thus, the final questionnaire had a total of three subcategories: *abuse*—emotional, physical, and sexual; *neglect*—emotional and physical; and *family dysfunction*—domestic violence, household substance abuse, household mental illness, parental separation or divorce, or household criminality. Exhibit 1.1 shows the wording and scoring of the original questionnaire. The major findings are summarized next.

ACE Study Results

The initial findings surprised everyone. The results indicated that ACEs are common, cooccur, and have cumulative effects, effects previously not seen in epidemiological surveys. Because the data on Kaiser Permanente patients was so comprehensive, the ACEs study provided a rare opportunity to assess the effects of childhood traumas on current health problems and behavioral risk

EXHIBIT 1.1

Original Adverse Childhood Experiences Study Questionnaire Items

Emotional abuse. Two questions from the Conflict Tactics Scale (CTS) were used: "How often did a parent, stepparent, or adult living in your home

1. swear at you, insult you, or put you down?
2. threaten to hit you or throw something at you but didn't do it?"

Responses of *often* or *very often* to either item defined emotional abuse in childhood were scored.

Physical abuse. Two questions from the CTS were used: "How often did a parent, stepparent, or adult living in your home

1. push, grab, slap, or throw something at you?
2. hit you so hard that you had marks or were injured?"

A respondent was defined as having been physically abused during childhood if the response was either *often* or *very often* to the first question or "sometimes, often, or very often" to the second.

Sexual abuse. Participants were asked the following four questions (Wyatt, 1985) about whether an adult, relative, family friend, or stranger who was at least 5 years older than themselves ever

1. had touched or fondled their body in a sexual way,
2. had them touch his or her body in a sexual way,
3. attempted to have any type of sexual intercourse with them (oral, anal, or vaginal), or
4. actually had any type of sexual intercourse with them (oral, anal, or vaginal).

Subjects were classified as having been sexually abused during childhood if they responded affirmatively to any of these questions.

Emotional neglect. Five statements were reverse-scored and summed:

1. "There was someone in my family who helped me feel important or special."
2. "I felt loved."
3. "People in my family looked out for each other."
4. "People in my family felt close to each other."
5. "My family was a source of strength and support."

These five items from the CTS scale were reverse scored and summed; respondents with a score of 10 or higher (moderate to extreme) were considered to have experienced emotional neglect.

Physical neglect. Five statements were scored and summed, with Questions 2 and 5 reverse-scored:

1. "I didn't have enough to eat."
2. "I knew there was someone there to take care of me and protect me."
3. "My parents were too drunk or too high to take care of me."
4. "I had to wear dirty clothes."
5. "There was someone to take me to the doctor if I needed it."

Items 2 and 5 from the CTS scale were reverse scored and combined with Items 1, 2, and 4; respondents with a summed score of 10 or higher (moderate to extreme) were considered to have experienced physical neglect.

EXHIBIT 1.1

Original Adverse Childhood Experiences Study Questionnaire Items (Continued)

Domestic violence. Four questions were used, all of them preceded by the following statement: "Sometimes physical blows occur between parents. While you were growing up in your first 18 years of life, how often did your father (or stepfather) or mother's boyfriend do any of these things to your mother (or stepmother):

1. push, grab, slap, or throw something at her;
2. kick, bite, hit her with a fist, or hit her with something hard;
3. repeatedly hit her for at least a few minutes; or
4. threaten her with a knife or gun, or use a knife or gun to hurt her?"

A positive indication for witnessed domestic violence was a response of *sometimes*, *often*, or *very often* to at least one of the first two questions or any response other than *never* to at least one of the last two questions.

Household substance abuse. Two questions: "While you were growing up in your first 18 years of life, did you

1. live with anyone who was a problem drinker or alcoholic?
2. live with anyone who used street drugs?"

Subjects were classified as experiencing household substance abuse if they responded affirmatively to either question.

Mental illness in household. Two questions: "While you were growing up in your first 18 years of life,

1. was a household member depressed or mentally ill?
2. did a household member attempt suicide?"

Subjects were classified as experiencing mental illness in the household if they responded affirmatively to either question.

Parental separation or divorce. Participants were asked whether their parents had ever separated or divorced during their first 18 years.

Criminal household member. If anyone in the household had gone to prison during the respondent's childhood, the respondent was defined as having been exposed to a criminal household member.

Note. Data from Dong, Giles, et al. (2004, p. 1763) and Dube, Anda, Felitti, Edwards, and Croft (2002, pp. 715–717).

factors (Felitti, 2019). Each of the major findings is described in the following subsections.

ACEs Are Common

One of the most surprising initial findings of the original ACEs study was the prevalence of childhood abuse, neglect, and family dysfunction. Two-thirds of the well-educated, middle-class, middle-aged sample of adults had at least one ACE. The most commonly reported ACE was being physically abused

FIGURE 1.1. Prevalence of Adverse Childhood Experiences by Category

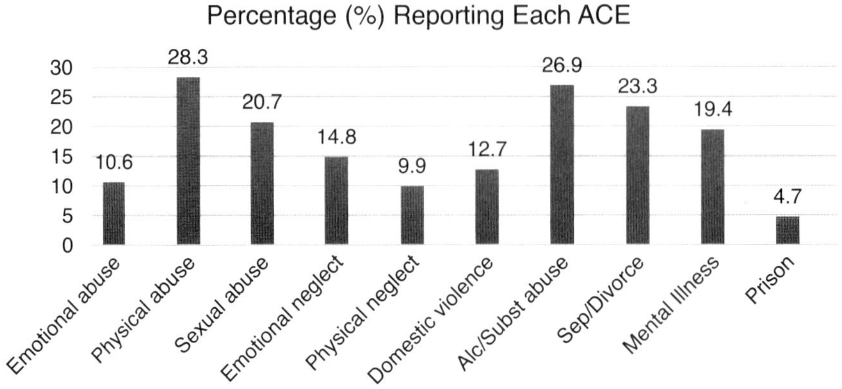

Percentage (%) Reporting Each ACE

(28.3%), followed closely by parental substance or alcohol abuse (26.9%). Figure 1.1 shows the percent of the Kaiser respondents reporting each ACE category.

ACEs Are Interrelated

Most clinicians and social service providers are only too aware that clients and participants in intervention programs have experienced multiple forms of mistreatment. However, most research on child abuse and neglect, family risk factors, and other types of adversity tends to focus on one, or perhaps several, categories of adversity. The ACEs study was the first large-scale study to document that adversities tend to cooccur: having suffered one form of adversity significantly increases the likelihood of having had at least one other form of adversity (Dong, Anda, et al., 2004). For example, drug abuse frequently cooccurs with criminality, domestic violence, and other forms of abuse and neglect.

ACEs Have Cumulative Impact

Kaiser survey respondents were routinely asked about their past and current involvement in risky health behaviors; those responses were then linked with their health and clinic records. Analyses controlled for the potentially confounding effects of age, sex, race, and educational attainment on the relationship between ACEs and health behaviors and health status using logistic regression. For nearly every risk factor and health outcome studied, the results of these analyses indicated a strong, graded relationship, or "dose–response" effect. Thus, the higher the ACEs score, the higher the chance of risky behaviors and health problems. In 18 outcome categories, the odds ratios (ORs) depicting the increased risk of the behavior or health status show a pattern of increased risk with each added ACE (Anda et al., 2006). Figure 1.2 presents the mean number of cooccurring (comorbid) outcomes for each ACE score. The average number of comorbid outcomes in the full sample (Wave 1 + Wave 2) was 2.1. The increased risk is significant; the vertical bars represent 95% confidence intervals.

FIGURE 1.2. Mean Number of Comorbid Outcomes by Adverse Childhood Experiences Score

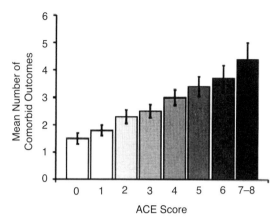

From "The enduring effects of abuse and related adverse experiences in childhood: A convergence of evidence from neurobiology and epidemiology," by R. F. Anda, V. J. Felitti, J. D. Bremner, J. D. Walker, C. Whitfield, B. D. Perry, S. R. Dube, and W. H. Giles, 2006, *European Archives of Psychiatry and Clinical Neuroscience, 256*, p. 179. Copyright 2006 by Springer Nature. Reprinted with permission.

ACEs Increase Behavioral Risk Factors

The cumulative effect of ACEs on behavioral risk factors is illustrated in Figure 1.3, which graphs the percentage of individuals reporting four risky behaviors by number of reported ACEs. This dose–response effect, or stairstep pattern, of increasing ACEs corresponding with increasing health-harming behavior is evident. For example, individuals with four or more ACEs have double the risk of smoking, their risk of alcoholism increases 7-fold, illicit drug use increases 4.5-fold, and having early intercourse increases 6.6-fold.

ACEs Affect Health Status

ACEs were also significant predictors of major chronic diseases and health problems in the Kaiser sample. As was seen for behavioral risk factors,

FIGURE 1.3. Adverse Childhood Experiences Score and Health Behavior Risk

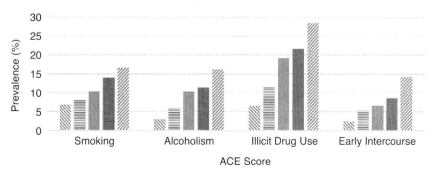

a dose–response relationship was observed for ACEs and chronic health problems, with the greatest risk for those with ACE scores of four or greater. Adjusted for age, sex, and educational attainment, having four or more ACEs was associated with a 90% increased risk of cancer, a 60% increased risk of diabetes, a 2.2-fold risk of ischemic heart disease, a 2.4-fold increased risk of stroke, and a 3.9-fold risk of chronic obstructive pulmonary disease (Felitti et al., 1998). Subsequent research documents other health problems associated with ACEs, including autoimmune disease (Dube et al., 2009), frequent headaches (Anda, Tietjen, Schulman, Felitti, & Croft, 2010), and liver disease (Dong, Dube, Felitti, Giles, & Anda, 2003). HIV and sexually transmitted illnesses also increase with higher ACEs (M. J. Brown et al., 2017), at least in part because of increased rates of risky sexual behaviors (Hillis, Anda, Felitti, & Marchbanks, 2001).

ACEs Predict Mental Health Problems

The risk of lifetime or current depression increased incrementally with ACE scores (Chapman et al., 2004). With ACE scores of four or more, depression increases 4.6-fold (Felitti et al., 1998), high perceived stress doubles, difficulty controlling anger quadruples, perpetrating intimate partner violence increases 5.5-fold, and suicide attempts increase 12.1-fold (Anda et al., 2006). Dose–response effects were also found for mental health problems, as well as for the co-occurrence of multiple physical and mental health problems (Anda et al., 2006).

ACEs and Societal Problems

The ACEs database has also been used to assess the relationship between early life adversity and later ability to function in society. Individuals with more ACEs experienced more residential mobility in childhood; the risk of moving eight or more times during childhood increased threefold with three ACEs, fourfold with four or five ACEs, and nearly sixfold with six or more ACEs. ACEs have also been associated with a significantly increased likelihood of both being a victim and perpetrator of intimate partner violence (Whitfield, Anda, Dube, & Felitti, 2003). The likelihood of unintended (Dietz et al., 1999) and adolescent pregnancies (Hillis et al., 2004) increases as ACEs scores climb, as does the risk of fetal death for both first and second pregnancies (Hillis et al., 2001). Even when adjusted for potential confounders (age and marital status at first pregnancy), unintended pregnancies are 50% more likely among women with four or more ACEs, particularly if their ACEs include emotional or physical abuse and witnessing intimate partner violence (Dietz et al., 1999). Analyses also show that the psychosocial problems linked with adolescent pregnancy (family, job, and anger problems, as well as high stress) also incrementally increase with ACEs.

ACEs Affect All-Cause Mortality

In 2009, the CDC, Kaiser Permanente, and other researchers published the effects of ACEs on premature death (Brown et al., 2009). Using records from the National Death Index, deaths were identified during the period between baseline appointment date and December 31, 2006. The results were sobering, revealing that, on average, individuals with six or more ACEs died nearly 2 decades earlier (at 61 years) than individuals with no ACEs (at age 79). ACEs also significantly increased the likelihood of a family member dying prematurely (i.e., before age 65). For every ACE item reported, the risk of family member's premature death increased by 13% (Anda et al., 2009).

ACEs STUDIES IN OTHER POPULATIONS

Since the 1998 publication of the Kaiser study, many researchers have replicated these findings, investigating the prevalence and effects of ACEs in other populations and expanding the scope of adversity and outcome types. Using the original eight- or 10-item ACEs questionnaire, or creating facsimile measures using comparable questions in existing databases, studies have now been conducted with a number of large-scale population groups (Bellis, Lowey, Leckenby, Hughes, & Harrison, 2014; Campbell, Walker, & Egede, 2016; Danese et al., 2009), and more distinct subgroups, such as adolescents (Balistreri & Alvira-Hammond, 2016), juvenile offenders (Baglivio et al., 2014), and those in developing countries (Ramiro, Madrid, & Brown, 2010). Results of these studies consistently confirmed the findings of the Kaiser Permanente and CDC researchers: *Adverse childhood experiences are prevalent, are cumulative, and have enduring negative effects on a multitude of health and developmental outcomes in diverse populations.*

Global ACEs

A large systematic review and meta-analysis of ACEs and subsequent risk calculated pooled odds ratios from 37 published studies with a total of 253,719 participants from around the world (Hughes et al., 2017). All studies used data from the general (nonclinical, low-risk) populations, with risk estimates for 23 health outcomes. The majority of participants across all studies reported at least one ACE (57%), and 13% reported at least four. Pooled ORs compared the risk between individuals with no ACEs and those with four or more. Analyses revealed a significant predictive effect of ACEs on every health-related behavior or outcome studied, ranging from relatively slight risk (increasing the risk of obesity by 39% and of diabetes by 52%) to moderate risk (more than doubling the likelihood of heart disease or cancer, and quadrupling the risk of adolescent pregnancy and depression), to truly staggering odds (raising the risk of drug abuse 10-fold and the risk of attempting suicide 30-fold). These data demonstrate that ACEs are common globally, a finding supported by a recent study of the prevalence of past-year victimization from physical, sexual, emotional, or multiple types of abuse for children aged 2 through 17 years. Globally, it is estimated that more than one billion children have experienced ACEs—that is, more than 50% of the world's future adults—with children in Asia, Africa, and North America having the highest prevalence (Hillis, Mercy, Amobi, & Kress, 2016).

British Cohorts

In 2018, investigators in the United Kingdom obtained survey responses from a representative sample of 3,885 British adults, using a questionnaire that included items from the original ACEs study and additional items related to British health policy (Bellis et al., 2014). Although prevalence rates were slightly lower than found in the original ACEs study, many of the findings replicated the Kaiser Permanente and CDC study findings. Controlling for sociodemographic variables, ACEs incrementally increased the likelihood of major risk behaviors, with increased adjusted odds ratios of numerous health-harming behaviors for those with four or more ACEs compared with none. These outcomes included smoking (OR = 3.3), binge drinking (OR = 2.1), using cannabis (OR = 6.2), having sex before age 16 (OR = 4.8), unintended teenage pregnancy (OR = 5.9), violence victimization (OR = 7.5), violence perpetration (OR = 7.7), lifetime incarceration (OR = 11.3), and poor dietary habits (OR = 2.0).

Data from the 1958 National Child Development Study (NCDS) birth cohort provided an opportunity to assess the effects of ACE-type items on premature mortality in another large British sample (Kelly-Irving et al., 2013). The NCDS included all live births in Great Britain occurring during 1 week in 1958. A measure of ACEs was developed using items from the ACEs study in the United States and childhood adversity research in other countries (Anda, Butchart, Felitti, & Brown, 2010; Benjet et al., 2009; Dong, Anda, et al., 2004; Rosenman & Rodgers, 2004). Responses to these items were then extracted from data collected at earlier assessment periods. Death records were obtained through December 2008 for all participants who were alive at the 16-year-old assessment in 1974. Analyses were run separately for males and females and controlled for demographic variables (e.g., maternal education). Overall, premature mortality was increased in both males (57%) and females (80%) who had two or more of the study's six ACE items. This relationship remained after controlling for early adulthood mediating factors, such as social class, education level, alcohol and tobacco use, body mass index (BMI), and depression (Kelly-Irving et al., 2013). The strengths of this study include its prospective design, with ACE-type items drawn from contemporaneous observations and assessments rather than participant recall.

U.S. State Surveys

An increasing number of U.S. states have added ACEs questions to their annual Behavioral Risk Factor Surveillance System (BRFSS) survey, a cross-sectional, random-digit dialing telephone survey coordinated by the CDC and conducted by state health departments. In 2011, nearly 50,000 adults in five states responded to a survey that included 11 ACEs items and other questions assessing health risk and comorbid conditions (Campbell et al., 2016). The findings from this sample confirm previously observed patterns: ACEs are prevalent, interrelated, and have cumulative negative effects on behavior and health. Fifty-five percent of respondents reported at least one ACE. Consistent with other studies, after adjusting for age, race, gender, marital status, education, employment, income, and region, ACEs significantly increased the odds of risky behaviors (binge and heavy drinking, smoking, high-risk HIV behavior), depression, and disability caused by poor health.

As more states include ACE items in their BRFSS surveys, it becomes possible to establish population-based estimates of ACE prevalence rates, assess trends over time, and identify differences in prevalence rates by demographic, racial/ethnic group, and other characteristics. CDC researchers (Merrick, Ford, Ports, & Guinn, 2018) analyzed data from a nationally representative telephone survey of 214,157 adults in 23 U.S. states. Respondents were asked if they had experienced the following eight ACE items: physical, emotional, or sexual abuse; household mental illness; incarceration; substance use; domestic violence; parental separation or divorce. Answers yielded ACE scores from0 to 8; the percentage that reported experiencing 0, 1, 2, 3, or 4 or more are compared with the original ACEs sample in Table 1.1. Results suggest that the prevalence of ACEs is remarkably consistent across a 20-year time period. In the most recent BRFSS survey, individuals reported having experienced 1.57 ACEs, with women reporting slightly more than men. Other groups who reported higher average ACEs included younger respondents (1.87 and 1.95 for 18- to 24- and 24- to 35-year-olds, respectively); respondents identifying as bisexual (3.14) or gay/lesbian (2.19); respondents without a high school education or GED (1.97); respondents who were unemployed (2.30), unable to work (2.33), or with less than $15,000 in annual income (2.16); and respondents identifying as multiracial (2.52). This study provides the largest and most diverse assessment of ACE exposure in the United States available to date. It indicates an association between ACEs and adult employment and economic outcomes that parallels the ACEs associations previously observed with health behaviors and chronic health conditions.

The original ACEs findings were drawn from a middle-aged, middle-class, and well-insured sample. Recent investigations have assessed ACEs in samples with less education attainment and lower income levels, in more racially and

TABLE 1.1. ACE Exposure in 1998 California Sample and 2018 Multistate Sample

ACE exposure(s)	Kaiser Permanente sample 1995–1997[a] (*N* = 17,337)	BRFSS 23-state sample 2018[b] (*N* = 214,157)
0	36.1	38.5
1	26.0	23.5
2	15.9	13.4
3	9.5	8.8
4+	12.5	15.8

Note. ACE = adverse childhood experience; BRFSS = Behavioral Risk Factor Surveillance System.
[a]Data from Anda et al. (2006).
[b]Data from Merrick, Ford, Ports, and Guinn (2018).

ethnically diverse samples, in socially marginalized groups, and in children and adolescents (Austin, Herrick, & Proescholdbell, 2016; Baglivio et al., 2014; Balistreri & Alvira-Hammond, 2016; Koss et al., 2003; Wade, Shea, Rubin, & Wood, 2014). A growing body of research is beginning to identify similarities and differences across different population groups, providing a better understanding of how prevalence rates vary and whether the effects of ACEs have similar effects on development and health outcomes in different populations.

ACEs IN CHILDREN AND ADOLESCENTS

With a few notable exceptions (Finkelhor & Kendall-Tackett, 1997), before the ACEs study was published, research on adversity in childhood typically focused on a single type of trauma or adversity, such as the effects of divorce or sexual abuse or parent substance use. More recently, investigators have incorporated multiple types of adversity, sometimes using ACEs factors and sometimes constructing similar items, to assess the proximal effects of exposure for multiple types of abuse, neglect, and family dysfunction. Outcome measures include commonly occurring health diagnoses or general health ratings (e.g., asthma), physiological responses to stress (e.g., cortisol), behavioral problems, cognitive development and learning, and emotion regulation and other aspects of executive function (attention, memory, and self-regulation).

ACEs in U.S. Children

Depending on the definition of the adversity, national samples of children and adolescents in the United States revealed that an estimated 20% to 48% have experienced multiple adverse experiences (Saunders & Adams, 2014). Using the National Survey of Children's Health (NSCH) database, researchers surveyed more than 33,000 parents of 12- to 17-year-olds and found the pattern of ACEs in adolescents similar to that observed in adults (Balistreri & Alvira-Hammond, 2016). ACEs were common, with 56% having already experienced at least one; interrelated; and have cumulative effects. Each ACE experienced increased the odds of reported poor health by 9% and the odds of emotional problems by 32%. Notably, for both health and emotional problems, family functioning—as measured by self-reported positive parenting behavior, frequent parent–child interactions, and low parent stress—influenced the effects of ACEs so significantly that their negative consequences were reduced in more high-functioning families. This suggests an ameliorating effect, as we discuss in Chapter 2.

Dr. Christina Bethell and colleagues (Bethell, Newacheck, Hawes, & Halfon, 2014) also used the 2011–2012 NSCH to assess the effects of ACEs on child and adolescent (ages 6–17 years) outcomes. Prevalence rates were comparable to the analyses of 12- through 17-year-olds, with 48% of parents in this sample reporting at least one of nine ACEs for their children and 22.6%

reporting two or more. The dose–response effect on health outcomes observed in previous studies was also found for children, as were social and learning difficulties. Children with two or more ACEs were nearly 3 times more likely to have repeated a grade in school than children with no ACEs, even after adjusting for demographic and health factors. Children with two more adverse experiences were also more likely to be at high or moderate risk for developmental, behavioral, or social delays. One of the study's more interesting findings was the significant differences in prevalence rates by state, with New Jersey reporting the lowest percentage of children with two or more ACES (16%) and Oklahoma reporting the highest (32%). Oklahoma has a history of trauma and adversity: the Dust Bowl of the 1930s (Arthi, 2014; Egan, 2006), the Tulsa Race Massacre of 1921 (Messer, Shriver, & Beamon, 2017), and the forced relocation of Native American tribes (Evans-Campbell, 2008). This may be one reason for the high prevalence of ACEs. We discuss the effects of historical trauma on families and communities in Chapter 7 and explore the challenges and opportunities for communities as a whole to heal from ACEs.

Although originally focused primarily on poverty, Gary Evans (2003) began a longitudinal research study of low-income rural children in the early 2000s that also assessed the effects of multiple types of adversity on physiological measures of stress regulation. Parents of 9-year-olds were asked about their children's exposure to six adverse conditions: noise, crowding, other housing problems, family turmoil, separation from family, and exposure to violence. Stress regulation (or dysregulation) was calculated from six separate measures, including three stress hormones (cortisol, epinephrine, and norepinephrine), systolic and diastolic blood pressure, and BMI. In the initial study, cumulative risk (i.e., multiple types of adversity) predicted increased physiological measures of dysregulation and psychological distress and decreased child reported self-worth and lower observed delay of gratification. Follow-up research with these children and their families found persistent effects of early adversity on physiological stress responses when the children were 13 but only for children whose mothers were low in responsiveness (Evans, Kim, Ting, Tesher, & Shannis, 2007). This again indicates the buffering effects of positive family functioning, which we discuss in later chapters.

ACEs in British Children

Using prospective data from the U.K. Avon Longitudinal Study of Parents and Children, Slopen, Kubzansky, McLaughlin, and Koenen (2013) assessed whether five types of early adversity (measured at seven times between birth and 8 years of age) predicted physiological measures of stress during childhood and adolescents. In this British cohort, cumulative risk during the first 8 years of life predicted C-reactive protein, a measure of inflammation associated with adult heart disease, at 10 and 15 years by cumulative risk during the first 8 years of life. Similarly, Essex and colleagues (2011) used salivary cortisol, a stress hormone produced by activation of the hypothalamic-pituitary-adrenal [HPA] axis, to assess the effects of multiple adversities experienced in infancy and toddlerhood on physiological stress responses in later childhood. Salivary cortisol was collected at morning, afternoon, and evening because cortisol levels normally are highest in the morning and lowest in the evening, unless dysregulated by prolonged stress exposure. Differences between morning, afternoon, and evening levels were calculated at ages 9, 11, 13, and 15 to assess deviations from the normal pattern. Results indicated that adverse experiences in infancy and early childhood were associated with either high (hyperaroused) or low (hypoaroused) cortisol responses, with less normal variation throughout the day, indicating the dysregulating effects of adversity on child and adolescent stress responses.

ACEs and Child Poverty

Children growing up in poverty are at increased risk of experiencing other forms of adversity (Evans & Kim, 2007). Dr. Nadine Burke Harris (2018), whose book *The Deepest Well: Healing the Long-Term Effects of Childhood Adversity* describes her experience applying ACEs science in a low-income urban pediatric clinic, writes eloquently about the effects of trauma and adversity (N. J. Burke, Hellman, Scott, Weems, & Carrion, 2011). Chart reviews of 701 pediatric patients in this clinic revealed that two thirds had already experienced at least one of nine ACEs. Having one or more ACEs increased the risk of having a diagnosed learning or behavior problem 10-fold, and having four or more increased the risk more than 32 times.

Data from the Fragile Families and Child Wellbeing Study (FFCW) revealed a number of similar patterns affecting a sample of young children from low-income families (Hunt, Slack, & Berger, 2017). The FFCW is a population-based, longitudinal birth cohort of 4,898 children born in large U.S. cities between 1998 and 2000 (Reichman, Teitler, Garfinkel, & McLanahan, 2001). Participants were disproportionately (3:1) nonmarital to marital births and more likely to be of minority race and/or ethnicity, with lower educational attainment and income than the general population. Eight ACEs were assessed at age 5, and behavior problems were assessed at age 9. Results revealed that three quarters of the children (77%) had at least one ACE by age 5, with parental anxiety or depression the most prevalent (44%) adversity experienced. Race and ethnic differences were observed, with Black children having the highest reported prevalence of emotional and physical abuse and parental incarceration; White children having the highest rates of parental substance abuse, anxiety, or depression; and Hispanic children having the highest prevalence of domestic violence exposure. Children with three or more ACEs were at significantly greater risk of externalizing behavior (e.g., aggression), internalizing problems (e.g., anxiety, depression), and having an attention-deficit/hyperactivity disorder diagnosis by age 9.

Also using data from the FFCW cohort, researchers (Jimenez, Wade, Lin, Morrow, & Reichman, 2016) analyzed data for 1,007 children who had teacher-reported outcomes at the end of the kindergarten year, as well as parent-reported information on ACEs at age 5. A majority had experienced at least one ACE, and 12% had experienced three or more. After adjusting for child age, gender, race, ethnicity, family income, maternal education, and parent relationship status at child's birth, ACEs significantly predicted teacher-reported ratings of academic, literacy, and behavior problems. Compared with children with no ACEs, the odds of having teacher-reported social and behavioral problems doubled for children with three or more ACEs, and attention problems were 3.5 times greater. ACEs also significantly contributed to poorer literacy and math skills.

In one of the first longitudinal studies investigating the effects of adverse experiences assessed in infancy and toddlerhood on later school performance in childhood, McKelvey, Edge, Mesman, Whiteside-Mansell, and Bradley (2018) analyzed data from the Early Head Start Research and Evaluation Project (Raikes, Brooks-Gunn, & Love, 2013). Information collected from parents when children were 1, 2, and 3 years old was used to construct a 10-item ACEs scale. Exposure to ACEs was common in this sample of infants and toddlers, with only one out of five having no ACEs during their first 3 years. ACEs predicted school performance at age 11, with the odds of having an individualized educational program (IEP) more than double for children with three or more ACEs compared with none, and double the odds of being retained a grade for those with two or more ACEs. As was observed in older children, exposure to ACEs increased the likelihood of having clinical behavior problems, with the risk of externalizing behavior nearly 3 times higher for children with two or more ACEs and more than 5 times higher for children with three or more ACEs. Similar results were observed for internalizing problems and for being diagnosed with attention-deficit disorder during schooling.

Children in the Child Welfare System

As may be expected, children whose families have been referred to Children's Protective Services (CPS) are more likely to have been exposed to abuse, neglect, and family dysfunction, even in the absence of actionable cases of abuse or neglect (Clarkson Freeman, 2014). The first National Survey of Child and Adolescent Well-Being (NSCAW I) looked at a nationally representative sample of young children whose families were investigated by CPS. The prevalence of ACEs was high, with 42% of children already having four or more ACEs during the first 6 years of life. The dose–response effect between number of ACEs and risk of later problems, previously observed in adults, was also seen in this sample. Compared with children with no ACEs, having four or more adverse experiences during the first 6 years of life increased the later child-hood risk of having externalizing problems by 3.5 times, and the risk of inter-nalizing problems increased nearly 5 times. This pattern was also found for children in the second NSCAW II cohort, collected in 2008–2009 from parents of children 18 to 71 months (Kerker et al., 2015). A decade after the first survey, an even larger percentage (98%) of children was found to have at least one ACE, with cumulative effects on behavior problems, social development, and chronic medical conditions.

Children in the Juvenile Justice System

Not surprisingly, one of the most at-risk groups of youth is those already in the justice system. Researchers in Florida used data from juvenile offenders to investigate the prevalence of ACEs and their effect on risk of reoffending (Baglivio et al., 2014). Almost 65,000 youth were included; all had received full assessment screenings and aged out of the system (turned 18) between 2007 and 2012. The 10 original Kaiser–CDC ACE categories were extracted from existing assessment data. As expected, adversity prevalence in this population was considerably higher than in nationally representative populations, with almost all teens (97% of males and 98% of females) reporting at least one ACE. Nine out of 10 males and 92% of females reported multiple ACEs, with significantly more ACEs reported by females (average of 4.29) than males (average of 3.48). Witnessing family violence was the most frequently rated adversity for both males (81%) and females (84%). As observed in other studies, ACEs had cumulative effects, with each ACE incrementally and significantly predicting reoffending risk for males and females.

Children From Violent Neighborhoods

To assess the effects of ACEs in a cohort of young adults who grew up in low-income urban neighborhoods, Mersky, Janczewski, and Topitzes (2017) analyzed data from the Chicago Longitudinal Study. The cohort included 1,539 children (93% African American, 7% Hispanic), born in 1979 or 1980 to low-income urban families. Using data from public databases and surveys of parents, teachers, and participants conducted since 1985, they constructed eight ACE variables: (a) CPS record of abuse or neglect, (b) victim or witness of violent crime, (c) parent substance abuse, (d) prolonged absence of parent, (e) divorce, (f) death of close friend or relative, (g) frequent family conflict, and (h) family financial problems. The ACE items were used to predict outcomes for participants who were surveyed between the ages of 22 and 24. Prevalence of ACEs was higher than that observed in the Kaiser Permanente sample, with four of five participants experiencing at least one ACE and nearly half reporting multiple ACEs. In this sample, as seen in previous studies, ACEs had a cumulative, dose–response effect on poor health, poor mental health, and substance use.

Youth-Defined ACEs

Seeking to understand the experiences that at-risk youth themselves perceive as adverse, researchers conducted and analyzed responses from a series of focus groups with 105 young adults who grew up in low-income neighborhoods in Philadelphia (Wade et al., 2014). Participants were asked to list their five most stressful childhood and adolescence experiences. Their responses included all the traditional 10 ACEs minus having a mentally ill caregiver or divorce/separation, reporting single parenthood as a factor instead. They added a number of unique adverse experiences, with stressful family relationships the most frequently reported general category of adversity. Substance abuse in the home was also frequently mentioned, followed by death and illness of family members, single-parent homes, and violence among family members. Participants frequently commented that their families lacked love, support, strong parenting, and guidance. Neighborhood violence and crime was the second most frequent response category; it was described as persistent and pervasive. These findings suggest that different population groups may experience adversities not captured in the original ACEs questionnaires and that self-reported adversities are similar to what is captured in the original questionnaire.

DEFINING ACEs

As seen in the Philadelphia young adult study (Wade et al., 2014), there may be childhood events and experiences not included in previous or current ACE questionnaires that have negative consequences on later health and development. These experiences may differ by culture, geography, and age of exposure. For example, the World Health Organization (2012) compiled a list of adverse childhood experiences more prevalent in developing countries and in countries experiencing internal strife or warfare. This measure, the Adverse Childhood Experiences International Questionnaire (ACE–IQ), includes many of the same items in the original ACEs questionnaire (parent mentally ill, abusing substances, or incarcerated, divorced or separated; verbal, sexual, and physical abuse). Other items tap into different types of adversities, such as peer bullying, physical fighting, witnessing community or neighborhood violence, being a refugee, or being victimized by soldiers, militia, gangs, or police. Although relatively little research has been conducted using the ACE–IQ, it remains a valuable tool for assessing communities and populations who experienced war or community violence.

Dr. Christina Bethell, director of the Child and Adolescent Health Measurement Initiative at Johns Hopkins University, and her colleagues recently identified and compared 14 methods to assess ACEs among children and families within research, population surveillance, and clinical contexts (Bethell, Carle, et al., 2017). There was considerable overlap in content among measures, and all showed cumulative effects of ACEs exposure and poorer outcomes. The authors conclude with two relevant points for researchers and clinicians alike: *Assessing ACEs is acceptable to parents and families when done in clinical and research contexts* and *addressing ACEs can promote healing from trauma associated with family relationships and promote resilience in children with ACEs trauma.* The therapeutic use of ACEs screening with children and families is discussed in more detail in Chapter 7.

Dr. Martin Teicher and colleagues assessed the impact that age of exposure to trauma and adversity has on various outcomes by developing and testing new items and scales (Teicher & Parigger, 2015). The Maltreatment and Abuse Chronology of Exposure (MACE) scale was developed using item response theory and evaluated with a sample of 1,051 healthy young adults. The researchers followed a rigorous process, statistically selecting and eliminating items, assessing test–retest reliability and convergent validity, identifying clinical cutpoints, making comparisons with ACEs and the Childhood Trauma Questionnaire (CTQ; Bernstein, Ahluvalia, Pogge, & Handelsman, 1997; Bernstein et al., 2003), and assessing differences in age of exposure by maltreatment type (Teicher & Parigger, 2015). The resulting scale assesses emotional neglect, nonverbal emotional abuse, parent physical abuse, parent verbal abuse, peer emotional abuse, peer physical bullying, physical neglect, sexual abuse from family or peers, witnessing interparental violence, and witnessing violence done to siblings. Items are rated by severity, and age of occurrence is noted. This scale produces two types of scores: The MACE Multiplicity score indicates the number of types of abuse or neglect, ranging from 0 to 10, much like ACE scores, and correlates .70 with ACE scores. The MACE Severity score sums individual scores and ranges from 0 to 100; it correlates .74 with the CTQ. Initial results indicated that different types of maltreatment are associated with distinct developmental patterns. These patterns exert significant effects on brain development and subsequent clinical symptomatology (Andersen & Teicher, 2008), a topic we explore in Chapter 3. Both the MACE and a related scale, the Maltreatment and Abuse Exposure Scale, which consists of 52 items without age of exposure, are available through open access to facilitate their use as research tools (Teicher & Parigger, 2015).

KNOWING ONE'S ACE SCORE

Researchers, clinicians, and others working to reduce children's exposure to ACEs or to create programs and environments that protect and help children, adolescents, and adults recover from them have an obligation to address personal childhood experiences that may help or hinder those goals. If you have not already taken the ACEs questionnaire, we invite you to do so (see Figure 1.4).

Despite the grim statistics presented in this chapter that link ACEs with negative health and developmental outcomes in large samples, ACE scores do not predict individual outcomes. ACE scores are estimates of probabilities of population risks not meant to predict individual risk. However, identifying our own ACEs can alert us to potential concerns. ACEs serve as a marker of stress we have undergone and remind us that stress may still be influencing our bodies, our brains, and our behavior. When we count our ACEs, we review the experiences that have shaped us. Reviewing these experiences is not,

FIGURE 1.4. ACEs Questionnaire

Adverse Childhood Experiences (ACEs)

While you were growing up, during your first 18 years of life:

1. Did a parent or other adult in the household often or very often: YES   NO

   Swear at you, insult you, put you down, or humiliate you **OR** act in a way that made you afraid that you might be physically hurt?

2. Did a parent or other adult in the household often or very often: YES   NO

   Push, grab, slap, or throw something at you **OR** hit you so hard that you had marks or were injured?

3. Did an adult or person at least 5 years older than you ever: YES   NO

   Touch or fondle you or have you touch their body in a sexual way **OR** attempt or actually have oral, anal, or vaginal intercourse with you?

4. Did you often or very often feel that: YES   NO

   No one in your family loved you or thought you were important or special **OR** your family didn't look out for each other, feel close to each other, or support each other?

5. Did you often or very often feel that: YES   NO

   You didn't have enough to eat, had to wear dirty clothes, and had no one to protect you **OR** your parents were too drunk or high to take care of you or take you to the doctor if you needed it?

6. Was your mother or stepmother or father or stepfather: YES   NO

   Often or very often pushed, grabbed, slapped, or had something thrown at her/him **OR** sometimes, often, or very often kicked, bitten, hit with a fist, or hit with something hard **OR** ever repeatedly hit for at least a few minutes or threatened with a knife or gun?

7. Were your parents ever separated or divorced?   YES   NO

8. Did you live with anyone who was a problem drinker or alcoholic or who used street drugs or prescription drugs not as prescribed?   YES   NO

9. Was a household member depressed or mentally ill or did a household member attempt suicide?   YES   NO

10. Did a household member go to prison?   YES   NO

Other? _____   YES   NO

Data from Centers for Disease Control and Prevention (2018).

or does not need to be, an invitation to reexperience terror or distress. Some-times this occurs and is an indicator that additional support and professional guidance is needed. There are mental health resources listed in the Appendix. In most cases when we have asked groups to take the ACEs questionnaire, individuals respond with hope and gratitude—that they have endured, have coped, are resilient, and will continue to recover and heal. Specific strategies to process and move on from childhood trauma and stress are described in Chapter 5. Becoming more cognizant of physiological responses to stress and behavioral patterns that may result from childhood adversity increases self-awareness, promotes continued growth, and offers opportunities to practice compassion for the others coping with the consequences of ACEs.

2

Protective and Compensatory Experiences

The Antidote to ACEs

. . . if we want children to live up to their developmental potential and to lead meaningful lives, we must afford them that opportunity by limiting their exposure to adversity: we must ensure that their brains receive the types of experiences that foster healthy brain development (and at the right times in development); and we must be mindful of the fact that deviations from the expectable environment during critical periods of development can lead to particularly egregious outcomes.

—CHARLES NELSON, 2017, p. 266

It was a beautiful spring day in Tulsa, Oklahoma, and Amanda was driving through the trendy, revitalized downtown area with Dr. Ann Masten, a renowned resilience researcher from the University of Minnesota. Along with scholars from across the country, she had come to speak about research on resilience and the role of the family (Criss, Henry, Harrist, & Larzelere, 2015). Amanda knew Ann from other conferences and several years before they visited the Oklahoma City memorial together. Amanda was eager to discuss her new interest in adverse childhood experiences (ACEs) and to get Ann's thoughts on how they fit in with resilience and developmental psychology.

Amanda described an ACEs conference that she and Jennifer had attended in Philadelphia the previous summer and about the power of the work presented. Several aspects of that conference had made a big impact. First, it was the first scientific conference she had attended where several speakers talked about *love*. Psychologists talk about emotional attachment, the parent–child

http://dx.doi.org/10.1037/0000177-002
Adverse and Protective Childhood Experiences: A Developmental Perspective, by J. Hays-Grudo and A. S. Morris

23

bond, and positive parenting, but no one really talks about love at developmental conferences. Second, she had been struck by the lack of discussion about developmental science and concepts known about resilience, that is, the ways that parents and other elements of children's environments can buffer the effects of ACEs. It was as if this information was completely unknown to the fellow conference participants. Of course, she did not have to tell Ann that there are literally decades of research on how children overcome adversity (Masten, 2001; Masten et al., 1990; Werner, 1995) nor about the importance of relationships and resources for healthy development (Huston, 1991; Sroufe, 2000). Ann agreed that developmental science has many of the answers to ACEs and that it would not be too difficult to develop a comparable measure to ACEs focused on factors that build resilience, and the seed was planted. Several months later, Amanda and Jennifer sat down and compiled a list of experiences that are known from research to promote resilience in the face of adversity. These items were whittled down to become the Protective and Compensatory Experiences (PACEs) scale.

In this chapter, we describe those 10 PACEs and outline the basic scientific support for their inclusion. We begin with the list of PACEs and then review the foundational research to support PACEs. We end the chapter with a discussion of our research on PACEs and the importance of assessing PACEs with ACEs in both research studies and clinical practice.

PACEs: RELATIONSHIPS AND RESOURCES

Along with other scholars (Luthar, 2015; Masten, 2015; Rutter, 1987; Ungar, 2004; Zeanah, 2009), we argue that protective and compensatory experiences during childhood lead to greater resilience and emotion regulation, whereas adverse childhood experiences lead to greater risk for social and mental health difficulties and emotion dysregulation (Morris, Treat, et al., 2018). Early experiences set the stage for later development. Evidence indicates that both relationships and resources provide the nurture and stability needed for success (G. J. Duncan & Brooks-Gunn, 2000; Korenman, Miller, & Sjaastad, 1995; Masten & Coatsworth, 1998; McLoyd, 1998; Shonkoff, 2010), and relationships and resources provide the foundation for the PACEs framework.

Relationship factors we identify as PACEs include (a) unconditional love from a parent (or other primary caregiver such as a grandparent serving in a parental role), (b) having a best friend, (c) volunteering in the community, (d) being part of a social group, and (e) having the support of an adult outside of the family (e.g., coach, mentor). *Resources* we identify as PACEs include (f) living in a clean and safe home with enough food; (g) having the resources and opportunities to learn (good school, other educational experiences); (h) having an engaging hobby, artistic, creative, or intellectual pursuit; (i) being part of organized sports or having regular physical activity (or both); and (j) being part of a family with routines and fair, consistent rules. Note that by resources, we are not merely talking about the absence of poverty; we are referring to quality resources and access to enriching opportunities. For example, the opportunity to have a hobby or belong to a team can provide a protective experience and is considered a resource in our PACEs model. Much like ACEs, PACEs tend to cooccur. In addition, like ACEs, PACEs are experiences that occur before age 18. In Chapter 6, we discuss specific PACES for young children (ages 0–5), although the basic framework remains the same.

1. Unconditional Love

The first PACE we identified is unconditional love from a caregiver. Although love is often discussed in terms of attachment and nurturing, thinking about it in "unconditional" terms is in accord with developmental science. Decades of research have confirmed that responsive, nurturing parenting is one of the strongest predictors of child adjustment and well-being (Baumrind, 1971; Morris, Cui, & Steinberg, 2013; Steinberg, 2001). Beginning in the first year of life, children form attachments to a parent or another primary caregiver (grandmother, aunt, sitter), and this attachment sets the foundation for their social, emotional, and cognitive development (Ainsworth, 1989; Bowlby, 2008; Brumariu & Kerns, 2010). Not only do children need to be nurtured and loved, the love needs to be unconditional. Children need to *feel* loved and know that they are cared about absolutely, no matter what. This contrasts sharply with love and acceptance that is conditionally based on behavior. When parents withdraw love because a child misbehaves or performs poorly in school, they send a message that love is contingent on behavior and performance. Imagine the guilt and shame this can induce in a child; over time, this guilt and shame can lead to depression and anxiety (Barber, 2002; Barber & Harmon, 2002). Children need to understand that parents may not approve of a behavior, but it does not mean that they are not loved. Love—free-flowing or used as a reward or punishment—sets the foundation for self-esteem, character, and confidence. From an evolutionary perspective, it can be argued that when children are young and helpless, bonding with a caregiver is as critical for survival as being fed and clothed (Dozier, 2000). Research on parent–child attachment (described later in this chapter) supports this idea and has illustrated the long-term effects of the parent–child relationship on later development. For children with ACEs, responsive and sensitive caregiving fosters healing, as we discuss more in Chapter 6.

2. Having a Best Friend

We know that having a best friend protects children from peer rejection, bullying, and victimization (C. L. Fox & Boulton, 2006; Hodges, Boivin, Vitaro, & Bukowski, 1999). As children develop into adults, they must transition from their family of origin to their own family or supportive peer network. When children are young, friends provide opportunities to learn through play and social interaction. Children can try out new skills and learned behaviors among equals (Tudge, 1992; Vygotsky, 1978). Friends also reduce stress and provide fun, social support, and acceptance. Children with a best friend have someone they can turn to outside of their family in times of need. Peer relationships are also important in social and emotional development. Researchers studying the protective effects of friendship have found an inverse relationship between having a best friend and experiencing negative life events, such as peer victimization, maternal hostility, harsh discipline, and stress or abuse (Adams, Santo, & Bukowski, 2011; Schwartz, Lansford, Dodge, Pettit, & Bates, 2013).

3. Volunteering in the Community

Helping others provides a sense of connection to the community; volunteering helps children learn about the needs of others and see a world outside their own. Many studies associate volunteer work with prosocial development and lasting positive developmental outcomes (N. Eisenberg, Morris, McDaniel, & Spinrad, 2009; C. W. Moore & Allen, 1996; Yates & Youniss, 1996). Giving of one's time cultivates empathy, altruism, and perspective and helps children learn that being kind and generous is part of living well. As pediatrician and trauma scholar Dr. Kenneth Ginsburg has argued, when people help others and understand that helping is not done out of pity, it allows individuals to take help from others when needed (Ginsburg & Jablow, 2005). Helping others also provides an opportunity for leadership and making a difference, encouraging confidence as children learn they have something valuable to give. Notably, research indicates that volunteering is particularly impactful among youth who volunteer with their parents, where parents model giving of themselves to others (Janoski & Wilson, 1995).

4. Being Part of a Group

Membership in a group or organization fosters a sense of belonging outside the family. Similar to volunteering, group involvement allows children and teens to learn about themselves in different contexts and provides opportunities for friendship and leadership. This sense of connection and belonging can provide support in times of need and can be an outlet for stress reduction. Participating in scouts, faith-based, or other groups means that children are spending time in positive activities. Although we want children to have some downtime, it is important to note that being active and engaged is associated with better academic achievement and improved self-esteem (Gerber, 1996). Group membership can also facilitate identity development and help children establish their own values and morals (N. Eisenberg et al., 2009). Extracurricular school activities are also beneficial (Fredricks & Eccles, 2006, 2010). For example, a large-scale longitudinal study found that participation in extracurricular activities was associated with lower rates of school dropout and arrests among both boys and girls considered high risk. However, this was true only among those youth whose social group participated in those activities as well (Mahoney, 2000). In another longitudinal study of 1,500 youth, researchers found that participation in school clubs and sports was positively associated with academic success, positive psychological adjustment and behavior, and lower rates of substance abuse (Blomfield & Barber, 2009). One explanation for these positive effects is that friendships and relationships are cultivated from such participation (Simpkins, Eccles, & Becnel, 2008).

5. Having a Mentor

Another identified PACE is having an adult (not a parent) who can be trusted and counted on for help or advice. Teens with caring adults in their lives are less likely to experience psychological distress and academic difficulties (Woolley & Bowen, 2007). Studies show that relationships with caring adults can protect children from engaging in high-risk behaviors (Keenan, 1992; Resnick, Harris, & Blum, 1993) and are related to positive outcomes such as academic success currently and over time (DuBois, Felner, Brand, Adan, & Evans, 1992; Masten, 2014). Having an adult to trust and rely on is particularly important when the parent or primary caregiver is not providing the love, support, and limit-setting that children need. Research shows that a coach, teacher, or relative can protect children in troubled families and can compensate for many negative outcomes associated with poor parenting (Lerner et al., 2014; Woolley & Bowen, 2007). Even if children have exemplary parents, an adult outside the home provides an additional source of information about the world, an alternate role model to which children can aspire, and a reminder that someone else loves and cares about them. An adult advocate or mentor can also be someone a child turns to for advice when it is not comfortable to ask a parent (e.g., dating, bullying) or for information about topics their parents may know less about (e.g., how to get into college, choosing a particular career).

6. Living in a Home That Is Clean and Safe, With Enough Food

It is important to note that we recognize three items within this one PACE; we did this purposely to reflect the importance of meeting primary needs. To thrive, children must have their basic needs met and live in a safe home (Maslow, 1943). Chaotic and unpredictable home environments are associated with harsh and inconsistent parenting and more negative responses to children's emotions, leading to academic difficulties, externalizing problems (i.e., acting out behaviors such as aggression and delinquency), and increased anxiety and depression in children (Deater-Deckard, Wang, Chen, & Bell, 2012; Evans & English, 2002; Jaffee, Hanscombe, Haworth, Davis, & Plomin, 2012; Valiente, Lemery-Chalfant, & Reiser, 2007). Research indicates that children who live in homes that are cluttered and unclean have worse outcomes than children living in clean, organized homes (Evans & English, 2002; Vernon-Feagans, Willoughby, Garrett-Peters, & The Family Life Project Key Investigators, 2016). Keeping their environment neat and clean teaches children to respect their home and possessions and can instill good values and habits that extend into adulthood. Children also deserve to live in a home that is safe inside and out. Children exposed to violence in the home and in the community are at risk for a host of problems, such as aggression, delinquency, school dropout, and depression (Turner, Shattuck, Finkelhor, & Hamby, 2016).

It is well documented that adequate nutrition is important for brain health and development (Prado & Dewey, 2014). Children should not have to worry about food. Despite this basic concept, one of every six children in the United States does not have consistent access to food (Feeding America, 2018). Unpredictability or lack of food can negatively affect physical, social, and emotional development (Kleinman et al., 1998). Children without enough food are more likely to have health problems, suffer from chronic medical conditions, and experience academic difficulties and internalizing behaviors such as anxiety and depression (Rose-Jacobs et al., 2008; Slopen, Fitzmaurice, Williams, & Gilman, 2010). It is also noteworthy that many studies have found that children and adolescents who regularly eat dinner with their families are less likely to be overweight, use drugs, drop out of school, or experience other problems (Fulkerson et al., 2006). When mealtimes are part of a home routine, the family has a time and place for communication, sharing, and fostering supportive relationships. Note that family meals can also be considered part of the last PACE *having rules and routines*.

7. Getting an Education

In the same way that a safe and predictable home can protect against risk, having the opportunity to learn and be educated in an environment that provides clear and consistent boundaries and rules can do the same. Having the resources and opportunities to have positive academic experiences, such as active learning, engaged teachers, and a quality curriculum, help children learn. Doing well in school opens doors and provides opportunities for later learning and more career options (Lleras, 2008). When children attend a good school, they are typically among peers who do well in school who are from families that value education. Students tend to fall or rise in performance based on those around them; being among achieving peers amplifies students' performance (Steinberg, Dornbusch, & Brown, 1992; Wentzel & Caldwell, 1997). Families may value different school experiences such as diversity, specialized curricula, home schooling, or advanced college prep programs; regardless of these nuances, evidence across many disciplines (e.g., psychology, economics, sociology) finds that quality education is one of the best predictors of later success and happiness (Heckman, 2011).

In early childhood specifically, studies indicate that there is a 7% to 13% return on investment for quality early childhood educational programming serving low-income children (Heckman, 2015), such as Head Start. A number of longitudinal studies with low-income families found that participation in high-quality early childhood programs improves adult health and educational outcomes, reduces use of welfare and social intervention programs, lowers arrest rates, and increases earnings (Reynolds, Temple, Ou, Arteaga, & White, 2011; Reynolds et al., 2007). In fact, research indicates that participating in quality early childcare programs builds resilience among children who have already experienced ACEs, such as children in foster care (Pecora et al., 2017).

8. Having a Hobby

Having a creative or intellectual pastime either alone or in a group is another PACE. Protective activities can be any positive recreational pursuit that a child chooses, such as playing an instrument, dancing, judo, reading, chess, robotics, or art. Organized activities teach discipline and self-regulation and can lead to a sense of mastery, competence, and self-esteem (Zarobe & Bungay, 2017). Creative hobbies provide an outlet for expression and identity exploration and allow children to have a voice and be recognized for their efforts. Hobbies also provide social connections and teach children persistence and coping skills for the challenges related to their hobby or developing skill (Sanders, Munford, Thimasarn-Anwar, Liebenberg, & Ungar, 2015). Hobbies can also provide a sense of routine and consistency that comes from adhering to a schedule, providing increased security and mastery motivation (Jennings, 1993). Daily practice can be part of a routine that helps children learn the value of repetition and improvement. Research also indicates that building competence and connections through hobbies and shared activities can be an effective treatment for children with a history of trauma (Blaustein & Kinniburgh, 2018).

9. Being Physically Active

Organized sports and physical activity can provide a sense of mastery and social connection. Young children need to engage in active, physical play and exploration every day to facilitate learning (Becker, McClelland, Loprinzi, & Trost, 2014; Vygotsky, 1967). Physical activity is important for health; it helps children handle the physiological effects of stress on the body and improves mood and mental health (K. R. Fox, 1999; Penedo & Dahn, 2005). Exercise helps our bodies manage stress (Edenfield & Blumenthal, 2011) and lessens the likelihood that children will grab a package of chips or lash out to relieve stress. Playing a team sport, working together toward a goal, is an opportunity for social development and connection. Sports can also lead to better self-regulation, competence, and self-esteem (Fraser-Thomas, Côté, & Deakin, 2005; Lakes & Hoyt, 2004). In a recent study of adults with ACEs, team sports participation during adolescence was associated with better mental health outcomes, suggesting long-term effects of participating in group sports among individuals with a history of adversity (Easterlin, Chung, Leng, & Dudovitz, 2019).

10. Having Rules and Routines

Security comes when children know what to expect and when caregivers enforce clear rules and limits. Children with no rules or limits (victims of "permissive parenting") tend to engage in risky behaviors as teens, do poorly in school, and often grow up to be irresponsible adults (Dornbusch, Ritter, Leiderman, Roberts, & Fraleigh, 1987; Hoeve et al., 2007). Children cannot parent themselves; they need high expectations, consistency, and parental involvement. During early childhood, this means parents should establish and enforce bedtime and other routines, redirect children when they misbehave, and explain the effects of behavior on others as children grow older. Routines are particularly important during childhood because they help children know what to expect and provide comfort (Spagnola & Fiese, 2007). During adolescence, parents need to know where their teens are, who they spend time with, and what they are doing. This is often called *monitoring* or *behavioral control* in the parenting literature and has been linked to less aggression, less drug and alcohol use, and higher academic achievement (Barnes & Farrell, 1992; Pettit, Laird, Dodge, Bates, & Criss, 2001).

Rules should be fair and consistent. The "fair" is critical as children grow: Children must have a say in the rules and be able to present their views. As the creator of a widely used parenting program, Dr. Michael Popkin (2014) said, "You may not get your way, but you always get your say" (p. 20). When a home has clear rules and limits and when a parent is ultimately in charge, children feel safer and more secure. When parents are disengaged or permissive, children often feel they do not matter and are not important. In a home with multiple children, a lack of parental involvement often puts undue stress on older siblings, who may try to step in to parent younger brothers and sisters.

PACEs FOUNDATIONAL THEORIES AND RESEARCH

There are many seminal developmental theories and research studies that ground our PACEs work. Most developmental scientists agree that children need nurturance and guidance, as well as clear rules and limits. Children need opportunities to grow and challenge themselves and to experience a variety of physical, mental, and creative activities that lead to a sense of competence. Developmental theories consider progression throughout development, with early experiences building on, and leading to, later experiences and growth trajectories.

Psychosocial Theory of Development

When teaching Erik Erikson's (1993, 1994) theory of psychosocial development, Jennifer tells her students that it is a blueprint for a good life. Erickson's theory focuses on resolving psychological conflicts that occur during different stages of development (see Table 2.1, with our addition of the positive

TABLE 2.1. Erikson's Stages of Development

Age	Stage	Virtue	Positive Outcome
Birth–18 months	Trust vs. Mistrust	Hope	Security *"I am loved"*
18 months–3 years	Autonomy vs. Shame & Doubt	Will	Self-Control & Exploration *"I am safe to explore"*
3–5	Initiative vs. Guilt	Purpose	Self-Efficacy *"I can do it"*
5–12	Industry vs. Inferiority	Competency	Self-Esteem *"I am good"*
12–18	Identity vs. Role Confusion	Fidelity	Independence & Self-understanding *"I know who I am"*
18–40	Intimacy vs. Isolation	Love	Companionship & Strong relationships *"I belong"*
40–65	Generativity vs. Stagnation	Care	Sense of Accomplishment *"I have done it and will help others"*
65+	Integrity vs. Despair	Wisdom	Satisfaction with Life *"I have lived a good life"*

Note. Data from Erikson (1993, 1994).

outcomes). These conflicts are resolved—or not—within the context of relationships and result in capacities or "virtues" that are carried into the next stage of development. Several of Erikson's stages are relevant to PACEs. The first stage, *trust versus mistrust*, posits that during the first year of life, infants develop a sense that the world is either a trustworthy, predictable place where needs are met or an unreliable, chaotic place where they are not. On the basis of these experiences, infants develop a relationship with caregivers that is either trusting and secure or mistrusting and unpredictable. Erikson's later stages focus on developmental milestones, such as achieving competence, identity formation, and intimacy. Several of the PACEs—being part of a group, having a hobby—are relevant to Erikson's *identity versus role confusion* stage, as discussed in the next sections. During each stage, caregivers and partners can work to facilitate positive outcomes through supportive behaviors and guidance.

Attachment Theory

In the first year of life, children begin to form attachments to caregivers, setting the foundation for later social and emotional development (Ainsworth, 1989;

Bowlby, 2008; Brumariu & Kerns, 2010). Attachment theory stems from evolutionary theories that argue attachment evolved as a species-specific response to ensure survival. Early researchers such as Harry Harlow (Harlow & Zimmermann, 1959) studied the effects of separating rhesus monkeys from their mothers. Harlow was particularly interested in determining whether attachment to the mother was the result of being fed by her, so he replaced the mothers with surrogates made of either cloth with no milk or wire mesh mothers with bottles of milk attached. When the infants were hungry, they went to the wire mothers for food; otherwise, they spent the majority of their time cuddling on the cloth-covered surrogates. When they were frightened or stressed, they went to the cloth mothers for comfort. This demonstrated that infants' need for maternal contact involved more than just satisfying hunger and basic needs; mothers provided comfort and security as well. These perspectives led to a more fully developed theory of infant attachment, which is commonly viewed as the joint work of John Bowlby and Mary Ainsworth.

Bowlby's ideas for attachment stemmed from his observations of young children's distress when separated from their mothers during the bombing of London in World War II (Bowlby, 1969). He proposed that mother–infant attachment is biologically driven to promote survival and that infants develop a *working model* of social relationships based on early experiences with a caregiver. Infants who experience caregivers as responsive, consistent, and nurturing develop a working model of the world and relationships as safe, secure, and predictable. In contrast, infants whose caregivers are unresponsive, inconsistent, or harsh develop a working model of the world and relationships as unsafe, insecure, and unpredictable (Bowlby, 1988). Although original attachment work was based on children and their mothers, it has been extended more recently to fathers and other caregivers, with similar findings (Grossmann et al., 2002; van IJzendoorn & De Wolff, 1997).

Ainsworth observed natural interactions between infants and their caregivers and introduced the important concept of the *secure base* into attachment theory. In healthy relationships, caregivers provide a secure base from which children branch out to explore and return to for emotional and behavioral needs to be met. Through her observations of these and related behaviors, Ainsworth created a standardized observational attachment classification system, the Strange Situation, used in research to identify children as securely or insecurely attached to a caregiver (Ainsworth & Bell, 1970; Bretherton, 1992). The Strange Situation is used for children 12 to 24 months of age and involves a series of separations and reunions with a caregiver. Importantly, a stranger is present during some of the episodes, and observers focus on the infant's behavior when the caregiver returns to classify attachment status.

In the Strange Situation, regardless of the distress level when the caregiver leaves, securely attached infants are able to be soothed by the caregiver upon return, and they exhibit a preference for the caregiver compared with the stranger. Infants classified as *insecure avoidant* are unresponsive to the caregiver and do not exhibit distress when the caregiver leaves. Moreover, these infants interact with the stranger and the caregiver in a similar way. Upon reunion, these infants avoid or are slow to respond to the caregiver. It is believed that insecure avoidant attachment occurs when infants have learned to soothe themselves because caregivers are not generally responsive to their needs. Infants classified as *insecure resistant* display clinginess and lack exploration before separating from the caregiver. They show distress when the caregiver leaves, and when reunited, they often cling to the caregiver while exhibiting anger or resisting comfort and continue to cry. It is believed that this dysfunctional attachment occurs when caregivers meet infants' needs inconsistently. The final insecure classification is *disorganized* attachment. This classification was added later by Main and Solomon (1986) on the basis of attempts to classify infants who did not fit into previous classifications. Infants with disorganized attachment display strange, unpredictable and sometimes disturbing behavior when reunited with their caregivers. They may freeze, hide, or look away from the caregiver while being held, or they may cry out after calming down. Disorganized attachment often occurs when a caregiver is abusive and represents abnormal patterns of interaction. Disorganized attachment is also associated with a number of later psychological problems (van IJzendoorn, Schuengel, & Bakermans-Kranenburg, 1999).

Many studies have found predictable associations between attachment classifications and child outcomes. Secure attachment in infancy is positively associated with emotion regulation, self-reliance, and social competence (Sroufe, 2005; Sroufe, Carlson, Levy, & Egeland, 1999). Children who do not form secure attachments with caregivers are more likely to have internalizing behaviors such as anxiety and depression or externalizing behaviors in the form of aggression or more serious conduct disorders (Allen, Porter, McFarland, McElhaney, & Marsh, 2007). Children who experience trauma early in life are at greater risk for negative outcomes and insecure attachments (Cook et al., 2005). Fortunately, having a secure relationship with a caring adult during childhood can buffer the negative effects of early maltreatment and neglect (Munson & McMillen, 2009; M.-T. Wang, Brinkworth, & Eccles, 2013), and this is discussed more in Chapter 6. Sadly, in the United States, only approximately 60% of children are typically classified as securely attached to a caregiver (Solomon & George, 2008), although rates vary somewhat depending on cultural background and caregiver history.

Parenting Styles

While Amanda was interviewing for graduate programs in developmental psychology, she was asked which researcher influenced her most during undergraduate training. Her confident reply: "Diana Baumrind and her research on parenting styles." Years later, Baumrind spoke at an Oklahoma State University conference. During a postconference reception at Amanda's home, Amanda vividly remembers Baumrind sitting at the "little kids" table in the corner of her playroom, visiting with other colleagues. Baumrind was an incredible, groundbreaking scholar, small in stature but certainly large in life.

In the 1960s, Baumrind recorded observations of preschool children and their parents at home (Baumrind, 1966, 1971; Baumrind & Black, 1967). On the basis of these observations, she was able to match patterns of parenting with children's behavior in school. She identified three types of parenting styles that can be thought of along two dimensions, *warmth* and *control* (see Figure 2.1). First, parents high in warmth and control were classified as *authoritative*, and their children were more likely to be competent, social, and well behaved in school. These parents had clear rules and limits but were also warm, nurturing, and responsive. Moreover, they listened to their children and allowed them to make choices. Second, parents who were high in warmth and low in control were *permissive*. In these households, the children—often spoiled—were in charge, but parents were nurturing and warm. In school, these children had behavior problems and difficulties with self-regulation. Third, parents low in warmth and high in control were *authoritarian*. Their children tended to be anxious and withdrawn at school. At home, authoritarian parents gave their children little autonomy or say in final decisions, and they did not display much warmth or nurturance. Years later, Maccoby and Martin (1983) identified a fourth parenting style, *neglectful*, which is low on both warmth and control. Much like disorganized attachment, this type of parenting is typically accompanied by abuse and neglect and is associated with a number of mental health problems, such as delinquent behavior, depression, and low self-esteem (Lamborn, Mounts, Steinberg, & Dornbusch, 1991).

Over the past 5 decades, Baumrind and others examined associations between these parenting styles and child outcomes, with similar results. For example, in a large study of adolescents, Steinberg and Dornbush found that authoritative parenting (high in warmth and control) predicted a number of positive outcomes in youth, such as self-esteem, academic achievement, and

FIGURE 2.1. Parenting Styles

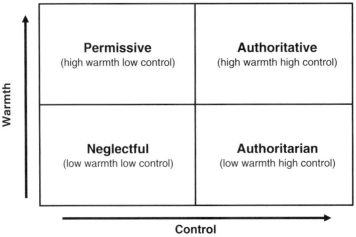

Data from Baumrind, 1966, 1971; Baumrind & Black, 1967.

prosocial behavior. Authoritative parenting was also associated with fewer negative outcomes such as aggression, delinquency, depressive symptoms, and peer problems (Steinberg, Lamborn, Darling, Mounts, & Dornbusch, 1994). Notably, they found that authoritative parenting consistently resulted in the best outcomes for children, regardless of ethnicity and income. As might be expected, a number of studies have found that the other parenting styles—authoritarian, permissive, and neglectful—are consistently associated with more negative outcomes such as school dropout, drug use, low self-esteem, and mental health struggles (Steinberg, 2001).

Authoritative parents resemble parents of securely attached infants—they are warm, supportive, and predictable. It is likely that children with authoritative parents have secure attachments, as much of the underlying parenting is similar in nature. Attachment theory and parenting styles provide the foundation for our first PACE, *unconditional love from a caregiver*. Unconditional love is a quality of secure parent–child attachment relationships and is displayed in parents with an authoritative parenting style, resulting in better child and adolescent outcomes concurrently and later in life. The last PACE, *having rules and routines*, is also reflected in authoritative parenting as parental control and in secure attachment as predictability.

Identity and Moral Development

As mentioned previously, Erikson's psychosocial stage during adolescence is *identity versus role confusion*. Developmentalists now recognize that identity development does not end during adolescence but continues into adulthood and that identities can change later in life. Nevertheless, James Marcia expanded on Erikson's theory and described four types of identity statuses that are based on various levels of commitment and exploration (Marcia, 1966, 1980). These concepts are helpful when considering the importance of some of the PACEs. First, Marcia described *foreclosure*. This occurs when adolescents or young adults commit to an identity without adequately exploring different beliefs, morals, and values. Often, they prematurely adopt the identity of their parents. Second, a *moratorium* occurs when teens actively seek out an identity and take time to explore different ideals of the self over a period of time, without actually committing to an identity. *Identity diffusion* is when adolescents and young adults switch back and forth between different identities and do not have a strong sense of self. Sometimes they adopt their parents' beliefs; sometimes they go against family norms. Finally, the ideal result of this stage, *identity achievement*, is reached when adolescents develop their own moral code and have a strong sense of self and personal values. Typically, when this occurs, adolescents integrate their parents' values into their own sense of morals and self.

Many of the PACEs, such as belonging to a group, volunteering, or having a hobby, are important because they facilitate identity development and exploration. For example, being in drama club or band exposes adolescents to different experiences and helps them identify with diverse groups (B. B. Brown & Klute, 2003). More recent research has focused on the development of self-concept, rather than identity per se. Self-concept reflects the way individuals see themselves in different domains such as social, physical, and intellectual (Harter, 1998). Experiences in various groups and settings influence how adolescents perceive themselves in these domains, support identity achievement, and often affect self-esteem. These beliefs can also be influenced by mastery of a certain skill or expertise in a specific area or through a hobby. Albert Bandura, a well-known psychologist known especially for his work on social learning theory, observational learning, and social cognitive theory, labeled this idea *self-efficacy*, a perception of success and competence that comes from practice, skill building, and positive experiences in a given domain (Bandura, 1997).

Seminal theories of moral development also provide a foundation for PACEs. For example, the work of psychologist Martin Hoffman stresses the value of parents and caregivers fostering empathy in children, and helping children gain perspective and understand the experience of others (Hoffman, 2001). This is relevant to several PACEs—volunteering, being part of a group, and having a best friend. Successful relationships with peers can foster empathy and understanding, and being part of a group exposes children to individuals outside their family of origin, allowing for the experience of knowing people with different views and perspectives. As mentioned previously, research on volunteering in the community, particularly when parents are involved, has been associated with several positive outcomes, including helping behavior and social competence (Janoski & Wilson, 1995; Yates & Youniss, 1996).

Resilience

People are always fascinated by stories of individuals who overcome hardship, thrive in the face of disaster, or persist in physical challenges despite setbacks. Developmental scientists have termed such phenomena *displays of resilience*, or the ability to bounce back from trauma or adversity. Masten (2014) defined resilience as "the capacity of a dynamic system to adapt successfully to disturbances that threaten system function, viability, or development" (p. 10). This broad definition can be applied to multiple systems, such as schools, ecosystems, or communities. Luthar, Cicchetti, and Becker (2000) note that resilience requires two critical conditions. First, there must be exposure to threat or severe adversity. Second, positive adaptation must occur despite significant attacks on development. Clearly, such concepts are important when understanding the potential effects of ACEs. However, conceptual issues are inherent in defining resilience; examples include how much adversity or risk is needed for resilience to occur, and how should scientists assess and define adaptation? Regardless of these and similar issues, Luthar and colleagues concluded that "despite many challenges linked with studying this complex construct, the continuation of scientific work in this area is of substantive value" (p. 556). We agree and view PACEs as protective experiences that can influence resilience in the face of adversity (for more information on definitional issues related to protective factors, see Luthar et al., 2000; Luthar, Sawyer, & Brown, 2006).

Our work is grounded in the pioneering work of resilience scientists such as Norman Garmezy who led the way in the study of resilience (Masten, Best, & Garmezy, 1990); Emmy Werner, a developmental scientist who studied resilience in a cohort of children from infancy into adulthood on the island of Kauai (Werner & Smith, 1992); Sir Michael Rutter, one of the first to use the term *cumulative risk* to describe a cohort of boys growing up in a rough part of London (Rutter, 1987); and Arnold Sameroff who created the transactional model of development describing how experiences and biology interact to affect development over time (Sameroff, 1975; Sameroff & Fiese, 2000). A history of the research on resilience is beyond the scope of this book (for a review, see Masten, 2014); nevertheless, some of the principles of PACEs are built directly on seminal resilience studies.

In an extensive review of the resilience literature, Masten (2014) provided a "Short List of Widely Reported Factors Associated With Resilience." Her list includes "effective caregiving and quality parenting; close relationships with other capable adults; close friends and romantic partners; intelligence and problem-solving skills; self-control, emotion regulation, planfulness; motivation to succeed; self-efficacy; faith, hope, belief life has meaning; effective schools; and effective neighborhoods, collective efficacy" (p. 148). Our PACEs including parenting, mentors, best friends, and good schools are similar to factors on this list. However, in our PACEs work, we focus primarily on *modifiable* resilience factors and processes—relationships that can be developed and strengthened, as well as resources that can be provided or enhanced. As seen from Masten's short list, many resilience researchers have focused more on internal traits such as optimism and intelligence, whereas others have studied processes such as emotion regulation and coping.

Many argue that the current focus of resilience research examines processes across systems (e.g., biological, social, contextual, and familial; Henry, Morris, & Harrist, 2015; Masten, 2007). In the next section of our book, we describe many of these processes and systems, bringing together health, neuroscience, epidemiological, and developmental research to shed light on how protective and adverse experiences get "under our skin," become a part of our self, and promote or hinder our resilience.

OUR RESEARCH ON PACEs

Our work has been influenced by these foundational theories and studies. After creating the PACEs survey, we began to test and distribute the PACEs in our own research studies and during ACEs talks we gave in the community and at scientific conferences. The study of PACEs fit well with Amanda's research program on parenting and children's emotion regulation and with Jennifer's research on environmental conditions (e.g., poverty, adversity, culture) that affect health. Our first study specifically examining PACEs was part of Amanda's Undergraduate Research Methods course. Students administered ACEs, PACEs, and other surveys to friends, family members, and other students. Analysis of that study revealed that higher PACEs were associated with lower ACEs and higher education and income, and it also showed that PACEs protected against negative parenting attitudes among individuals with high ACEs (Hays-Grudo & Morris, 2018; Morris et al., 2015). This study provided initial evidence that PACEs protect against the negative effects of ACEs (specifically harsh parenting attitudes) and that PACEs were associated with more resources and education. Next, we gave the PACEs survey to more than 900 adults across the United States, using an online survey method. Results replicated our previous finding that PACEs were negatively correlated with ACEs. We also found that PACEs were associated with greater self-reported adult attachment security, mental well-being, and higher income and education (Morris et al., 2016). From a research perspective, these results were especially significant as they demonstrated reliability and validity for the PACEs—reliability because people from different backgrounds answered the PACEs questionnaire in an internally consistent way, and validity because PACEs were associated with expected factors such as ACEs, depressive symptoms, and parenting attitudes and behaviors (Morris, Treat, et al., 2018).

Several years ago, in preparation for this book, we wrote several blogs on ACEs and PACEs and shared them with students in an undergraduate Introduction to Human Development and Family Science class to test some of our concepts. We presented the basic information to the students, had them complete the ACEs and PACEs surveys, and then provided weekly blogs for their feedback and reflection. Their responses were often striking, sometimes sad (many had high ACEs), sometimes hopeful, and sometimes naive. Our students reflected that "knowing your PACE score is just as important as knowing your ACE score," "it is important to know about ACEs and PACEs because it helps you better understand yourself and relate to others," "learning about ACEs and PACEs made me feel blessed and grateful," and "knowing this information makes me want to continue to grow my personal PACEs and to reach out to my friends and loved ones who might not be as fortunate as I am." Following that semester, we conducted several studies with OSU students, comparing ACEs and PACEs scores with students' mental and physical health. We recruited students who had a history of trauma and adversity. Results match much of what we discussed in Chapter 1: 13% had four or more ACEs, and ACEs were associated with depression, general health, and fewer PACEs (Ratliff et al., 2019; Roberts et al., 2015).

We continue to use PACEs in our research, particularly on parenting interventions and adversity, and continue to find similar results and themes. We always present PACEs when we present ACEs at conferences, and audience members are universally struck by the importance of including PACEs as the counterpoint to ACEs. We present the ACEs questionnaire on one side of the page and the PACEs questionnaire on the other. One audience member recently shared that she had known about ACEs research for years but that turning the page over and seeing the PACEs items changed her life. She never thought there might be an antidote to ACEs. Learning about PACEs gave her encouragement and hope. The following story describes a similar experience.

KNOWING ONE'S PACE SCORE

Several years ago, at a meeting with civic and foundation leaders, Jennifer presented background information on ACEs and our initial work on PACEs. In doing so, as we routinely do, she gave the audience the two questionnaires on one double-sided sheet of paper. The group was riveted by the research. It prompted them to think about their own experiences and how ACEs explain many problems and conditions in their lives and in those around them, and how PACEs suggest new approaches to social problems in our community. One member of the group, a well-respected and much-admired community leader, shared her experience, saying, "Wow. My ACE score is high. If I had only taken the ACEs and not the PACEs, I would have felt broken." For her, learning about ACEs without PACEs would have been devastating, but PACEs helped her make sense of her life, creating a more complete narrative.

We maintain that it is critical to present PACEs along with ACEs. You completed the ACEs survey in Chapter 1; now we invite you to complete the PACEs questionnaire (see Figure 2.2). As with ACEs, there are PACEs that may not be on our list. We chose our items on the basis of developmental research, and we focused on childhood experiences that are relevant to most individuals. However, other PACEs may have been important in your life, such as having a close relationship with a pet, being attached to a sibling, or experiencing another culture. When taking the survey, feel free to identify other protective factors you experienced before age 18.

FIGURE 2.2. Protective and Compensatory Experiences (PACEs)

When you were growing up, prior to your 18th birthday:

1. Did you have someone who loved you unconditionally (you did not doubt that they cared about you)?   YES   NO

2. Did you have at least one best friend (someone you could trust, had fun with)?   YES   NO

3. Did you do anything regularly to help others (e.g., volunteer at a hospital, nursing home, church) or do special projects in the community to help others (food drives, Habitat for Humanity)?   YES   NO

4. Were you regularly involved in organized sports groups (e.g., soccer, basketball, track) or other physical activity (e.g., competitive cheer, gymnastics, dance, marching band)?   YES   NO

5. Were you an active member of at least one civic group or a non-sport social group such as scouts, religious group, or youth group?   YES   NO

6. Did you have an engaging hobby—an artistic/creative or intellectual pastime either alone or in a group (e.g., chess club, debate team, musical instrument or vocal group, theater, spelling bee, or did you read a lot)?   YES   NO

7. Was there an adult (not your parent) you trusted and could count on when you needed help or advice (e.g., coach, teacher, minister, neighbor, relative)?   YES   NO

8. Was your home typically clean AND safe with enough food to eat?   YES   NO

9. Overall, did your schools provide the resources and academic experiences you needed to learn?   YES   NO

10. In your home, were there rules that were clear and fairly administered?   YES   NO

11. Additional PACEs: _____   YES   NO

From "Integrating research and theory on early relationships to guide intervention and prevention," by A. S. Morris, A. E. Treat, J. Hays-Grudo, T. Chesher, A. C. Williamson, and J. Mendez, in A. S. Morris and A. C. Williamson (Eds.), *Building Early Social and Emotional Relationships With Infants and Toddlers* (p. 21), 2018, Cham, Switzerland: Springer. Copyright 2018 by Springer. Reprinted with permission.

II

HOW EARLY EXPERIENCE INFLUENCES THE BODY, BRAIN, AND BEHAVIOR

. . . how many mental health problems, from drug addiction to self-injurious behavior, start off as attempts to cope with unmanageable emotions. Stifling inner cries for help does not stop the mobilization of stress hormones.

—BESSEL VAN DER KOLK, 2016, p. 268

INTRODUCTION

In the previous two chapters, we described the evidence for the enduring effects of adverse childhood experiences (ACEs) and the theoretical and research findings for the protective and compensatory experiences (PACEs) that may help explain the positive developmental outcomes achieved by many despite having experienced high levels of adversity. The data linking ACEs and subsequent development, health, and health-harming behavior across cultures and regions of the world are compelling and perturbing. They suggest that rates of childhood adversity have been grossly underestimated and that ACEs have been overlooked as a major source of costly chronic health conditions, societal problems, and other forms of human misery. There can be no question that childhood trauma and adversity are powerful predictors of development and health, and that positive relationships and resources have the power to promote resilience and healthy outcomes.

Given the *what*—the effects of ACEs—the questions we address in this section relate to the *how*—the behavioral and neurobiological processes that are beginning to emerge as explanations for these effects. These questions also address the processes at work in protective experiences: What explains the evidence that warm and supportive relationships and enriched environments mitigate the effects of adversity? These are complex questions, and are being investigated from many different fields using multiple perspectives and models. Creating a comprehensive picture of the problem and its potential solutions requires delving into disciplines about which many of us have had limited exposure or only basic knowledge—disciplines such as immunology and stress biology, neuroscience and neuroimaging, epigenetics and genetics, comparative behavior, as well as infant mental health, parenting, and developmental psychology, among others.

We pose and discuss these questions because by seeking a fuller understanding of the neurobiological effects of trauma and stress on the developing child, we are better able to develop and evaluate protective and therapeutic environments and interventions. In the next two chapters, we summarize and discuss the proverbial elephant who was described by a team of blind-folded scientists: All of us are able to "see" the part of the elephant in front of us, none of us the whole. Our goal is to integrate the various approaches and explanatory evidence linking early life adversity and protective factors with health and behavioral outcomes and so improve the odds for children at risk.

3

Effects of Early Life Adversity on Neurobiological Development

. . . it shouldn't require molecular genetics or neuroendocrinology factoids to prove that childhood matters and thus that it profoundly matters to provide childhoods filled with good health and safety, love and nurturance and opportunity. But insofar as it seems to require precisely that sort of scientific validation at times, more power to those factoids.

—ROBERT SAPOLSKY, 2017, p. 222

In Romania in 1966, to increase his country's population, communist leader Nicolae Ceauşescu outlawed all forms of contraception. At the same time, his dictatorial regime devastated the economy, and many families could not afford to keep their babies. The horrifying result was approximately 170,000 children raised in 700 government-run, overcrowded institutions and orphanages. The Romanian children languished in their cribs most of the day, with little care-giver interaction, stimulation, or toys. Many ended up with stunted growth, delayed language, and odd social behaviors. The children would raise their arms to be picked up but would then push adults away. The children self-soothed by rocking back and forth in their cribs and were disturbingly quiet (Nelson, Fox, & Zeanah, 2014; Zeanah et al., 2003).

In 1989, the regime was overthrown, and the world discovered the crushing neglect these children experienced. Child psychiatrists and developmental scientists in the United States were involved in the creation of foster care and an adoption system, obtaining funding from the National Institutes of Health to assess the effects of early deprivation and therapeutic foster care (Zeanah

http://dx.doi.org/10.1037/0000177-003

Adverse and Protective Childhood Experiences: A Developmental Perspective, by J. Hays-Grudo and A. S. Morris

45

et al., 2003). Because there were not enough high-quality foster homes, they randomized 136 infants to either quality foster homes or care as usual. Another group of Romanian infants who were never institutionalized were included as a normative comparison group. Using multiple assessment methods, researchers found deficits in almost every domain examined in children who remained institutionalized. They had low levels of brain activity and reduced levels of gray matter (neuronal cell bodies, dendrites, and synapses) and white matter (fatty white myelin sheath surrounding the axons connecting gray matter). In addition, they also demonstrated profound patterns of dysregulation in their responses to distress, extreme impairment in IQ, problems with attention, reduced telomere length (an indicator of premature cellular aging), significant problems in social and emotional development, and greater mental health problems. The researchers concluded that these differences were not caused by malnutrition or poverty but by lack of human contact and connection—the absence of a responsive, consistent caregiver. In general, children placed in the newly created foster homes before age 2 had better outcomes than those placed in foster care after age 2, suggesting the importance of early intervention. The fostered children also showed fewer brain differences and delays (Nelson, 2013, 2017). The Bucharest Early Intervention Project illustrates our biological need for nurturance and love and the devastating developmental effects when these basic bonding needs are not met early in life (Nelson, Fox, & Zeanah, 2014).

MODELS OF BIOBEHAVIORAL RESPONSES TO CHILDHOOD ADVERSITY

In this chapter, we summarize what is known about the effects of early life adversity on the body and the brain. Stress has direct effects on the developing body via the immune, metabolic, and endocrine systems, as well as indirect effects through the multiple stress-regulating hormones that affect brain development and, thus, cognitive, social, and emotional development and behavior. A number of models have been proposed to help organize the complexity of the body and brain's response to stress. We describe the primary models and theories that have shaped our understanding of the observed effects of adverse childhood experiences (ACEs) on health and development. We examine human and animal studies and the findings that support these models and generate new research questions and clinical applications. We conclude with a new model that accommodates and integrates these multidisciplinary findings and provides a framework for future prevention, intervention, and policy initiatives.

The ACEs Pyramid

When the original ACEs study was published in 1998 (Felitti et al., 1998), the authors included a pyramid-shaped model to explain the relationships they observed between ACEs and health behavior and between ACEs and chronic health conditions. At the base of the pyramid (see Figure 3.1; Centers for Disease Control and Prevention, 2018) are ACEs, and in successive layers building on them are their proposed sequelae: Social, Emotional and Cognitive Impairment; Adoption of Health-Risk Behaviors; Disease, Disability, and Social Problems; topped off by Early Death. An arrow on the left denotes the *Whole Life Perspective*, from conception to death. Versions of this model were also posted on the Centers for Disease Control and Prevention's (CDC's) ACEs website and include two arrows on the right labeled *Scientific Gaps* between the layers linking ACEs with developmental impairments and risky health behavior. Because Felitti had heard patients describe direct links between experiencing abuse and adopting health-risk behaviors, such as overeating, there was reason to believe traumatized individuals might cope with adversity by adopting short-term solutions that had long-term health-harming consequences. At the time, however, little was known about this process. Even less was known about the relationship between ACEs and cognitive, social, emotional, and developmental milestones.

In 2018, we had an opportunity to ask Dr. Robert Anda, coauthor of the original ACEs study, about this model when he came to consult with our research center. When asked if he remembered the Scientific Gaps version of the model, which is sometimes still found on various websites, he laughed and said, "Of course I remember! I put them there!" He elaborated that the Kaiser Permanente and CDC research team hypothesized the relationships but had no data in the late 1990s that supported the model. At that point they

FIGURE 3.1. Early Adverse Childhood Experiences Model

Reprinted from "Adverse Childhood Experiences Presentation Graphics," by Centers for Disease Control and Prevention, 2018 (https://www.cdc.gov/violenceprevention/childabuseandneglect/acestudy/ace-graphics.html). In the public domain.

were still convincing people their data were correct, as no one initially believed the strength of the study findings linking ACEs and subsequent health outcomes. The CDC epidemiologists ran the analyses several times to convince themselves and their colleagues, and they had to submit the original paper to multiple journals before it was finally accepted by the *American Journal of Preventive Medicine*. Now with 2 decades of replicating results, we realize how revolutionary these findings were in 1998. Who would have believed that a single number from a 10-item nonmedical questionnaire would be a more powerful predictor of cancer than any other known risk factor? Not only cancer, but heart disease, chronic lung disease, stroke, diabetes, fractures, early death, depression, drug use, suicide attempts, and so on. No theoretical framework existed at that time that could explain these findings.

The ACEs pyramid model currently depicted on the CDC website and elsewhere (see Figure 3.2; CDC, 2018) differs little from the initial model developed more than 20 years ago. It is essentially a life-course model, depicting the proximal and distal consequences of ACEs in a cumulative and interrelated process. It can be summarized as follows: Adverse experiences have immediate and enduring effects on neurobiological development, resulting in deficits in cognitive skills, social relationships, and emotion regulation, increasing the likelihood of adopting short-term coping behaviors that have

FIGURE 3.2. Current Adverse Childhood Experiences Model

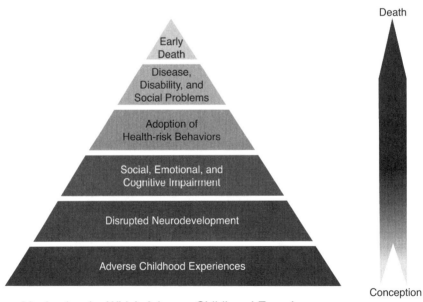

Mechanism by Which Adverse Childhood Experiences
Influence Health and Well-being Throughout the Lifespan

Adapted from "Adverse Childhood Experiences Presentation Graphics," by Centers for Disease Control and Prevention, 2018 (https://www.cdc.gov/violenceprevention/childabuseandneglect/acestudy/ace-graphics.html). In the public domain.

negative health consequences, which in turn increase the risk of chronic diseases and social problems, ultimately culminating in premature mortality.

Although no model explained the connection between early adversity and later health problems before the ACEs model, there were several decades of research documenting the effects of early life trauma and stress on behavior and development. Researchers in the field of child abuse and neglect had shown that abused and neglected children were more likely to have problems with aggression and impulse control (Cole & Putnam, 1992; van der Kolk, Perry, & Herman, 1991), attentional and dissociative problems (Chu & Dill, 1990; Teicher et al., 2003; van der Kolk et al., 1996); and difficulty with social relationships (Cicchetti & Schneider-Rosen, 1984; Finkelhor & Kendall-Tackett, 1997; Finkelhor, Ormrod, & Turner, 2007).

There was evidence of a causal link between early adversity and later health-harming behaviors and chronic health conditions (Anda et al., 2006). What was not well understood or agreed on were the mechanisms and processes instrumental in producing these effects. Were the negative effects of adversity the result of learned behavior (you get hit, you hit)? Were they the result of genetic aberrations passed from parent to child? With the publication of the ACE study results, it became clear that diverse childhood adversities had cumulative effects that were not fully explained by existing theories, particularly those that focused on nature versus nurture. Scientific theories are frequently overhauled or abandoned as new data accumulate that are not well explained by existing theories (Kuhn, 1963). We began to realize the need for an integrative model that encompasses the interplay between biology and behavior, genes and environment, to explain the complex and enduring effects of early life experience (Halfon, Larson, Lu, Tullis, & Russ, 2014).

Allostasis and Allostatic Load

In 1998, the same year in which ACEs data were first published, Dr. Bruce McEwen's paper in the *New England Journal of Medicine* vastly improved our understanding of the effects of acute and chronic stress. Drawing from experimental research in his and others' labs using primarily animal models (Sapolsky, 1992; Sapolsky, Krey, & McEwen, 1986), McEwen (1998) developed a model of the body's stress response using the concepts of allostasis and allostatic load. *Allostasis* is defined as the body's coordinated response to a threat or stressor from multiple biological systems, and *allostatic load* is the cumulative "wear and tear on the body and brain resulting from prolonged activation of stress-response systems that are normally used in brief, crisis-response type situations" (p. 37). In response to an existential threat, all systems mount a coordinated response to ensure survival.

Imagine that you are hiking in the woods on a beautiful sunny day. As you stop to pick some berries from a giant blueberry bush . . . BEAR! *BEAR!* ***BEAR!*** What happens in your body even as you only imagine this scene is a small glimpse of what actually occurs when the danger is present and immediate.

Your adrenal glands immediately begin to pump out adrenalin, making your heart beat faster so you can jump higher and run faster; the hypothalamic–pituitary–adrenal (HPA) axis delivers cortisol, a long-acting hormone, to enhance your cardiovascular function and raise blood sugar for the energy you will need for a prolonged fight or foot race; and your immune system dumps a variety of cytokines (small proteins that enable your immune system to communicate within its own network and with other organs) into your blood system just in case the bear gets his claws into you. This *fight, flight,* or *freeze* response works. We are the descendants of generations and generations of humans who outran bears and other threats to survive, but the system did not evolve to cope with prolonged stress (see Figure 3.3). In this model, the brain perceives and coordinates responses to threats and stressors, sometimes even before we are aware of them (e.g., changes in ambient temperature or atmospheric pressure). Individual differences based on genes, development, and experience influence behavioral responses, which subsequently influence future physiological responses depending on whether the behaviors help (e.g., exercise) or hinder (e.g., substance abuse) the body's response to stress (Doan, Dich, & Evans, 2014). When our stress response is overused, allostatic load results. Allostatic load explains the paradox of how the stress response, which can keep us alive, can also kill us.

Allostatic load can play out in several ways. In Figure 3.4, the top graph depicts the normal response, with an immediate physiological reaction (e.g., measured heart rate, stress hormones, respiration rate), followed by a recovery period when the threat or stress is over. In experiments with animals exposed to a variety of stressors, four types of allostatic load have been found: (a) repeated "hits," (b) lack of adaptation, (c) prolonged response with no recovery, and (d) inadequate responses. Indicators of allostatic load include high blood pressure (prolonged response) and a "flattened" (either high

FIGURE 3.3. Stress Response and Development of Allostatic Load

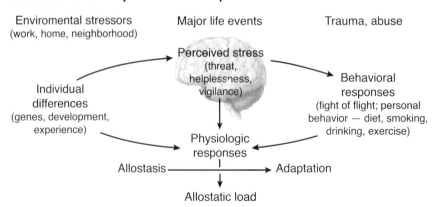

From "Allostatic Load Biomarkers of Chronic Stress and Impact on Health and Cognition," by R.-P. Juster, B. S. McEwen, and S. J. Lupien, 2010, *Neuroscience & Biobehavioral Reviews, 35*, p. 3. Copyright 2010 by Elsevier. Reprinted with permission.

FIGURE 3.4. Four Types of Allostatic Load

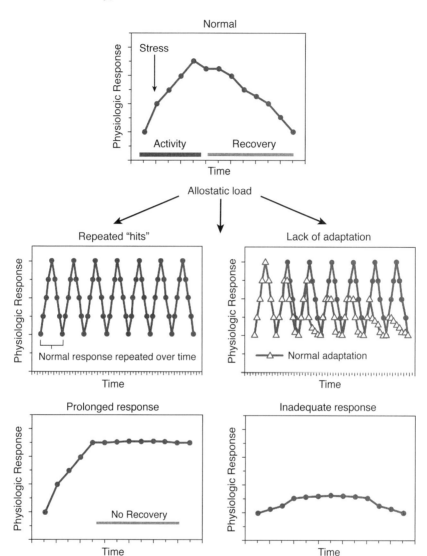

From "Allostatic Load Biomarkers of Chronic Stress and Impact on Health and Cognition," by R.-P. Juster, B. S. McEwen, and S. J. Lupien, 2010, *Neuroscience & Biobehavioral Reviews, 35*, p. 4. Copyright 2010 by Elsevier. Reprinted with permission.

or low) diurnal pattern in cortisol, a hormone produced in response to stress that is normally higher in the morning, helping us rise and shine, and lowest at bedtime, allowing us to wind down and sleep. These physical effects may be accompanied by strong feelings of anxiety and depression or an exaggerated response to risk and a diminished response to reward.

Allostatic load provides a plausible argument for the causal relationship between early life adversity and its attendant stress with multiple types of health problems. In experimental studies with animals and in clinical and epidemiological research with humans, the effects of repeated and prolonged stress have been shown to damage multiple systems, including neurological (brain structure and function and cognitive and affective function; Pechtel & Pizzagalli, 2011), endocrine (cortisol and other stress hormones that affect bone loss and other systems), immunological (measures of inflammation such as C-reactive protein; Deighton, Neville, Pusch, & Dobson, 2018; Taylor, Lehman, Kiefe, & Seeman, 2006), cardiovascular (blood pressure; Lehman, Taylor, Kiefe, & Seeman, 2009), and coronary calcification (Juonala et al., 2016). Allostatic load damages multiple biobehavioral systems, and the effects are even more detrimental when the stress exposure and response occur during development (Danese & McEwen, 2012; Moffitt, 2013).

Toxic Stress

The term *toxic stress* is sometimes confused with allostatic load but involves more than physiological wear and tear on the body. Toxic stress was coined by the National Scientific Council on the Developing Child, a group of researchers convened by Dr. Jack Shonkoff to help translate scientific development concepts into language for policy makers. Toxic stress in childhood is serious and sustained stress that is experienced without adequate adult support, damaging the developing body and brain (Shonkoff et al., 2012). It differs from positive stress, which is short term and can be adaptive, and from tolerable stress, which is more prolonged and potentially damaging but is buffered by supportive relationships. This concept is a particularly useful addition to the study of ACEs and allostatic load because it highlights the important role of supportive and nurturing relationships in mitigating the damaging effects of exposure to severe and prolonged stress during childhood.

Biological Embedding of Stress

As more data from animal and human studies have documented the profound effects of stress on development, researchers began to characterize the process as stress "getting under the skin" or becoming *biologically embedded* (Berens, Jensen, & Nelson, 2017; Miller, Chen, & Parker, 2011; Nelson, 2018). Biological embedding occurs when (a) experiences alter biological and developmental processes; (b) systematic differences in experiences, especially in childhood, lead to systematically different biological and developmental states; (c) resulting differences are stable and long term; and (d) these differences have the capacity to influence health, well-being, learning, or behavior over the life course (Hertzman, 2012).

   Ample evidence indicates that childhood adversity meets the conditions for biological embedding, with stable and long-term changes occurring in multiple biological systems, including brain structure and function (McEwen, 2012), neuroendocrine responses (Bruce, Gunnar, Pears, & Fisher, 2013), autonomic functioning (El-Sheikh et al., 2009), immunity and inflammation (Slopen,

McLaughlin, Dunn, & Koenen, 2013), and metabolic functioning (Maniam, Antoniadis, & Morris, 2014; for a more detailed review, see Berens et al., 2017). These modifications affect health, learning, and behavior (Krugers et al., 2017). Miller and colleagues (2011) proposed a developmental model synthesizing behavioral and biological research on adversity and stress; it includes components and concepts drawn from models described previously, including the Barker hypotheses (described in Chapter 4, this volume), life-course models emphasizing trajectories (Hertzman, 2012), allostasis and allostatic load (McEwen, 2012), and the Risky Families model and research documenting the enduring effects of psychosocial environments (Repetti et al., 2002).

This amalgamated model proposes that childhood stress "programs" immune system cells to behave in a hypervigilant manner, resulting in detrimental outcomes. For example, specialized immune cells, such as macrophages, normally behave as sentinels out in the various organs and tissues to alert the rest of the immune system of infection or injury. In addition to helping clean out infected tissue, they play an important role by sending warning signals to nearby blood vessels, other immune cells, and the brain that there is an infection or danger. This is an essential and beneficial process called inflammation that has helped humans survive. However, problems arise when childhood stress wires these cells to be more easily excitable and more likely to release "proinflammatory" danger signals, even in the absence of infection or injury. This physiological "crying wolf" results in a chronic inflammatory state and contributes to chronic diseases associated with aging, such as heart disease, stroke, cancer, and osteoporosis. Making matters worse, these proinflammatory tendencies are exacerbated by behavioral tendencies (e.g., hypervigilance, social isolation, poor emotion regulation) and hormonal dysregulation (particularly stress hormones, such as cortisol) that are themselves the result of early life stress. Of particular note for our discussion, researchers using this approach have found that maternal warmth (retrospectively reported) may offset some of these negative health consequences in adulthood (Chen, Miller, Kobor, & Cole, 2011), a topic we discuss more fully in Chapters 4 and 6.

This model has had a major effect on the study of early life adversity. As one of the first psychological models to incorporate information from diverse fields such as biomedical and life-course epidemiology, clinical medicine, pathophysiology, and animal models, it has greatly influenced the way that we think about how childhood disadvantage and maltreatment influence current and future health and development. However, this model, with its focus on inflammation and chronic diseases related to aging, does not easily accommodate the multiple reciprocal effects of ACEs, nor does it address the effects of positive or compensatory experiences promoting resilience. Understanding the mechanisms underlying adversity's damaging effects on healthy development requires a second generation of research, one that emphasizes the multidirectional transactions among biological systems. Miller and colleagues (Nusslock & Miller, 2016) recently proposed a *neuro-immune network hypothesis*. This framework emphasizes the multiple bidirectional pathways that link inflammation with brain regions involved in threat, reward, and executive control, thus explaining the link between ACEs and risky health behaviors—that is, adopting short-term coping strategies with disastrous long-term consequences. As with previous models, however, it does not incorporate protective factors or propose processes to account for resilience.

EPIGENETICS AND CHILDHOOD ADVERSITY

As psychologists who study the importance of context and relationships, we are particularly intrigued with the idea of epigenetics, that is, environmental influences that turn genes "on and off." *Epigenetics* literally means "on top of the genes" and refers to changes in the way genes are expressed (phenotype) without changing DNA itself (genotype). This relatively new field of research has generated compelling evidence for a causal relationship between early life experiences and physiological systems, adult behavior, and even the physiology and behavior of future generations.

The Basics of Epigenetics

All cells contain chromosomes with long double strands of DNA that contain genes. These DNA strands contain information, stored as a chemical code, which is transcribed in the form of RNA and goes on to create the various functional proteins produced inside cells (see Exhibit 3.1 for definitions of terms used in this section).

EXHIBIT 3.1

Definitions of Genetic and Epigenetic Terms

DNA (deoxyribonucleic acid): a self-replicating material that is present in nearly all living organisms as the main constituent of chromosomes. It is the carrier of genetic information.

RNA (ribonucleic acid): a nucleic acid present in all living cells. Its principal role is to act as a messenger carrying instructions from DNA.

Epigenetics: A term first used (Waddington, 1942) to describe stress-induced changes in the phenotype (gene expression) without changes in the genotype (DNA sequencing code).

DNA methylation, which occurs when a *methyl group* (an organic compound of one carbon atom bonded to three hydrogen atoms) attaches to the DNA, making it more difficult to be read and transcribed into RNA. Methylation typically functions as the "dimmer switch."

Histones are bundles of proteins that the DNA is wound around. *Histone modification* relaxes histones, making it easier to read the DNA.

MicroRNAs are molecules regulating the steps involved in translating RNA to proteins.

Epigenetic changes occur when chemical compounds, such as methyl groups, attach themselves to parts of the DNA strands, to histones (bundles of proteins around which DNA are wound), or to the promoter regions of microRNA genes (molecules that regulate the steps involved in turning RNA into protein). A schematic of this process if provided in Figure 3.5. Early life adversity activates different epigenetic responses that are based in part on genetic makeup as well as previous generational epigenetic markings. This process leads to immediate or short-term alterations in the body's reactivity to stress, as well as to longer term adaptations via epigenetic changes to genes that regulate neural networks, hormones, neurotransmitters, and neuropeptides. Ultimately, this results in behaviors that increase or decrease adaptation to the individual's environment (Gröger et al., 2016). There is considerable evidence for the broad framework of this process in both animal and human research.

Much of this research, especially studies with humans, focuses on DNA methylation. DNA methylation is often referred to as an "on–off" switch, but it actually functions more like a dimmer switch because the silencing of the gene varies with the amount of methylation occurring. An excellent explanation of these processes can be found in Lester, Conradt, and Marsit's (2016) introduction to the special section on epigenetics in *Child Development*. Although many in the social and behavioral sciences are relatively unfamiliar with the science of epigenetics, understanding these biological reactions to environmental experiences creates exciting new opportunities for preventing and treating childhood adversity.

Epigenetic Research With Animal Models

The first research on the epigenetic effects of early maternal care on adult health and behavior was conducted in the rodent labs of Drs. Michael Meaney and Moshe Szyf (for reviews, see Doherty & Roth, 2016; Szyf, McGowan, & Meaney, 2008). They observed that naturally occurring individual differences in maternal care during the first few weeks of life were associated with individual differences in both the behavioral and biological responses to stress in the offspring (Francis, Diorio, Liu, & Meaney, 1999; Liu et al., 1997). As adults, the offspring of high-maternal-care dams (i.e., high levels of licking and grooming), compared with the offspring of low-maternal-care dams (i.e., low levels of licking and grooming) were less fearful when placed in novel surroundings (exploring more) and had reduced production of the hormones that activate the HPA system. Moreover, the low-maternal-care offspring had higher levels of DNA methylation, reducing the expression of the glucocorticoid receptor (GR) gene promotor in the hippocampus. Reducing the GR gene promotor is important for stress regulation because it results in a lack of negative feedback in the HPA system, thus exaggerating the rodents' stress responses as adults (Weaver et al., 2004).

In animal research, the epigenetic effects are reversible by injecting chemicals that interfered with the methylation process or by changing the

FIGURE 3.5. Interplay of Gene × Environment Response to Stress

```
                    ┌─────────────────────────────┐
                    │        Environment          │
                    │  Early life stress (timing, │
                    │            type)            │
                    │           Gender            │
                    └─────────────────────────────┘
                                  ↓
                    ┌─────────────────────────────┐
                    │    Genetic/epigenetic       │
                    │       predisposition        │
                    │    Vulnerable vs. resilient │
                    └─────────────────────────────┘
                                  ↓
                    ┌─────────────────────────────┐
                    │     Short-term effects      │
                    │  Acute/dynamic epigenetic   │
                    │          changes            │
                    │ Alterations in endocrine    │
                    │      hormone systems        │
                    │ Acute changes in gene       │
                    │        expression           │
                    └─────────────────────────────┘
                                  ↓
                    ┌─────────────────────────────┐
                    │   Long-term adaptations     │
                    │      Neuronal networks      │
                    │   Stress hormone systems    │
                    │     Transmitter systems     │
                    │    Neuropeptide systems     │
                    │   Stable epigenetic marks   │
                    └─────────────────────────────┘
                Positive                      Negative
     ┌───────────────────────┐    ┌───────────────────────┐
     │   Adapted behavioral  │    │      Maladapted       │
     │       strategies      │    │  behavioral strategies│
     │       Resilience      │    │  Dysfunctional behavior│
     │                       │    │     Psychopathology   │
     └───────────────────────┘    └───────────────────────┘
```

From "The Transgenerational Transmission of Childhood Adversity: Behavioral, Cellular, and Epigenetic Correlates," by N. Gröger, E. Matas, T. Gos, A. Lesse, G. Poeggel, K. Braun, and J. Bock, 2016, *Journal of Neural Transmission*, *123*, p. 1045. Copyright 2016 by Springer Nature. Reprinted with permission.

environment, often by cross-fostering. *Cross-fostering* is a type of adoption process in which researchers switch the newborn offspring of mothers high in maternal care to low-maternal-care mothers, and vice versa. In cross-fostering studies, resulting patterns of DNA methylation at a GR promotor gene in the offsprings' hippocampi were associated with the foster mothers, not the birth mothers (Francis et al., 1999). In other words, the methylation patterns of pups born to neglecting mothers who had been fostered by nurturing dams were indistinguishable from pups born to and raised by the nurturing dams; the behavior of the nurturing foster mother overcame the biology of the birth mothers. Researchers have also experimentally manipulated rodent pups' exposure to stress during the first few weeks of life—for example, through daily maternal separation. Even brief maternal separation resulted in epigenetic alterations that increased stress reactivity via HPA axis activity and in memory deficits, decreased stress coping (Murgatroyd et al., 2009), and increased freezing behavior in response to stress (Toda et al., 2014; for a review, see Blaze & Roth, 2015).

Genes related to brain plasticity are also highly sensitive to early maternal care. Dr. Tania Roth and colleagues investigated the effects of stressed and abusive maternal care in rodents on methylation of the *BDNF* gene, which is important in neural plasticity and neuron health. In these studies, stressed maternal caregiving was induced by placing dams in an unfamiliar environment with limited bedding material shortly before introducing pups into the environment for nursing (Blaze & Roth, 2013; Roth, Lubin, Funk, & Sweatt, 2009; Roth & Sweatt, 2011). In the stressed conditions, the dams were more likely to step on, drag, or actively avoid pups, and were lower in normative maternal care, such as licking and grooming. The pups' brief exposure to this stressed and adverse caregiving resulted in changes in DNA methylation of the *BDNF* gene, which persisted into adulthood. Months after this exposure, the grown pups still had significantly lower levels of *BDNF* mRNA in the prefrontal cortex (PFC) and increased methylated *BDNF* DNA (Roth & Sweatt, 2011). These studies consistently found enduring negative behavioral responses and epigenetic alterations across the life span of the offspring, particularly changes that upset brain regions and systems involved in regulating and adapting to stress—that is, the PFC, amygdala, and hippocampus (Doherty & Roth, 2016). What is especially noteworthy about this research is the finding that altered *BDNF* methylation patterns were also found in the offspring of the generation that experienced early mistreatment, a generation never exposed directly to adverse conditions (Roth et al., 2009). This and other research on the intergenerational transmission of epigenetic and behavioral responses to adversity and stress are described more in Chapter 4, this volume.

Epigenetic Research With Human Populations

Animal experiments provide compelling evidence that early life adversity alters genes across the life span and in subsequent generations. A growing number of studies has also documented the critical role of epigenetic pro-graming in the enduring effects of adverse childhood experiences in humans (Gershon & High, 2015), although the role of human intergenerational epigenetic transmission is less understood at this time.

Epigenetic changes have been observed in response to a variety of maternal stresses during the prenatal period, including wartime famine (Heijmans et al., 2008), natural disasters (Cao-Lei et al., 2014) and maternal depression and stress (Braithwaite, Kundakovic, Ramchandani, Murphy, & Champagne, 2015; Nemoda et al., 2015). Oberlander and colleagues (2008) were among the first to link prenatal exposure to maternal depressed mood with methylation of *NR3C1* (a human GR gene in newborns), even at nonclinical levels of depression. Methylation status was also associated with infant stress cortisol reactivity at 3 months, suggesting that prenatal maternal depression is related to infant stress responsiveness via an epigenetic link involving *NR3C1* methylation. This is a plausible mechanistic explanation because cortisol is produced by HPA axis activity in response to stress. Glucocorticoid receptors bind to cortisol in the blood stream, reducing further HPA activity and preventing more cortisol from being produced. When *NR3C1* is silenced or diminished, fewer glucocorticoid receptors are available for binding to cortisol and removing it from the system, exaggerating the stress response.

Researchers found different patterns of *NR3C1* methylation when they compared postmortem hippocampal samples from suicide victims with and without a history of childhood abuse and to control subjects who died suddenly of unrelated causes (McGowan et al., 2009). This study was the first to translate findings from animal models to humans by comparing brain tissue and epigenetic changes with known early life stress histories. They found reduced hippocampal volume in individuals with a history of child abuse that were associated with epigenetic changes in a major GR gene promotor, replicating research done in animal models.

Childhood adversity has been found to affect other genes as well. For example, researchers identified associations between childhood stress and methylation of *SLC6A4*, a gene that regulates serotonin exposure (Montirosso et al., 2016), and between childhood abuse and methylation of the oxytocin receptor (Smearman et al., 2016). Another research strategy has been to conduct genome-wide scans to identify associations between childhood adversity and novel DNA methylation patterns (Papale, Seltzer, Madrid, Pollak, & Alisch, 2018). Essex and colleagues (2013) collected extensive data from mothers and fathers during their children's infant and preschool years and buccal epithelial cells (cells from cheek swabs) for DNA analyses from their children at age 15. Findings revealed that DNA methylation in midadolescence was associated with maternal stress during infancy and with paternal stress during the preschool years. Sex differences were observed, with mothers' stress related to epigenetic changes in both boys and girls, whereas fathers' reported stress was associated more with changes in girls.

There is mounting evidence that the epigenetic changes observed in animal models of early life adversity are also operating in cases of childhood adversity.

These changes, primarily methylation of genes that regulate the stress response systems, again illustrate that short-term adaptations to ensure survival in a hostile or disadvantaged environment program the body in ways that are maladaptive in other contexts. This adaptation to adversity is also evident in the development of the brain.

EFFECTS OF CHILDHOOD ADVERSITY ON BRAIN STRUCTURE AND FUNCTION

There is no denying that childhood maltreatment and trauma impair development and mental health. It has been estimated that maltreatment accounts for almost half of childhood psychiatric disorders, and general childhood adversity accounts for a significant percentage as well (Green et al., 2010). As discussed earlier in the chapter, stress affects the physiological systems controlled by the brain, resulting in physical changes and developmental deficiencies. Stress hormones, such as cortisol, change the structure of neurons and dendrites and can suppress and influence the formation of new neurons (McEwen, 1998). Such changes are more evident during sensitive periods of increased brain plasticity and in regions that develop later and are rich in stress hormone receptors (e.g., glucocorticoids; Teicher & Samson, 2016). These differences can be measured by examining the structure of brain regions (e.g., volume of gray and white matter) and functional patterns and connectivity during tasks designed to elicit certain responses. In most studies of maltreatment, researchers examine differences in maltreated versus nonmaltreated participants while controlling for the effects of variables such as age, gender, and income levels in analyses. The Romanian orphan story at the beginning of this chapter illustrates such a study and shows how deprivation and trauma affect psychological, social, and brain development. The photo in Figure 3.6 displays computed tomography scans of the brains of two 3-year-old children. The image on the left is from a healthy child with an average head size (50th percentile). The image on the right depicts the results of severe sensory-deprivation neglect (Perry, 2002). Such evidence underscores how adversity alters the brain, as well as biological systems controlled by the brain.

Neuroscience research draws significantly on animal studies and models of the brain. However, advances in the study of the human brain over the past 3 decades have allowed more research on adversity and trauma in humans. These studies have greatly advanced our understanding of the effects of stress and adversity on the brain. Unlike animal studies in which the brain can be manipulated through surgeries, hormones, and even genetic programming, human studies must use noninvasive methods. Moreover, many experimental manipulations are designed to study the effects on the brain postmortem; this is not possible in human research for obvious reasons.

We study the brain in two primary ways: neuroimaging and electroencephalography (EEG; see Exhibit 3.2; see also Galván, 2017). Human neuroimaging studies began in the 1990s, with an explosion of imaging

FIGURE 3.6. Computed Tomography Scan Comparing Brain Structures of a Nonneglected Child (left) Versus a Severely Neglected Child (right)

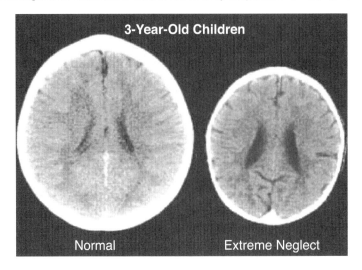

From "Childhood Experience and the Expression of Genetic Potential: What Childhood Neglect Tells Us About Nature and Nurture," by B. D. Perry, 2002, *Brain & Mind*, *1*, p. 93. Copyright 2002 by Springer Nature. Reprinted with permission.

EXHIBIT 3.2

Primary Ways to Study the Brain

Technique and definition	Output	Advantages	Disadvantages
Magnetic resonance imaging (MRI) MRI measures brain structure (sMRI), white matter tracts (diffusion tensor imaging, or DTI), brain function (fMRI, rsMRI, or resting state MRI), and patterns of connectivity. Participants are in a scanner and a strong magnetic field and radio waves are used to create images.	• Multidimensional picture of the brain • Changes in magnetic resonance signal, a hemodynamic response, corresponds to neuronal activation	• Examines deep brain structures • Examines structure and function • Relatively safe (no radiation) and can be repeated	• 4- to 6-second delay after stimulus • Participants cannot move in scanner • Costly • Scanning cannot occur if there is any metal in the body, which interferes with signal
Electroencephalography (EEG) Measures brain activity using electrical signals. Signals are detected through electrodes, metal disks, and wires attached to the scalp.	• Electrical signals graphed on a computer screen • Different wave forms represent different cognitive processes	• Neural feedback collected in real time • Less expensive than MRI • Participants can move	• Only measures cortical activity • Deep structures, such as the amygdala or hippocampus, cannot be examined

research in the early 2000s. Imaging examines brain structure, function, and patterns of neural connectivity. EEG is an entirely different technique that examines brain activity via electrical signals produced close to the brain's surface when neurons communicate with one another.

Effects of Maltreatment on Brain Structure and Function

Many studies have used EEG to examine the effects of adversity on brain activity. These studies typically examine patterns of brain activity across regions (coherence), and brain responses to different stimuli, such as angry, fearful, happy, and neutral faces (Belsky & de Haan, 2011). In general, studies of maltreated and institutionalized children show altered, less developed patterns of brain connectivity and complexity; some studies also find that institutionalized children display an overall pattern of delayed development and less activation (Moulson, Fox, Zeanah, & Nelson, 2009; Parker, Nelson, & Bucharest Early Intervention Project Core Group, 2005a, 2005b). Studies of maltreated children also suggest atypical emotion processing (Pollak, Cicchetti, Klorman, & Brumaghim, 1997) and hypervigilance to expressions of anger (Belsky & de Haan, 2011; Pollak, Messner, Kistler, & Cohn, 2009; Pollak & Tolley-Schell, 2003).

In an extensive review of research on the neurological effects of maltreatment using neuroimaging methods, Teicher and Samson (2016) came to several conclusions. First, maltreatment has consistent, negative effects on structural and functional brain development. This is also supported by animal research as well as many studies reporting a dose–response relationship with greater negative effects resulting from more severe abuse. Second, the type of abuse matters: Specific types of abuse selectively target pathways and sensory systems known to process related experiences. Third, age of abuse is significant. Evidence points to sensitive periods of exposure in brain regions including the hippocampus, amygdala, and PFC, although timing between exposure and brain changes is somewhat unclear. Fourth, there is evidence for gender differences in patterns of effects, with some regions more adversely affected in males and some functional differences seen in females. Fifth and finally, differences are likely an adaptive, neurologically specific response to environmental conditions and not a general stress-induced response. Teicher and Samson argued that brain changes are adaptations to a dangerous, unpredictable world and that abuse initiates a cascade of stress-related hormonal effects and consistent negative structural and functional brain alterations. Next, we specify several specific brain regions that have been implicated in numerous studies of the effects of maltreatment on the brain, and we briefly review the supporting research.

Responsible for the formation and retrieval of memories, the *hippocampus* is densely populated with GRs. Thus, it is highly susceptible to damage from excess levels of stress hormones such as cortisol (Sapolsky, Krey, & McEwen, 1985). Overexposure to glucocorticoids can lead to dendrite atrophy, neurogenesis suppression, and smaller hippocampal volume (Frodl & O'Keane,

2013; Sapolsky, 1996). There is strong evidence that adults with a history of maltreatment have smaller hippocampi than nonmaltreated adults (Teicher & Samson, 2016). Research on children and adolescents is less clear, suggesting that there may be a "silent period" between maltreatment exposure and neurobiological differences, with effects becoming more obvious postpuberty (Andersen & Teicher, 2004). Larger hippocampal volume is associated with better cognitive skills, such as attention processing (Frodl et al., 2006) and memory (Pohlack et al., 2014). Thus, maltreatment may cause reductions in hippocampal volume that then affects learning and cognitive functioning. Studies documenting lower hippocampal volume in individuals with depression and posttraumatic stress disorder further associate this region with mental health problems and trauma (Geuze, Vermetten, & Bremner, 2005).

Maltreatment also affects the structure and function of the *amygdala*. The amygdala is an almond-shaped structure responsible for processing responses to threat, fear, and emotion. Think of it as a smoke alarm, signaling danger (van der Kolk, 2015). Like the hippocampus, the amygdala has a high density of glucocorticoid receptors. Studies of amygdala volume have produced mixed results, with increased amygdala volume documented primarily in children with early exposure to abuse and decreased volume in older adolescents or adults who have longer histories of abuse and mental health problems. This suggests that early exposure to abuse may sensitize the amygdala to later stress, resulting in a reduction in amygdala volume in late adolescence and adulthood (Teicher & Samson, 2016). Several studies have also associated maltreatment with heightened amygdala responses to threat and diminished responses to reward (Fareri & Tottenham, 2016). In both children and adults, maltreatment is associated with increased amygdala responses to pictures of faces demonstrating different emotions (Teicher & Samson, 2016). This hyperalertness can be compared to malfunctioning sensors on a car; instead of only alerting the driver to a close obstacle, the system beeps when bugs and birds fly by.

Circuits that regulate reward and threat are another set of brain pathways and regions that differ in maltreated versus control groups. Part of this circuit is the *striatum*, which is involved in processing reward. In several studies, researchers used a monetary incentive delay (MID) paradigm in which participants win or lose money by completing a simple task. Before each trial, they are told how much money they can win or lose. In general, participants who experienced early life adversity demonstrate a diminished response to reward in the MID (Mehta et al., 2010), including children who had been in institutional care and adults who were abused as children (Dillon et al., 2009). Fareri and Tottenham (2016) pointed out that accelerated amygdala development interferes with functional interactions between the amygdala and the ventral striatum, and they argued that early life stress impedes the ability of amygdala processing to reach the ventral striatum. As a result, emotions may be blunted, which may lead to increased risk-taking behavior to feel positive or negative emotions.

The *cerebral cortex*, like the amygdala and hippocampus, is dense in GRs, particularly in infancy and early childhood (Sarrieau et al., 1986) and in late adolescence and early adulthood (Sinclair, Webster, Wong, & Weickert, 2011), suggesting two periods of heightened vulnerability to stress. In general, children who experienced abuse and children raised in institutions have reduced cortical gray and white matter volumes, primarily in regions of the *prefrontal cortex* (anterior cingulate cortex, dorsolateral PFC, and the orbitofrontal cortex). These areas of the PFC are important in emotion regulation and decision-making, suggesting that physical alterations due to maltreatment affect socioemotional development and cognitive functioning. Moreover, patterns of cortical network organization and connectivity between prefrontal and limbic regions in maltreated individuals suggest difficulties in regulating emotions and impulses and a heightened experience of emotions and self-centered emotional thinking (Teicher & Samson, 2016; L. Wang et al., 2014).

One particular region of the PFC, the inferior frontal gyrus (IFG), has been the focus of several studies. The IFG is important in emotion regulation and impulse control, with studies of nonhuman primates showing a high density of GRs in the IFG (Patel, Katz, Karssen, & Lyons, 2008). In a longitudinal study of children beginning at ages 3 to 6 who participated in neuroimaging at ages 7 to 12, Luby, Barch, Whalen, Tillman, and Belden (2017) examined ACEs and brain structure, specifically the IFG, and emotional and behavioral outcomes at ages 9 to 15. Higher ACE scores were associated with emotional and physical health problems in late childhood and early adolescence. Moreover, the IFG region was negatively affected by ACEs. Smaller IFG volume also mediated relations between emotional awareness (i.e., labeling feelings) and later physical health symptoms and severity of depression, suggesting a possible pathway through which ACEs affect brain structure and subsequent physical and mental health. In a study using the same sample, more ACEs predicted increased internalizing symptoms (anxiety, depression) and externalizing problems (aggression, attention/hyperactivity), and altered IFG connectivity predicted greater externalizing symptoms in middle childhood and early adolescence (Barch, Belden, Tillman, Whalen, & Luby, 2018). Taken together, these studies suggest that early adversity negatively affects a brain region critically important to emotional and behavioral regulation and that these alterations affect later physical and mental health.

One consistent finding from research on maltreatment in children and adults is reductions in white matter area in the *corpus callosum*, the area connecting the brain hemispheres and facilitating communication between brain regions (Belsky & de Haan, 2011). This difference may be more pronounced in boys compared with girls (Teicher & Samson, 2016). Reductions in corpus callosum thickness have also been documented in children with mental health problems such as ADHD (Luders, Narr, et al., 2009) and in children and adults with bipolar disorder (Arnone, McIntosh, Chandra, & Ebmeier, 2008), underscoring the importance of this region for mental well-being. Importantly, at least one study found that the longer the duration of maltreatment, the smaller the total corpus callosum, implying a dose–response relationship (De Bellis et al., 1999).

An interesting line of research demonstrates that specific forms of abuse affect areas of the brain related to processing the aversive experience. It appears that severe exposure to parental verbal abuse results in different patterns of white matter tracts in language processing circuits (Rilling et al., 2008), as well as increased density in auditory processing regions of the brain (Tomoda et al., 2011). Evidence also suggests that children who witness multiple episodes of domestic violence have differences in visual processing regions and related white matter tracts (see Teicher & Samson, 2016). In a study of cortical thickness of women who were sexually abused in childhood, Heim and colleagues found an association with gray matter volume in the part of the visual cortex responsible for facial recognition and processing, as well as thinning of the part of the somatosensory cortex representing the genitals (Heim, Mayberg, Mletzko, Nemeroff, & Pruessner, 2013). These studies suggest that specific brain alterations may be due to specific types of abuse, as opposed to just a general stress response to adversity (Teicher & Samson, 2016). Heim and colleagues suggested that this cortical adaptation may actually shield a child from sensory processing related to a specific form of abuse.

In summary, these studies further substantiate that childhood maltreatment, that is, ACEs—cause structural and functional changes in the brain. Moreover, many mental health problems in adults may actually stem from early life adversity, and brain abnormalities attributed to mental illness may in fact be a consequence of early trauma and abuse, although not all maltreated individuals suffer from psychopathology (Teicher & Samson, 2016). Early adverse experiences increase individual risk for psychopathology and brain changes. In another stunning paradox, maltreatment changes the brain in ways that are adaptive responses to current adversity, protecting the body and promoting survival by altering the stress response system. These changes shift approach and avoidance tendencies to maintain survival. These short-term adaptations to adversity, however, have their own long-term health consequences.

Effects of Poverty on Brain Structure and Function

Many children experiencing ACEs also live in poverty (Bellis, Lowey, Leckenby, Hughes, & Harrison, 2014). Approximately one in five children in the United States lives in poverty, and 40% live with insufficient resources (National Center for Children in Poverty, 2018). Worldwide, 385 million children live in poverty (UNICEF, 2017). Children living in poverty are more likely to experience malnutrition, exposure to environmental toxins, instability in housing, and developmental delays, among other risks. They are also less likely to go to college and more apt to drop out of school (Brooks-Gunn & Duncan, 1997), leading to intergenerational poverty and related problems. The effects of poverty on the brain may help explain how this happens (see also Blair & Raver, 2012).

Using animal models, the first studies examining the effects of early life adversity on the developing brain focused primarily on poverty or deprivation. In summarizing 50 years of animal studies on the effects of an enriched versus deprived rearing environment, Johnson, Riis, and Noble (2016) documented changes in brain function and structure as well as gene expression in animals reared in deprived circumstances. Animals raised in environments that included toys, novelty, and social stimulation had better learning and memory and more brain plasticity, and they adapted more easily in different behavioral situations. In studies of children in poverty, researchers found key structural and functional changes in the PFC (reductions in volume and surface area and in gray and white matter), the amygdala (deficits in emotion processing and differences in volume), and the hippocampus (less volume; Barch et al., 2016; Brito & Noble, 2014; Duval et al., 2017; Tottenham & Sheridan, 2010). Shortfalls in language and reading-related brain regions (left occipitotemporal and left perisylvian regions) have been documented as well; children in higher income families had greater neural specialization in reading-related regions (Noble et al., 2015; Noble, Wolmetz, Ochs, Farah, & McCandliss, 2006). In a longitudinal study using imaging to examine normal brain development in children, Hair, Hanson, Wolfe, and Pollak (2015) found poverty associated with structural differences (less gray matter) in brain areas implicated in school readiness skills, and these changes affected academic achievement. Poverty has also been linked to the volume and surface area of these regions (Hair et al., 2015; Noble et al., 2015), as well as with different patterns of cortical activation (D'Angiulli et al., 2012).

There is evidence that nurturing caregiving can protect against poverty's negative effects on the brain. For example, a longitudinal study of preschoolers (Luby et al., 2013) found that early childhood poverty was related to less cortical gray matter and smaller white matter, hippocampal, and amygdala volumes in late childhood and early adolescence. Supporting our ACEs–PACEs theory, this study found that the effects of poverty on hippocampal volume were mediated by maternal support, providing evidence that positive parenting may alter the negative effects of poverty on children's brain development.

Threat Versus Deprivation

Margaret Sheridan, Katie McLaughlin, and colleagues (Duffy, McLaughlin, & Green, 2018; McLaughlin & Sheridan, 2016; McLaughlin, Sheridan, & Lambert, 2014; Sheridan et al., 2018) have proposed a model delineating the effects of threat and deprivation on brain development. They tie their model back to the ACEs literature and argue that early life stress alters neurocircuitry involved in emotion processing, cognitive control, and threat and reward processing. Alterations lead to problems in executive functioning (working memory, attention, delay of gratification) and emotional reactivity and to a blunted response to reward–risk behaviors such as smoking, alcohol use, and overeating. This model aligns with theories discussed previously but focuses more on neural mechanisms. Specifically, the authors argue that deprivation (absence of environmental inputs and stimulation) and threat (experiences that threaten one's safety) may be linked to different neural mechanisms. Animal and human studies suggest that threat changes the structure and function of the amygdala, PFC, and hippocampus, resulting in long-term changes in threat and reward circuitry as well as changes in connectivity between these regions and the PFC. In contrast, deprivation is associated with reductions in thickness and volume of the association cortex (the region that processes cognitive stimuli) because of overpruning of synaptic connections and reduced dendritic branching, likely from a lack of cognitive stimulation. Sheridan and McLaughlin have argued that these adaptations to the environment result in adaptive learning that is protective in short-term survival, but, without intervention, deleterious in the long run.

PUTTING IT ALL TOGETHER: THE ICARE MODEL

In Figure 3.7, we present an integrative and comprehensive synthesis of the effects of childhood stress on biobehavioral systems, developmental processes, and associated outcomes that can be used to guide future research, summarizing what we know to date. The model begins with an assumption that there is a balance of adverse and protective experiences in children's lives. ACEs increase physiological stress responses and PACEs buffer stress, resulting in a balance of stress exposure. Decades of research on allostatic load, developmental origins of disease, and neurobiological effects of childhood stress document that the resulting stress exposure produces adaptations in biological systems' response to stress, including neurological, endocrine, immunological, and metabolic. Short-term activation of these physiological responses is evolutionarily programmed to increase survival in the short term. However, these sustained stress responses and adaptations negatively affect developmental systems, including executive function, threat and reward responses, impulse control, emotion regulation, arousal, attachment, and language. Detrimental changes in developmental systems can have a wide range of negative behavioral, health, and social consequences. Affected systems may include behavior (e.g., alcohol, drug abuse, overeating, smoking), mental health (e.g., depression, anxiety), physical health (e.g., heart disease, cancer, dementia), and societal (e.g., school dropout, delinquency, teen pregnancy, domestic violence). These developmental systems are continuously influenced by external environmental stressors (horizontal bars at the top) but may also be modified or buffered through preventive programs, resilience-promoting relationships and resources, and therapeutic interventions (horizontal bar along the bottom). As we discuss in Chapter 4, these responses and adaptations to environmental stress and threats may be transmitted to future generations through a variety of behavioral and biological pathways.

FIGURE 3.7. Intergenerational and Cumulative Adverse and Resilience Experiences (ICARE) Model

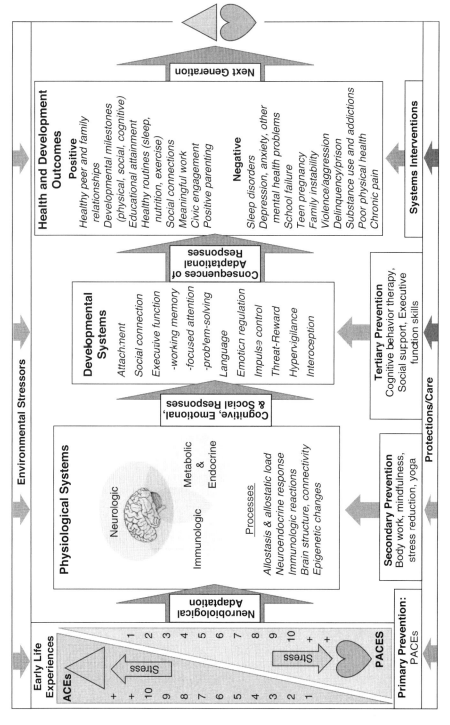

4

The Intergenerational Transmission of ACEs and PACEs

The roots of parenthood lie in the child's relations to his own parents in his earliest years. The love which a mother has for her children is a reflection of the love which she received when she was a little girl. The love which a father has for his children is a reflection of the love which he received when he was a little boy. It is in childhood that we learn to love
—JOHN BOWLBY, 1953

The transmission of adversity across generations is not a new idea. It is embedded in the Ten Commandments, stating that worshiping other gods will result in "visiting the iniquity of the fathers upon the sons to the third and fourth generation" (Exodus 20:5). It appears in the writings of Euripides, "The gods visit the sins of the father upon the children," and in Shakespeare's *The Merchant of Venice*, "The sins of the father are to be laid upon the children." Yet research has only recently begun to delineate the processes and pathways through which adversity and suffering are visited upon the children. In this chapter, we present findings supporting an intergenerational transmission of ACEs through both biological and behavioral pathways. Building on the Intergenerational and Cumulative Adverse and Resilience Experiences (ICARE) model presented in the previous chapter, this chapter discusses research from both animal models and human studies supporting the age-old observation that the so-called sins of fathers (and mothers) are passed to their offspring, sometimes for generations.

http://dx.doi.org/10.1037/0000177-004
Adverse and Protective Childhood Experiences: A Developmental Perspective, by J. Hays-Grudo and A. S. Morris

PSYCHOSOCIAL TRANSMISSION OF ADVERSITY AND RESILIENCE

An *intergenerational cascade of adversity* is a useful way to conceptualize these generational patterns. Developmental cascades are used to acknowledge the snowballing effects that occur when failures or delays in one domain derail further development in that domain or others. Masten and Cicchetti (2010) described them as "the cumulative consequences for development of the many interactions and transactions occurring in developing systems that result in spreading effects across levels, among domains at the same level, and across different systems or generations" (p. 491). We saw evidence in Chapter 3 that the stress of child abuse, neglect, and family dysfunction challenge and over-work the many response systems evolutionarily programmed to respond to environmental threats. Prolonged activation of these stress-response systems has long-term effects on immune function, metabolic systems, and neuro-endocrine hormones. We also saw evidence that trauma and adversity change structural components and neural connections in the developing brain. These effects impede cognitive, social, and emotional development in childhood and adolescence, which increase the risk of behavior problems, learning difficulties, school failure, peer relationship difficulties, and inadequate work-force preparation. We propose that intergenerational cascades occur when inadequate developmental outcomes in one generation lead to poor adult functioning and parenting, compromising developmental outcomes for the next generations. In addition, childhood adversity may be transmitted inter-generationally via biological processes, specifically through epigenetic changes in response to childhood adversity. This chapter summarizes the research on the intergenerational transmission of adversity, drawing from a number of scientific fields and theoretical frameworks, including infant mental health (IMH), the neurobiology of attachment and parenting, and epigenetics.

Infant Mental Health

Psychotherapists and mental health practitioners have observed and addressed the intergenerational transmission of trauma in clinical settings for many years. IMH specialists have been particularly focused on intergenerational trauma, as first described by Selma Fraiberg and her colleagues as "ghosts in the nursery." Emphasizing the necessity of exorcising the ghosts of traumas past to protect the next generation, they wrote:

> In every nursery, there are ghosts. They are the visitors from the unremembered past of the parents; the uninvited guests at the christening. Under all favorable circumstances the unfriendly and unbidden spirits are banished from the nursery and return to their subterranean dwelling place. The baby makes his own imperative claim upon parental love and, in strict analogy with the fairy tales, the bonds of love protect the child and his parents against the intruders, the malevolent ghosts. . . . But how shall we explain another group of families who appear to be possessed by their ghosts? The intruders from the past have taken up residence in the nursery, claiming tradition and rights of ownership.

They have been present at the christening for two or more generations. While no one has issued an invitation, the ghosts take up residence and conduct the rehearsal of the family tragedy from a tattered script. (Fraiberg, Adelson, & Shapiro, 1975, pp. 387–388)

Not all patterns from the past are harmful, however; some experiences and feelings that parents pass down are protective, nurturing, and beneficial. These are the remembered and not remembered actions of benevolent and loving caregivers that are also present within the new parent. Expanding on the metaphor of ghosts in the nursery, Lieberman, Padrón, Van Horn, and Harris (2005) called our attention to forgotten but internalized feelings of love, safety, and delight that lie beneath the surface and can be harnessed in caring for the next generation:

> Angels emerge from childhood memories deeply connected to the phenomenology of care-receiving experiences that are characterized by intense shared affect between parent and child and provide the child with a core sense of worth and security. These messages of intrinsic goodness and unconditional love constitute the essence of the angel. As they enact scenes from their own past, parents unknowingly carry forth the angels from their childhoods into their babies' nurseries. In this way, the message of the "angels in the nursery" is transmitted to the next generation in the form of benevolent influences that guard the course of development. . . . In darker moments, these "angels in the nursery" square off against their more famous siblings, the ghosts (Fraiberg, Adelson, & Shapiro, 1975), doing battle with them to keep intact the protective shield of parental love that surrounds young children and endeavoring to repair the damage when malevolent influences from the past break through. (p. 506)

Fraiberg and colleagues (1975) constructed the theory and practice of IMH, a discipline that evolved into a worldwide campaign to provide parents and infants the "opportunity to enter into and sustain healthy attachment relationships, reducing the risk of delay or disorder and increasing the possibility of optimal development in infancy and early parenthood" (Weatherston, 2001, p. 44). Recall from Chapter 2, this volume, that the healthy attachment relationship is the foundation on which future development rests. It is the secure base from which children explore and the safe harbor to which they return when hurt, lonely, or afraid. Secure attachment relationships form the lens through which children observe themselves and others and promote motivation to please and connect with others, thus acquiring the cognitive, social, and emotional skills that they will need to join their communities. Parents' own adverse childhood experiences may jeopardize the quality or security of this attachment. IMH therapists focus on building strong and trusting relationships with parents, providing them with unconditional support and empathy as they recognize and address obstacles to attachment, serving as models of a secure attachment relationship.

IMH integrates many relevant theoretical perspectives, including classic psychoanalytic theory, newer formulations from Erikson, Bowlby, Ainsworth, Main, and Winnicott, and cognitive (Piaget) and contextual (Vygotsky, Bronfenbrenner) approaches (for a review of theories, see Weatherston, 2001).

The field of infant mental health provides valuable insight and evidence-based interventions, such as child–parent psychotherapy, for preventing the unwanted legacy of trauma across generations and building on strengths and benevolent childhood experiences and has yielded research findings that support these concepts. For example, a recent study of 185 low-income and ethnically diverse mothers of young children referred for child–parent psycho-therapy after the child's exposure to a traumatic event completed a standardized interview to assess angels in the nursery (e.g., a memory of feeling especially loved, understood, or safe as a small child). Results showed a significant relationship between these memories and maternal and child well-being, in that more positive and elaborated "angel memories" buffered maltreated mothers from experiencing clinical levels of posttraumatic stress disorder as adults and reduced the transmission of trauma to their children (Narayan, Ippen, Harris, & Lieberman, 2019).

Intergenerational Transmission of Parenting

The behavioral and developmental effects of ACEs also have implications for later parenting behaviors related to developmental outcomes of offspring. A recent review of ACE-related effects on parenting revealed a positive relation-ship between parental history of childhood adversity and current parenting stress, independent of income level (Steele et al., 2016). Parenting stress has been associated with children's problem behavior and difficulties in school (Anthony et al., 2005; Crnic, Gaze, & Hoffman, 2005) and with children's elevated cortisol levels (Essex, Klein, Cho, & Kalin, 2002). Moreover, studies of early life stress in animals and humans indicate that pervasive deficits in parenting behaviors, emotionality, and cognitive functioning are likely due to biological processes discussed previously. Caregivers with these deficits are often reactive, inattentive, aggressive, depressed, or uninvolved, resulting in volatile and insensitive parent–child interactions. This puts children at risk for a host of behavioral and emotional problems (Lomanowska, Boivin, Hertzman, & Fleming, 2017; Repetti et al., 2002). Research has also documented a negative relationship between parent ACEs and children's socio-emotional functioning (Wurster, Sarche, Trucksess, Morse, & Biringen, 2019). For example, in a study of families enrolled in an Early Head Start program in an American Indian community, researchers found that parent mental distress was a key moderator of this relationship and that high levels of parent emotional avail-ability buffered the relation between parent ACEs, mental distress, and chil-dren's socioemotional problems (Wurster et al., 2019). In contrast, studies of positive parenting show a healthy transmission of caregiving, with positive parenting related to children's social competence (Yamaoka & Bard, 2019) and to later positive parenting as adults (Raby et al., 2015).

As illustrated in the ICARE model (see Figure 3.7), executive function skills are a critical developmental pathway through which early life stress affects adult cognitive and emotional functioning and subsequent parenting.

Executive functions include cognitive capacity for working memory, cognitive flexibility, attention, and impulse control. Such skills are necessary for learning, academic achievement, and emotional and behavioral regulation (Deater-Deckard, 2014). Deficits in executive function may be due to stress and adversity experienced during key periods in childhood when the prefrontal cortex is maturing and developing these higher order cognitive processes. If adversity occurs during these developmental windows, there may be lifelong, cascading consequences, starting with difficulty in school, and leading to poor performance in later educational and work settings (Pechtel & Pizzagalli, 2011). There is also evidence that early adversity negatively affects emotion regulation and emotion processing (J. C. Young & Widom, 2014), which may result in impaired social relationships. In a review of the literature, Kirby Deater-Deckard (2014) argued that self-regulation (executive function, attentive behavior) is transmitted from parent to child through social interactions and biological mechanisms and that the broader family and home context (socioeconomic status, household chaos, and cultural factors) can alter these processes. Moreover, the family system can facilitate adaption and protection, or risk and vulnerability, because of the way emotions, behaviors, and stress are managed in the home (Henry, Morris, & Harrist, 2015).

Adult Attachment

Another pathway through which parenting is transmitted from generation to generation is through adult attachment. As described in Erik Erikson's psychosocial theory of development (see Chapter 2), the primary struggle of young adulthood is *intimacy versus isolation*. The goal of this stage is to share one's life with another person, to love selflessly—be it romantic love or friendship—and balance relationships with independence. Developmental scientists use Bowlby's theory of attachment (Bowlby, 1969) to help explain adult romantic relationships and success or struggles with intimacy. Recall from Chapter 2 that, on the basis of their childhood experiences, individuals develop *working models* of attachment—beliefs about relationships and how the social world works. Adult attachment is usually examined via retrospective interviews or surveys that assess adult perspectives on early relationships with caregivers and current beliefs about relationships (see Crowell & Treboux, 1995; Main, Kaplan, & Cassidy, 1985).

A number of studies of adult attachment suggest that individuals' descriptions of their early experiences with their parents are associated with attitudes and beliefs about intimate relationships (Crowell & Treboux, 1995; Feeney & Noller, 1990; Fraley & Shaver, 2000). Three primary adult attachment categories have been identified. *Securely attached* adults describe their parents as warm, loving, and supportive and view themselves as likable and open adults. They are comfortable with intimacy and rarely worry about abandonment or someone getting too close to them. Importantly, their relationships are typically characterized in terms of trust, happiness, and friendship. *Insecure dismissing/avoidant* adults describe their parents as demanding, disrespectful, and critical. As adults, they often focus on their own independence and may be emotionally distant, distrusting of partners, and concerned about excessive closeness. *Insecure preoccupied/anxious* adults describe their parents as unpredictable and often unfair. As adults, these individuals may have difficulties maintaining boundaries with a significant other and often fall in love quickly. At the same time, they worry that their intense feelings will overwhelm others who do not really love them. Their most important relationships are characterized as high in jealousy and in desperation about whether their partner will return their affection (Crowell & Treboux, 1995; Feeney & Noller, 1990). Research supports the premise that early adversity jeopardizes the formation of secure attachment relationships and negatively affects adult intimacy and parenting. For example, research examining adult attachment and parent–child attachment in a sample of mothers with a history of abuse and neglect found that 83% of their infants were classified as insecurely attached using the Strange Situation observation (Berthelot et al., 2015). In addition, there was a high concordance between child and maternal attachment classifications, suggesting intergenerational transmission. An adult attachment survey developed by psychologist Chris Fraley is available online and generates a report on one's attachment style (see Resources for website), particularly as attachment style relates to anxiety and avoidance (Fraley, Waller, & Brennan, 2000).

NEUROBIOLOGICAL TRANSMISSION OF PARENTING

Scientists argue that the emotional and behavioral dynamics of parent–child attachment and adult attachment are governed by the same biological systems (Feeney & Noller, 1990; Hazan & Shaver, 1987). Research supports the essential need for love from a caregiver, but what actually happens in the brain and body during early relationships? When babies are born, they know their mothers' smell and voice. They know their father's voice too, if he is involved with the mother during pregnancy (Bornstein et al., 2017; G. Y. Lee & Kisilevsky, 2014). Studies have also shown the sound of a baby's cry affects a caregiver's body (increases in blood pressure) and brain to motivate her to respond to the baby's needs (Bornstein et al., 2017; Frodi, Lamb, Leavitt, & Donovan, 1978).

Neurobiology of Love and Attachment

In the past decade, animal models of caregiving evolved to brain imaging and neuroendocrine studies in humans, documenting that brain circuits and regions (striatum, amygdala, hypothalamus, hippocampus, and social cognitive areas of the prefrontal cortex) and associated hormone systems are wired to promote parenting responses. These systems help parents manage stress and motivate nurturing behavior (Swain, Kim, & Ho, 2011). Several functional MRI studies have examined parents' brain responses to pictures of babies, sounds of babies crying, or pictures of babies smiling. Results show that specific brain circuits involved in empathy, motivation, and reward are activated during the presentation of baby stimuli (Swain, Lorberbaum, Kose, & Strathearn, 2007). In a recent review of studies from 11 countries that looked at maternal responses to crying infants, mothers displayed similar responses by picking up and talking to their babies (Bornstein et al., 2017). Moreover, imaging studies in multiple countries identified similar brain responses to infant cries, signifying an evolutionary reason for this response. Imaging studies also suggest structural changes in mothers' brains after birth (e.g., increases in gray matter volume in the midbrain), indicating a time of increased plasticity (Kim et al., 2010). In other words, the "mommy brain" is real, and these biological changes are priming parents for caregiving and attachment.

The Role of Hormones

During birth, the mother produces oxytocin, a hormone important in mother-child bonding and social relationships. Oxytocin is also released during breastfeeding, orgasm, cuddling, and even when playing with dogs (Magon & Kalra, 2011; Nagasawa, Kikusui, Onaka, & Ohta, 2009). Oxytocin promotes social bonding, trust, and even monogamy in some animals. Prairie voles, for example, who mate with one partner for life, have high levels of oxytocin receptor genes that influence reward centers of the brain. In contrast, montane voles, who have many partners, have fewer oxytocin receptor genes. Scientists believe the oxytocin in prairie voles is what makes them monogamous, rewarding them for mating and nesting with only one partner (Carter, Devries, & Getz, 1995). There is also evidence that oxytocin reduces hypothalamic–pituitary–adrenal axis activity in prairie voles, lowering stress hormone production; this decrease may account for the health benefits found in loving relationships among human mammals (Carter, 1998).

Parenting research documents that experiences with caregivers influence how and when genes are expressed. For example, girls raised in homes with a lot of conflict and violence, especially related to the father (or if the father is absent), often start puberty early. It is believed that chemical changes in the body initiate puberty so that these girls are ready to leave a conflicted home of origin sooner (presumably to start their own families). This phenomenon was evolutionarily adaptive hundreds of years ago, but it can be difficult for girls today (Belsky, Steinberg, & Draper, 1991; B. J. Ellis & Garber, 2000; B. J. Ellis, McFadyen-Ketchum, Dodge, Pettit, & Bates, 1999). Today, we think that these chemical changes in the body may be caused by an epigenetic sequence that triggers the early release of pubertal hormones.

Synchrony

The human reward system in the brain is similar to the prairie vole, and neurotransmitters such as dopamine (the pleasure chemical) and norepinephrine (which mobilizes the brain and body for action) are released during positive social interactions and bonding. Dr. Ruth Feldman developed a model describing the neurobiology of attachment in mammals, arguing that dopamine and oxytocin influences on the striatum (the reward center of the brain) prompt social motivation and interaction and physiological synchrony or attunement. Human attachments are characterized by the coupling of the partners' physiological and behavioral interactions, which are observed through behavioral synchrony, coupling of heart rate rhythms, coordinated hormonal release, and brain synchrony (Feldman, 2017; see Figure 4.1). This coupling promotes attachment and social interaction.

Similar to physiological synchrony, behavioral synchrony has been examined in numerous studies, usually with infants and mothers. Parent–infant synchrony is a social dance of sorts, with coordinated interactions between caregivers and babies. In infancy, synchrony is grounded in caregiver sensitivity and responsiveness to babies' needs, cues, and bids for attention. Positive relationships between infants and caregivers include synchronous interactions; asynchronous interactions suggest unhealthy relationships. Specific characteristics of synchrony include matched affect, contingent responding, joint engagement, and physiological synchrony of biological variables such as heart rate, cortisol, and brain activity (Feldman, 2017; Harrist & Waugh, 2002; Lindsey & Caldera, 2015; Morris, Squeglia, Jacobus, & Silk, 2018).

Tronick, Brazelton, and Als (1978) examined synchronous interactions between infants and their mothers using the *still face paradigm*. During this task, mothers are asked to play normally, face-to-face, with their babies, for a specified period of time. Then the mother is told to stop interacting with her baby and sit with a still face for 2 to 3 minutes. The infant's response to the mother's still face is observed and used to assess the synchrony of the dyad and the infant's recovery and reliance on the caregiver (Adamson & Frick, 2003). When using the still face paradigm with depressed mothers, researchers documented differences in maternal behaviors that affected their interactions. For example, depressed mothers were less engaged with their babies, less vocal, less emotionally consistent, and more intrusive. As a result, infants were more likely to withdraw from the interaction by averting their gaze or turning their head to help self-soothe (Reck et al., 2004).

In an epigenetics study, Conradt and colleagues (2015) compared *NR3C1* DNA methylation from placental samples at birth with infants' self-regulation during the still-face paradigm (Haley & Stansbury, 2003) at 4 months. As predicted, greater DNA methylation of *NR3C1* was related to greater cortisol reactivity in response to the still-face paradigm and to poorer infant self-regulation. This gene has also been linked to early childhood stress exposure in preschool-age children (Tyrka et al., 2015), previous maltreatment in school-age children (Romens, McDonald, Svaren, & Pollak, 2015), and childhood abuse and neglect in adults (Perroud et al., 2011). These findings support what we discussed in Chapter 2: When *NR3C1* is silenced or diminished, fewer glucocorticoid receptors are available for binding to cortisol and removing it from

FIGURE 4.1. Biobehavioral Synchrony in Human Attachments

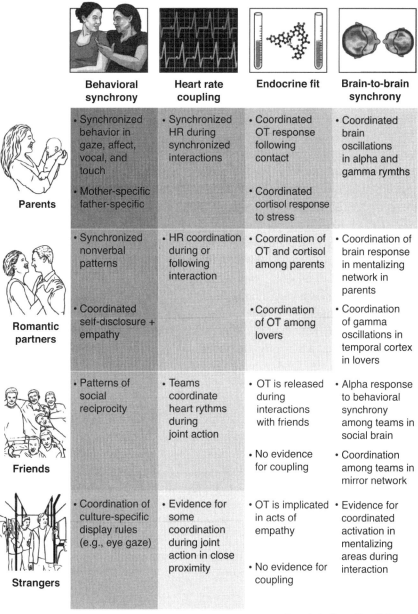

	Behavioral synchrony	Heart rate coupling	Endocrine fit	Brain-to-brain synchrony
Parents	• Synchronized behavior in gaze, affect, vocal, and touch • Mother-specific father-specific	• Synchronized HR during synchronized interactions	• Coordinated OT response following contact • Coordinated cortisol response to stress	• Coordinated brain oscillations in alpha and gamma rymths
Romantic partners	• Synchronized nonverbal patterns • Coordinated self-disclosure + empathy	• HR coordination during or following interaction	• Coordination of OT and cortisol among parents • Coordination of OT among lovers	• Coordination of brain response in mentalizing network in parents • Coordination of gamma oscillations in temporal cortex in lovers
Friends	• Patterns of social reciprocity	• Teams coordinate heart rythms during joint action	• OT is released during interactions with friends • No evidence for coupling	• Alpha response to behavioral synchrony among teams in social brain • Coordination among teams in mirror network
Strangers	• Coordination of culture-specific display rules (e.g., eye gaze)	• Evidence for some coordination during joint action in close proximity	• OT is implicated in acts of empathy • No evidence for coupling	• Evidence for coordinated activation in mentalizing areas during interaction

Trends in Cognitive Sciences

HR = heart rate; OT = oxytocin. From "The Neurobiology of Human Attachments," by R. Feldman, 2017, *Trends in Cognitive Sciences*, *21*, p. 89. Copyright 2016 by Elsevier. Reprinted with permission.

the system, exaggerating the stress response and increasing dysregulation and possibly impaired social interactions.

The Importance of Fathers

Most parenting research with humans has been done with mothers, but what about fathers? Fathers, and supportive others, are needed to take care of mothers and babies, particularly during times of transition and stress; we like to call this concept *holding the nest*. The image of nest-holding perfectly symbolizes how caregivers need support and protection in the wild and in life. Research on fathers' brains shows a pattern similar to that seen in mothers. In Abraham and colleagues' brain imaging and observational study of mothers, heterosexual fathers, and homosexual fathers, researchers observed a *parental caregiving neural network* across all caregivers (Abraham et al., 2014). Brain regions involved were associated with emotion processing, reward, motivation, social understanding, and empathy, and these brain structures were linked to oxytocin. In addition, some findings were more pronounced among fathers who spent more time caregiving. Like mothers, the brains of fathers were malleable and plastic, so there is a "daddy brain" too, especially when dads are highly involved.

What about synchrony among fathers and infants? Much like the early research on fathers in child development that demonstrated more "rough-and-tumble" play with dads (Smith, 1989), observational research on father–infant behavioral synchrony shows its own unique patterns. With moms, synchrony is coordinated and predictable, with moderate and low levels of infant emotionality. Dads, in contrast, display sudden bursts of positive affect and synchrony, with frequent peaks and high-intensity turns as play progresses (Feldman, 2003). (Who hasn't seen a mom gently rocking her baby in her arms, and the dad tossing the baby in the air?) This affirms that moms and dads both play an important role in social and emotional development, facilitating different components of emotion regulation—socially congruent and expected patterns of regulation versus unpredictable and intensely positive patterns of regulation.

NEUROBIOLOGICAL TRANSMISSION OF ADVERSITY AND RESILIENCE

We have shown that love actually starts in the brain, not the heart, and that love and nurturance, or lack thereof, have profound effects on the brain. This happens through stress-related changes in the endocrine system and in gene expression. Research also increasingly points to the role of epigenetic changes in development. Recall that *epigenetics* refers to the process of genes being "turned on" or "turned off" by environmental influences, such as caregiver interactions. The genes themselves do not change; rather, whether they are readily decoded and activated or suppressed is changed. For example, during mating, prairie vole oxytocin receptor genes are "turned on," which may be important in pair bonding. Studies of early life stress in animals and humans point to the role of oxytocin specifically in the intergenerational transmission of ACEs. In a review of the literature, Toepfer and colleagues argued that the oxytocin system interacts with the stress response system and inflammatory pathways, and these systems are sensitive to environmental stressors such as maltreatment. Moreover, genetic studies suggest that variations in oxytocin genes may affect biological susceptibility to early life adversity (Smearman et al., 2016; Toepfer et al., 2017). We next discuss the science behind the intergenerational transmission of ACEs in more detail, using animal and human studies to illustrate further how adversity is passed down from one generation to the next.

Developmental Origins of Disease Models

One of the first studies linking maternal and early life stress exposure and later adult health problems was published by British epidemiologists who observed that babies born during famine and deprivation following World War I (1921–1925) had higher than expected rates of heart disease 40 to 50 years later (Barker & Osmond, 1986). They hypothesized that the nutritional hardship and maternal stress that increased infant mortality rates also extended its reach into the adult lives of the surviving infants. The *Barker hypothesis* helped explain the growing body of research linking adverse conditions during fetal development with chronic diseases decades later. Initially focused on prenatal nutrition and subsequent obesity, metabolic syndrome, and heart disease, further research investigating the effects of different gestational and early life environments, such as high- versus low-income countries, supported the hypothesis in other contexts. The developmental origins of disease (DOoD) paradigm was developed to explain the increased risk of adult disease when the fetal environment did not match later living conditions (Gluckman & Hanson, 2004a). For example, the origins of metabolic diseases such as obesity and Type II diabetes are thought to develop when the fetus, deprived of adequate nutrients, makes a "predictive adaptive response" to efficiently store fat in utero, even though postbirth living conditions are rich in cheap and plentiful calories (Gluckman & Hanson, 2004b). DOoD theories focus on the enduring effects of environment during critical or sensitive periods of development and provide a foundation for more recent life course models of health that synthesize research from biological, behavioral, and social science disciplines (Halfon et al., 2014). Currently, researchers and policymakers alike are focusing on the perinatal period as a critical window for long-term health, focusing on the development of interventions for mothers with a history of complex trauma (Chamberlain et al., 2019).

Most early research adopting a life course approach, including the DOoD studies just described, focused on the effects of childhood poverty or deprivation rather than perinatal exposure to trauma on adult health. Because childhood poverty is more easily measured and available for large population groups, it has been widely used and is a well-established predictor of adult physical and mental health problems (Braveman & Barclay, 2009; Graham & Power, 2004; Wadsworth & Kuh, 1997; Yoshikawa, Aber, & Beardslee, 2012). Children raised in poverty are also more likely to engage in health-harming behaviors as adults (e.g., smoking, heavy alcohol use; Melchior, Moffitt, Milne, Poulton, & Caspi, 2007). Poverty is also known to have damaging effects on cognitive and intellectual development (Bradley & Corwyn, 2002; G. J. Duncan, Brooks-Gunn, & Klebanov, 1994; McCall, 1981; McLoyd, 1998) and socio-emotional development (G. J. Duncan et al., 1994; McLeod & Shanahan, 1996; McLoyd, 1998). Most research on the effects of childhood poverty focused on the physical characteristics of poverty, for example, the lack of books and cognitive enriching experiences (Bradley & Corwyn, 2002), an impoverished language environment (Hoff, 2003), poor quality diets encouraging obesity (Sobal & Stunkard, 1989), and lack of access to health care (Frank, Strobino, Salkever, & Jackson, 1991). Research has also documented the effect of poverty on socioemotional environments, including harsher, less responsive parenting styles (Bradley & Corwyn, 2002), and more hostility and conflict in the home (Grant et al., 2003; Repetti, Taylor, & Seeman, 2002; Taylor, Repetti, & Seeman, 1997). As more data accumulated on stress and allostatic load, stressors associated with childhood poverty were proposed as a "missing link" (Lupien, King, Meaney, & McEwen, 2001) between childhood poverty and poor health and developmental outcomes (Evans & Kim, 2007).

Epigenetic Transmission Across Generations

In Chapter 3, we reviewed the animal research documenting the effects of early life adversity on epigenetic changes to genes related to stress, including glucocorticoid receptor (GR) genes and *BDNF* genes that promote the production of the *BDNF* protein and support brain health and plasticity. Not only do epigenetic changes resulting from early life stress change brain structures and functions in the generations experiencing the adversity, but a growing number of studies have found that epigenetic and behavioral alterations are present in generations of offspring not directly exposed to trauma (Blaze & Roth, 2015; Champagne, 2008; Francis, Diorio, Liu, & Meaney, 1999; Franklin et al., 2010; Klengel, Dias, & Ressler, 2016).

Some of the earliest studies documented that female rodents who received low levels of maternal care as infants went on to exhibit low levels of care to their infant pups. This was originally thought to result from epigenetic changes in estrogen-related oxytocin binding (Champagne, 2008), but additional studies indicated that other processes were also involved. In one study, the research team bred a generation of normally reared mice, removed the male parent from the cage (who is not normally involved in rearing the pups), and exposed the offspring (first generation) to chronic and unpredictable maternal separation during the first 14 days of life (Franklin et al., 2010), which produced the predicted changes related to stress reactivity and depressive behavior (i.e., nonexploratory behavior in a new environment). The male offspring were then bred with normally reared females and removed from the cage, having no contact with the next (second) generation. When that generation reached adulthood, this process was repeated, with the second-generation male offspring again bred with nonstressed females, producing a third generation, also reared normally. Depressive behaviors (e.g., fearful, low exploration) were seen in the second and third generations, even without any direct exposure to stress or to the stressed parent or grandparent. Epigenetic changes were altered in the male germline of the first generation after early stress exposure, and some of these alterations were present in the second and third generations (Franklin et al., 2010). This same generational stress protocol was repeated with social anxiety and altered social memory as the outcome, and again, epigenetic effects in the first generation were observed in the next two generations (Franklin, Linder, Russig, Thöny, & Mansuy, 2011).

Dias and Ressler (2014) used olfactory fear conditioning in mice to investigate whether the olfactory experience of a parent might influence their offspring. In the fear conditioning procedure, 2-month-old naive male mice were conditioned by pairing mild foot-shocks with a chemical odor with known receptor sites (fear-conditioned group) or left in their home cage (control group). Both groups were paired with naive females (no adverse exposure) to produce a second generation; the male offspring of the second generation were paired with naive females producing a third generation. Neither group of male sires had any contact with the pups. The second and third generation mice exhibited the conditioned fear (i.e., startle) response to the odor without having experienced the fear conditioning. The authors also showed that the gene encoding for the olfactory receptor activated by the odor was hypomethylated (had fewer methyl groups attached to the DNA) in the sperm of the fear-trained generation and that this methylation pattern remained in sperm of the next two generations.

The animal studies clearly demonstrate that early life exposure to stress leaves enduring epigenetic alterations that influence gene expression in the exposed animal as well as its descendants. Research continues to identify the relative contribution of behavioral transmission (e.g., parental behavior affecting offspring phenotype through several generations) and germline transmission (e.g., epigenetic changes passing to subsequent offspring through either the maternal or paternal line), but there is strong evidence of intergenerational transmission of behavior and epigenetic alterations.

Our understanding of generationally transmitted epigenetic changes in humans is less complete than in animals, but recent studies suggest similarities (Buss et al., 2017). An epigenome-wide association study in Brazil found that women exposed to partner violence during pregnancy affected the DNA methylation of their *grandchildren* (Serpeloni et al., 2017). Investigating the effects of the Dutch famine during World War II on subsequent generations,

Painter and colleagues (2008) found that being briefly exposed to famine during pregnancy did not affect the birth weight or metabolic disease of off-spring, but it did predict increased neonatal adiposity (amount of body fat) and poorer health of the offspring's children—that is, the grandchildren of the women exposed during pregnancy and the children of their offspring exposed in utero. Extensive research on the offspring of Holocaust survivors suggests biological as well as behavioral effects of trauma in subsequent generations (Yehuda & Lehrner, 2018), with epigenetic alterations observed in both exposed parents and offspring (Yehuda et al., 2016).

Childhood exposure to trauma and stress is powerful, creating epigenetic alterations that change the affected individual's gene expression and behavior and, to some extent, those of their future offspring. The moderating role of nurturing parenting is also beginning to be recognized. Although little research has investigated epigenetic alterations from positive environments, several studies indicate that parenting behaviors may moderate the epigenetic effects on childhood stress. Conradt and colleagues (2016) found that depressed new mothers who were more nurturing and responsive during play had infants with less methylation across the genome than infants of depressed mothers who were less responsive with their infants. In one of the first studies to consider adolescence as a sensitive window for epigenetic change, Naumova et al. (2016) found that increases in perceived parental rejection across three points from midchildhood to adolescence predicted increased adult DNA methylation and that methylation patterns were also related to psycho-social adjustment problems in adulthood. These are promising avenues for future research.

CONCLUSIONS AND ACTIVITY: ACEs AND PACEs GENOGRAMS

Through a neurobiological lens, the model in Figure 4.2 illustrates these processes and the long-term impact of parenting on child development (Feldman, 2015). When babies are born in a positive environment, parent and infant brains are shaped by oxytocin and positive interactions, resulting in more synchronous interactions in infancy, as well as in positive adjustment in childhood such as emotion regulation, well-being, empathy, and stress management. These experiences prepare the adult brain for later positive parenting and attachment. When the system is disrupted through adversity or trauma, asynchronous behavioral and biological patterns emerge between infants and parents, leading to insecure attachment and difficulties in chil-dren's emotion regulation, socialization, and mental health. In adulthood, the pattern repeats itself with disrupted attachment relationships and possible "ghosts" in the nursery.

As we wrap up this section, in which we discussed the multiple approaches to researching the effects of early experience—both adverse and positive—on developing mental and physical systems, we also want to explore how this knowledge can be used to help individuals gain more self-awareness about

FIGURE 4.2. Long-Term Impact of the Adaptive Human Parental Brain on Children's Social Development

Key:
—— Verified links
····· Mediated links
····· Inferred links

• Maternal behavior • Physical contact
• Oxytocin • Breastfeeding

Newborn
Parent–infant contact

The adaptive human

• Memories of parental care
• Oxytocin increase during romantic bonding
• Mother–father brain synchrony

Adulthood
Sensitizing adult brain for parenting

Infancy
Parent–infant synchrony

Synchrony
• Behavioral
• Physiological
• Hormonal
• Brain-to-brain

Parental brain

Childhood
Socialization, stress/emotion regulation, well-being

Mediated by contact
• Stress management
• Physiologic organization
• Executive function
• Parent–child reciprocity

Mediated by oxytocin
• Reduced psychopathology
• Social reciprocity with peers
• Social engagement

Mediated by synchrony
• Empathy
• Social engagement
• Symbolic competence
• Emotion regulation

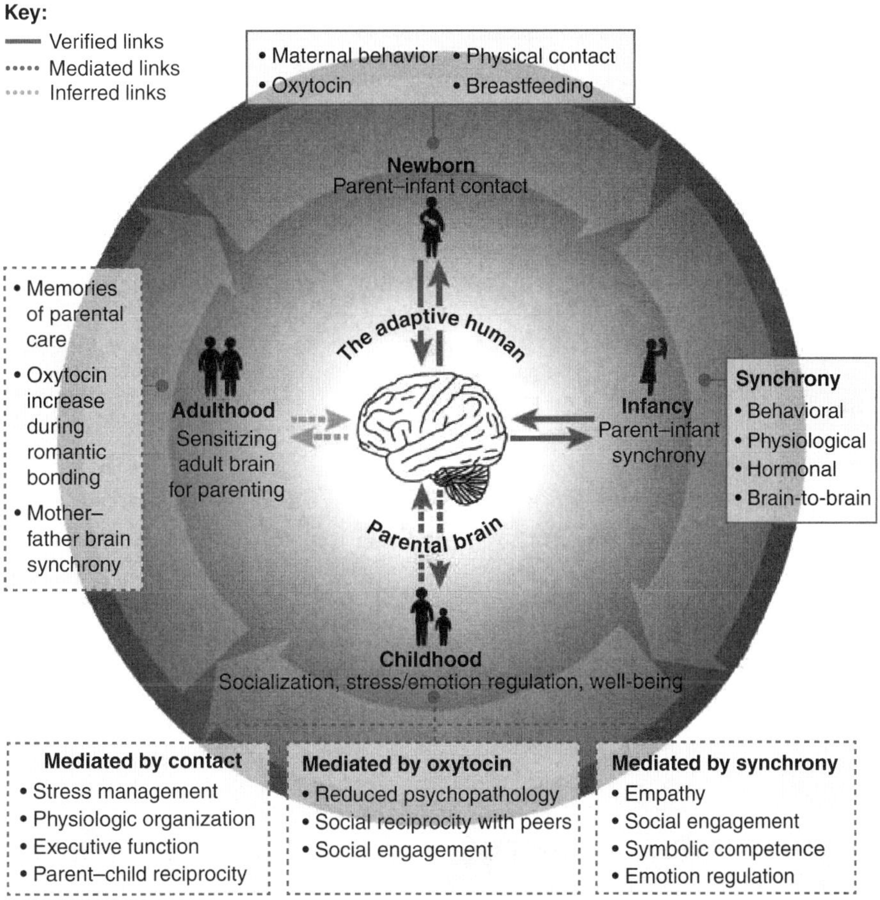

From "The Adaptive Human Parental Brain: Implications for Children's Social Development," by R. Feldman, 2015, *Trends in Neurosciences, 38*, p. 395. Copyright 2015 by Elsevier. Reprinted with permission.

the effects of ACEs and protective and compensatory experiences (PACEs) in their own lives—their thoughts, feelings, relationships, and health. Creating a world in which ACEs are uncommon rather than common, and in which PACEs are the norm and not the exception for all children, starts with creating individuals who have looked at their own histories of ACEs and PACEs, and those of their families. As we describe in the next few chapters, creating safe, trauma-informed cultures in which both children and adults who have experienced toxic stress from trauma and adversity begins with each of us.

Many psychologists, social workers, and others are familiar with family genograms. They are often used in medical research, where genetic pre-dispositions are of concern, and in family therapy to identify patterns of attitudes and behaviors that are no longer adaptive or cause pain. In this

FIGURE 4.3. Adverse Childhood Experiences (ACEs) and Protective and Compensatory Experiences (PACEs) Genograms

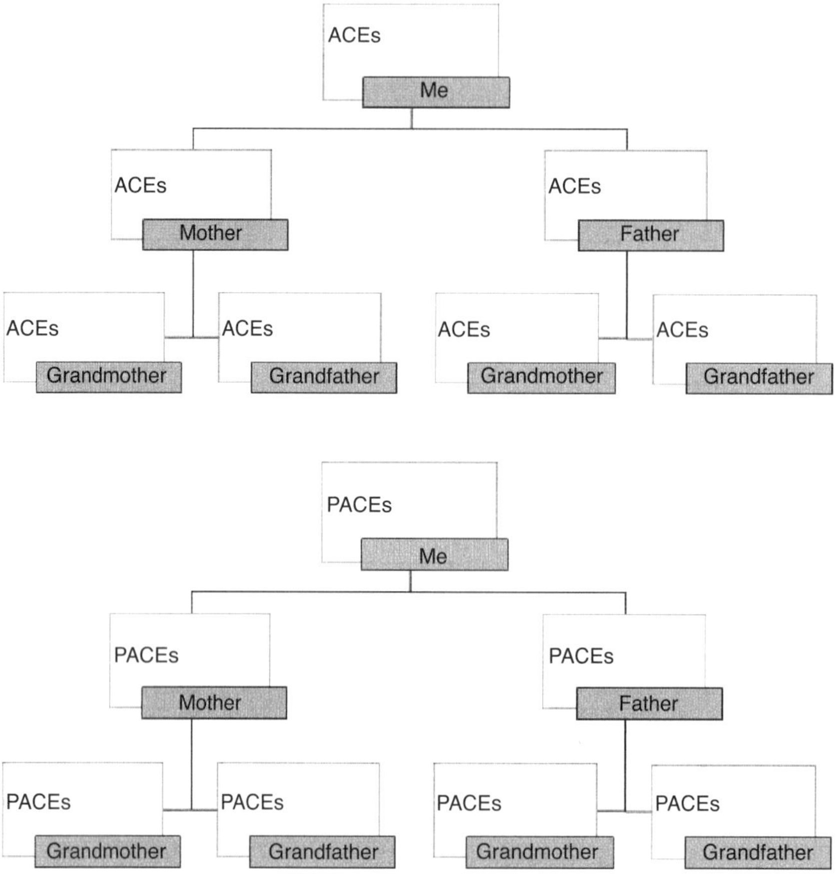

case, we have constructed ACEs and PACEs genograms to help individuals identify how their parents' and their parents' experiences—both positive and negative—may have been passed down through the generations. Simply put, a genogram is a like a family tree but with a focus on the adverse and protective relationships and resources that may form patterns in a family history. We have included a "family tree" with blanks for ACEs and the PACEs of parents and grandparents (see Figure 4.3). Other family members, such as stepparents, aunts, or foster parents, can be included by adding boxes. Note themes and patterns observed across generations. Although individuals may not discover anything they did not already know, this activity prompts most of us to look at our family history in a completely new way. It may also prompt a new type of conversation with other family members, in order to explore and share observations of patterns that stand out in both adverse and protective experiences. As we described at the beginning of the chapter, most of us were attended by ghosts and angels in our nurseries, and the ACEs and PACEs genograms can be useful tools for addressing them in a way that is constructive and therapeutic.

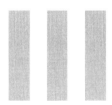

BREAKING THE CYCLE OF ACEs AND INCREASING PACEs

Public health problems are often unconsciously attempted solutions to personal problems dating back to childhood, buried in time, and concealed by shame, secrecy, and social taboos against certain topics.

—VINCENT FELITTI, 2018

INTRODUCTION

In the previous section, we provided evidence that adverse childhood experiences (ACEs) have powerful and enduring effects on neurobiological development, cognitive, social and emotional functioning, and subsequent behavior and health. We have also seen that this emotional and biological programming can be moderated by a variety of protective and compensatory experiences (PACEs). As illustrated by the ICARE Model (see Figure 3.7), the ACE–PACE balance plays a major role in determining the extent to which early life stress impedes the development of the childhood competencies on which adult capacities are based. ACEs are at the root of many of the problems facing individuals and society, problems that incur immeasurable human suffering and cost billions of dollars: preventable illness and chronic pain, violence and incarceration, drug and alcohol abuse, unmet potential and lost productivity, fractured relationships, mental illness, and suicide. Repairing the effects of ACEs and preventing their reverberations and repetition is vital for productive, well-functioning individuals, families, communities, and societies.

In the next three chapters, we provide an overview of emerging approaches to address this cascade of injury through programs and policies designed to prevent, mitigate, and treat the effects of ACEs in children and adults. In Chapter 5, we present evidence-based and promising interventions that are being used to help adults recover from the effects of early life stress and create environments and relationships that support continued recovery and growth. In Chapter 6, we describe preventive programs being used to decrease and mitigate the effects of adverse experiences in children and adolescents, with a particular focus on dual-generation interventions. In Chapter 7, we identify and describe policies and programs focused on creating resilient communities and organizations. In Chapter 8, we summarize the main points of the book and provide recommendations for implementation of policies and practices and moving the research field forward.

Our discussion of approaches to prevent, mitigate, and treat the effects of childhood adversity is grounded in theories and research from developmental psychology and related fields. Therapeutic interventions to address the enduring consequences of childhood trauma and stress have historically focused on one or perhaps several types of trauma, such as child abuse or neglect, exposure to violence, or parental drug and alcohol use. They have tended to focus on physical and health effects, psychological distress, or the behavioral and social problems resulting from early life stress but rarely on the combined and cumulative effects. This mind–body separation does a disservice to people recovering from ACEs, as well as anyone who has experienced both physical and psychological consequences of early life stress. Our goal is to include as many whole-person programs as possible, acknowledging and addressing the enduring physical consequences of ACEs and the inseparability of mind and body.

We do not have all the answers to the many questions about how to interrupt the cycle of ACEs and create systems that promote resilience and growth. We have, however, identified some encouraging prevention programs, intervention strategies, and policy initiatives that offer hope for improving the developmental trajectory for children and increasing the well-being and functioning of adults, families, and communities coping with the consequences of ACEs. In researching this section, we have encountered remarkable and inspiring individuals and organizations dedicated to this task. There is courage, compassion, and optimism within this movement.

5

Repairing the Effects of ACEs in Adulthood

Childhood adversity can tear you down but it can also be your single greatest impetus for growth. It takes tremendous courage and inner strength to transform the trauma of childhood adversity into a journey toward post-traumatic growth. But when you do reorient yourself, you open to the possibility of health.

—DONNA JACKSON NAKAZAWA, 2015, p. 227

We were struggling. All of us—the researchers, staff, and participants enrolled in EduCareers, a workforce training program for parents of children at Tulsa Educare early childhood centers (see https://www.educareschools.org/). EduCareers was one of several elements of the Tulsa Children's Project, a highly integrated set of interventions developed by a team of researchers from the University of Oklahoma in Tulsa, Harvard University's Center for the Developing Child, and the University of Texas. The aim was to interrupt the cycle of poverty in families with young children (Hays-Grudo, Slocum, Root, Bosler, & Morris, 2019). In the first two cohorts, the EduCareers program had helped more than 50 parents achieve career education goals. In the nursing training program, 100% of parents successfully passed the coursework and state exams to become certified nurse assistants. Successfully completing the next level of training, to become a licensed professional nurse, was proving difficult if not impossible for 80% of the parents, however. EduCareer staff provided every support element recommended by expert advisors and the parents themselves: weekly support

http://dx.doi.org/10.1037/0000177-005
Adverse and Protective Childhood Experiences: A Developmental Perspective, by J. Hays-Grudo and A. S. Morris

meetings led by skilled facilitators to build social support and life skills; tutoring sessions; and financial support for books, tuition, fees, transportation, and additional child care. Yet parents were failing classes, reporting that they could not remember what they studied, had difficulty planning ahead and flexibly adjusting their schedules for clinical rotations, and struggled to cope with the continual crises that occur when there is not enough money to make ends meet.

In developing the program, we had assumed that poverty was the problem, but as parents shared story after story of difficulties that required executive function skills (i.e., working memory, focusing attention, problem-solving, planning, and managing stress), we began to realize we had not considered the effects of adverse childhood experiences (ACEs). We assessed participants' executive function skills (LeJeune et al., 2010) and realized that these deficits were the source of the problem and that helping them develop these skills was fundamental—a crucial requirement for jobs with better pay, benefits, and opportunities for advancement in the health care sector. At that point, we revised the intervention, incorporating mindfulness-based stress management (MBSR) and executive function activities to improve the parents' biobehavioral responses to stress and build cognitive skills. Staff and parents embraced the practice of mindfulness, with parents reporting how MBSR was helping them manage stress and negative emotions and improve relationships with their children and other family members. More structured evaluations supported these reports, revealing significant gains in measures of mindfulness, self-compassion, stress, and hope (Hays-Grudo et al., 2019).

ACE-BASED SCIENCE AS A FOUNDATION FOR INTERVENTIONS

EduCareers had been designed using the existing best practices for building human capital in dual-generation programs—that is, it was embedded in a high-quality early childhood center, targeted appropriate economic workforce sectors, and addressed financial and social support needs throughout the program (Chase-Lansdale & Brooks-Gunn, 2014). However, our success was limited because our initial approach focused on the observable outcomes of childhood adversity—inadequate education and workforce training rather than the underlying neurobiological effects of ACEs. Because lack of job skills and financial resources are easily seen and measured, our intervention targeted these problems and deficits. As we became more aware of the negative effects of ACEs on self-regulation and other developmental outcomes, we recognized the need for interventions that focused on and improved biobehavioral regulation and executive function skills. We began to see the ACEs model more as an iceberg rather than a pyramid (see Figure 5.1), with the neurobiological and developmental deficits below the "water line," the submerged drivers of the more observable problems in functioning, unhealthy behaviors, and chronic conditions. Knowing the effects of ACEs pointed us toward new intervention targets.

FIGURE 5.1. Adverse Childhood Experiences (ACEs) Iceberg Model

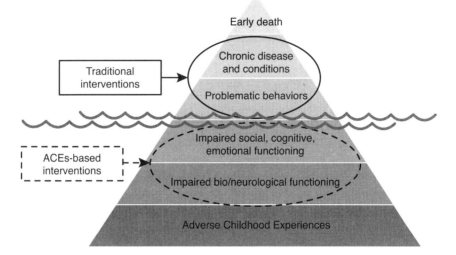

In this chapter, we describe what we and others have learned about helping adults with a history of childhood trauma develop the ability to manage and respond to stress and to acquire the cognitive, social, and emotional skills that may be impaired by early life adversity. Using the Intergenerational and Cumulative Adverse and Resilience Experiences (ICARE) model as a framework, we first discuss the research on mindfulness and other body-based programs that appear to "rewire" the neural connections compromised by childhood adversity, facilitating healthier neurobiological responses to stress. Next, we discuss more cognitive approaches that help individuals change the negative thought processes resulting from childhood trauma and create more appropriate coping strategies. Finally, we describe how using an adult protective and compensatory experiences (PACEs) plan can help individuals establish the relationships and resources in everyday life that sustain therapeutic outcomes and promote continued health and well-being (Table 5.1).

Improving Neurobiological Stress Regulation

The research reviewed in previous chapters leads us to conclude that among the most debilitating consequences of exposure to adversity during development is the dysregulation in both physiological and behavioral stress response systems. When a developing organism is exposed to persistent physical or psychological threats, the systems responsible for maintaining high levels of stress responses are programmed to respond to those threats. When the environment is hostile and threatening, maintaining high levels of vigilance and a quick fight, flight, or freeze response is adaptive. Unfortunately, as described by the allostatic load model, this prolonged stress response overloads these systems, resulting in hyper- or hyporesponsiveness, preventing

TABLE 5.1. ICARE Framework for ACEs-Based Interventions for Adults

Increasing positive neurobiological stress responses	Increasing adaptive behavior: cognitive, social, and emotional	Creating supportive and adaptive environments
Mindfulness-based stress reduction	Executive function skills training • Working memory games • Perspective-taking activities • Focused attention exercises	PACEs—Relationships • Unconditional love • Best friend • Volunteer • Mentor • Community or social group
Yoga	Expressive writing	
Body-based (bottom-up) activities • Floatation • Drama • Music • Dance • Martial arts	Trauma-focused cognitive behavior therapy	PACEs—Resources • Clean, uncluttered homes • Learning opportunities • Physical activity • Hobbies/recreation • Regular routines

Note. ACEs = adverse childhood experiences; PACES = protective and compensatory experiences.

the development of normal stress regulation. Thus, many of the interventions we describe have a focus on improving neurobiological responses to stress as well as developing the cognitive-behavioral and environmental supports to develop and maintain improved self-regulation.

Mindfulness-Based Programs

In previous chapters, we described the ways that childhood stress and trauma may compromise the development of executive functions and corresponding regions of the brain that are negatively affected by poverty (Luby et al., 2013) and early life trauma (Teicher & Samson, 2016). We know early life stress causes aberrant amygdala activation and is associated with anxiety (Stein, Simmons, Feinstein, & Paulus, 2007) and depression (Drevets et al., 1992). Mindfulness training appears to have positive effects on both these brain regions and their corresponding executive functions. Our decision to add MBSR training to the EduCareers curriculum was based on emerging evidence that MBSR had positive functional and structural effects on brain regions associated with the cognitive and self-regulatory skills that many of our participants lacked. For example, an early MBSR study suggested that participating in an 8-week program significantly affected perceived stress, which corresponded to decreased amygdala gray matter density (Hölzel et al., 2010).

Mindfulness and related practices have been valued by religious and spiritual traditions throughout history as a method for increasing self-awareness, self-control, and well-being. Mindfulness is characterized by objective and sustained awareness of physical sensations, perceptions, thoughts, and feelings with no corresponding judgment. A standard program to cultivate mindfulness to reduce stress and improve health and well-being was developed in the mid-1970s by Dr. Jon Kabat-Zinn at the University of Massachusetts. This program has demonstrated improved outcomes for patients suffering from a variety of chronic ailments (e.g., cancer, autoimmune disease, depression, and anxiety), as well as healthy individuals seeking skills to cope with the stresses of daily life (Gotink, Meijboom, Vernooij, Smits, & Hunink, 2016; Grossman, Niemann, Schmidt, & Walach, 2004; Kabat-Zinn, 2005). Training sessions cover particular exercises and topics, which are examined within the context of mindfulness, yoga postures, and homework assignments in the form of meditation practice and applying mindfulness to everyday situations (e.g., mindful eating or walking).

MBSR is a group-based program that provides guidance and opportunities to practice being mindfully present. There is little formal research using MBSR or similar programs specifically to ameliorate the effects of adverse childhood experiences in adults, but existing research with similar populations suggests that mindfulness-based programs may be particularly well suited for this purpose (Korotana, Dobson, Pusch, & Josephson, 2016). For example, randomized trials found that mindfulness-based interventions increased executive function, particularly focused attention, emotion regulation, and self-awareness (Gallant, 2016; Tang, Hölzel, & Posner, 2015), in nontraumatized adults as well as adults who experienced childhood abuse (Earley et al., 2014; Kimbrough, Magyari, Langenberg, Chesney, & Berman, 2010).

In the years since the EduCareers intervention, evidence continues to accrue that supports the use of MBSR to increase executive function skills and corresponding neural changes (Tang et al., 2015). In 2011, Hölzel and colleagues randomly assigned healthy adults to participate in an 8-week MBSR program or a control condition. They observed increased gray matter in brain regions involved in learning and memory processes, emotion regulation, self-awareness, and perspective-taking, and increased gray matter concentration in the left hippocampus in the MBSR group (Hölzel et al., 2011). A similar study of a 4-week mindfulness program found changes in cognitive functioning related to working memory and corresponding changes in the left hippocampus (Greenberg et al., 2019). Several recent reviews of the effects of MBSR on brain structure and function in healthy adults found consistent patterns of association between neural changes and enhanced executive function skills, including focused attention, emotion regulation, emotion processing, and self-awareness (Gotink et al., 2016; Hatchard et al., 2017; Tang et al., 2015). MBSR has also helped reduce symptoms in individuals with posttraumatic stress disorder (PTSD), anxiety, depression, and addiction (Paulus, 2016; Sedlmeier et al., 2012). Other studies show that mindfulness positively affected immunological and epigenetic mechanisms involved in mood and stress-related disorders (Daubenmier et al., 2012), with MBSR-practicing individuals demonstrating reduced inflammatory responses compared with controls (Rosenkranz et al., 2013).

Analyzing high-resolution MRI data of long-term meditators and matched controls, Luders, Toga, and colleagues (2009) found that experienced meditators had significantly larger volumes of the right hippocampus and other regions associated with emotion regulation and impulse control. Similar associations have also been found between brain regions and self-awareness and lower perceived stress in individuals rated high on "trait" or "dispositional" mindfulness (Lu et al., 2014; Prakash, Hussain, & Schirda, 2015). Prakash and colleagues (2015) found that emotion regulation mediated the relationship between dispositional mindfulness and perceived stress. Also investigating the link between dispositional mindfulness and well-being, Short and colleagues (2016) found that self-regulation and executive function, both independently and together, mediated the relationship between mindfulness and negative affect, whereas only self-regulation mediated the relationship between mindfulness and positive affect. Relatedly, dispositional mindfulness was found to temper the relationship between high ACEs and having multiple health conditions, poor health behaviors, and poor health-related quality of life in Head Start staff members (Whitaker et al., 2014) and between ACEs, alcohol use, and negative alcohol consequences in college students (Brett, Espeleta, Lopez, Leavens, & Leffingwell, 2018). Clearly, mindfulness has benefits for health and well-being.

Neurofeedback

Another newly emerging approach that may be appropriate for treating emotion regulation problems related to ACEs is neurofeedback. Using real-time functional MRI neurofeedback (rt-fMRI-nf), individuals can learn to control neural activity in regions of the brain associated with anxiety and depression. In a recent series of studies, Dr. Jerzy Bodurka and colleagues at the Laureate Institute for Brain Research demonstrated the effectiveness of rt-fMRI-nf for reducing symptoms of anxiety and depression, as well as corresponding changes in neural connectivity. In one double-blind, placebo-controlled trial, adults with depression learned to retrieve happy memories while focusing on increasing the hemodynamic activity in either the left amygdala (experimental group) or a segment of the intraparietal sulcus, a region putatively not involved in emotion regulation (control group; K. D. Young et al., 2017). Participants in the experimental group showed significant reductions in depressive symptoms, with one third meeting criteria for remission at the study end. They also increased their recall of specific positive events and decreased their recall of overly general memories, a cognitive deficit associated with depression.

Using a similar methodology, researchers in the Bodurka lab randomly assigned combat veterans with and without PTSD to either a control condition or an experimental condition. The goal was for participants to increase the feedback signal from the left amygdala (experimental group) or the intraparietal region (control group) by recalling happy autobiographical memories. The veterans in the experimental group learned to upregulate blood oxygenation level–dependent activity to the left amygdala and demonstrated significant and clinically meaningful reductions in PTSD symptoms and comorbid depression severity. Changes in symptoms significantly correlated with positive changes in functional connectivity between the left amygdala and the left dorsolateral prefrontal cortex (Zotev et al., 2018) and with connectivity increases in areas not targeted by the rt-fMRI-nf training tasks (Misaki et al., 2018). Although most research evaluating neurofeedback as a treatment for stress has focused on individuals with PTSD (Nicholson et al., 2017; Reiter, Andersen, & Carlsson, 2016), the technique has been shown to improve PTSD symptoms in adults with a history of childhood trauma or abuse (Gapen et al., 2016; Kluetsch et al., 2014), suggesting that similar neural mechanisms may be potential targets for intervention with ACEs.

Yoga

Yoga is one of the most widely practiced forms of mindful movement therapy in the United States and has been widely studied as a part of complementary and integrative medicine. The National Institutes of Health's National Center for Complementary and Integrative Health (NCCIH, 2018) describes yoga as

> an ancient and complex practice, rooted in Indian philosophy. It began as a spiritual practice but has become popular as a way of promoting physical and mental well-being.
>
> Although classical yoga also includes other elements, yoga as practiced in the United States typically emphasizes physical postures (*asanas*), breathing techniques (*pranayama*), and meditation (*dyana*). Popular yoga styles such as iyengar, bikram, and hatha yoga focus on these elements.
>
> Several traditional yoga styles encourage daily practice with periodic days of rest, whereas others encourage individuals to develop schedules that fit their needs. ("What Is Yoga and How Does It Work" section, paras. 1–3; italics in original)

In yoga, similar to MBSR, the focus of attention is on the sensory experience of breathing. However, yoga practice also includes awareness of the physical sensations brought about by changes in poses. The mindfulness aspect is hypothesized to increase emotion regulation by drawing attention to thoughts, feelings, and sensations, and the heightened body awareness promotes increased recognition of physiological responses to those feelings and thoughts (e.g., body tension, increased heartbeat, rapid and shallow breathing). As in MBSR, which incorporates yoga postures into its sessions, the goal is to observe these responses as they come and go without judgment, rather than avoiding them or holding on to them. Van der Kolk (2015) proposed that adults with a history of childhood trauma may find yoga more tolerable than MBSR because it provides physical movement and sensations as a target for focused attention rather than the more limited range of sensations experienced during seated meditation.

Studies on the efficacy of yoga for trauma and related mental health problems vary considerably in their scientific rigor, and evidence of its effectiveness is still preliminary (Cramer, Anheyer, Saha, & Dobos, 2018; Macy, Jones, Graham, & Roach, 2018). However, the results of several randomized clinical trials suggest that yoga should be considered at least as an adjunct to other therapies (Dick, Niles, Street, DiMartino, & Mitchell, 2014; Mitchell et al., 2014). For example, van der Kolk and colleagues (2014) randomized 64 women with chronic, treatment-resistant PTSD to either trauma-informed yoga or to a supportive women's health education program for 10 weekly 1-hour sessions. Both groups showed reduction in PTSD symptoms midway through treatment. However, posttreatment symptom levels returned to baseline for women in the supportive education group, whereas participants in the yoga group continued to have reduced symptoms of depression and PTSD, with effect sizes comparable to other effective treatments. The investigators extended these findings by examining the effects of a more intensive 20-week trauma-sensitive yoga program for women with treatment-unresponsive PTSD (Price et al., 2017). Although limited by a small sample size ($n = 9$), significant reductions in PTSD and dissociation symptoms were found, suggesting that long-term treatment may help manage chronic and severe forms of posttraumatic stress, with results comparable to other trauma-focused treatments.

Research on interventions such as MBSR and neurofeedback appear to improve outcomes by helping individuals increase the capacity to focus their attention, minimize judgments, and control negative thoughts. Not all survivors of ACEs may benefit from these therapies (van der Kolk, 2015). Some individuals find it too painful or difficult to sit still alone with their thoughts, and will benefit from more active forms of meditative action, such as yoga and other more physical and active forms of therapy.

Body-Based Interventions to Reduce Stress Responses

In his 2015 book *The Body Keeps the Score*, Dr. Bessel van der Kolk proposed that there is an understudied and underutilized category of interventions to help recover from childhood trauma. These are the "bottom-up" or body-based experiences that not only deal with effects of current or everyday stressors but also help excavate and shed the internalized stress from previous years. These activities allow "the body to have experiences that deeply and viscerally contradict the helplessness, rage, or collapse that result from trauma" (van der Kolk, 2015, p. 3). Many of these activities and experiences are widely available in most communities and provide a wide array of choices for adults struggling with the effects of childhood trauma.

Floatation-REST

A novel intervention for reducing anxiety and increasing self-awareness in individuals with anxiety or comorbid depression is floatation with reduced environmental stimulation (Floatation-REST; Feinstein, Khalsa, Al Zoubi, et al., 2018; Feinstein, Khalsa, Yeh, et al., 2018). Floatation-REST involves floating for 60 to 90 minutes in a shallow pool of water saturated with Epsom salt (magnesium sulfate) to create buoyancy. The experience is calibrated to remove all or most visual, auditory, olfactory, gustatory, thermal, vestibular, gravitational, and proprioceptive signals, as well as most movement and speech. In a study with 50 anxious and depressed patients who had a wide range of stress-related disorders, Feinstein, Khalsa, Al Zoubi, et al. (2018) found that a single 60-minute floatation session induced a strong reduction in state anxiety and a substantial improvement in mood. Floatation-REST is considered an evidence-based medical treatment in parts of Europe and "float tanks" are increasingly available, if not always inexpensive, in the United States at spas and other wellness centers. Consumers should be aware, however, that commercial establishments may exaggerate flotation benefits, and facilities can vary greatly in quality (Jonsson & Kjellgren, 2014).

Theater and Drama

Participating in amateur theater groups is not often recognized as a therapeutic modality to aid in the recovery from childhood trauma and adversity. However, this approach is becoming more widespread in urban communities and is nicely illustrated by an anecdote from van der Kolk's own family experience. In his 2015 book, van der Kolk described how his son's adolescent chronic fatigue-type illness left him isolated and self-hating until he joined an evening class in improvisational theater for teens. He observed a marked change in his son's demeanor as a result of "acting" like a strong, popular guy for a role in a play, and van der Kolk (2015) concluded that

> unlike his [son's] experience with the numerous therapists who had talked with him about how bad he felt, theater gave him a chance to deeply and physically experience what it was like to be someone other than the learning-disabled, oversensitive boy that he had gradually become. Being a valued contributor to a group gave him a visceral experience of power and competence. I believe that this new embodied version of himself set him on the road to becoming the creative, loving adult he is today. (p. 331)

Theater groups have been surfacing in other communities as a way to help teens and young adults come to terms with injuries sustained at the hands of their families and communities. For example, the Possibility Project in New York City provides after-school, evening, and Saturday sessions for teens to experience writing, acting, and directing their own material based on their adverse experiences. A recent 3-year evaluation by Dr. Michael Hanson at Teacher's College of Columbia University, found evidence of the program's impact on emotional support, conflict resolution, and self-disclosure in participating youth. Significantly, participants in the program specifically designed for youth in foster care are much less likely to become teen parents or be arrested or convicted of a crime 1 to 6 years following participation (see https://the-possibility-project.org/foster-care-research-report.)

Music and Dance

Collective movement and music are also avenues for managing stress and connecting with others, as evidenced by the use of communal musical and rhythmic activity in religious rituals, military drills, and even forced physical activity. Their effects simultaneously enhance individual dignity and social solidarity, and they increase individual and group survival (van der Kolk, 2015). Think about what is involved in doing something as ordinary as singing in a choir. First there are the rehearsals, which entail making a commitment to fit them into an already busy schedule, to be on time, to practice, to engage with others, and, most important, to listen to others, as you pitch your voice in harmony or add a counterpoint melody, making mistakes and starting again, overlooking others' mistakes and starting again. The shared space becomes an altered reality, where a kind of intimacy is required—people standing close together on the risers, listening to each other, breathing together in time, co-creating sounds and art that is beyond the capacity of any one individual. Then, there is the performance, drawing that first breath in front of the audience—a moment that would be incredibly, distressingly stressful if you were singing alone but is tolerable, even thrilling, when one's voice is joined with others' in concert (*concert* also means "to act jointly"). This same analogy can be used for chamber or symphony orchestras, jazz or marching bands, dance groups, and other musical and rhythmic activities. Research indicates that increasing musical activity (e.g., singing, improvising) can have beneficial effects on emotion regulation and self-awareness, along with corresponding neural activation (K. S. Moore, 2013). For example, group drumming improves immune function in healthy adults (Bittman et al., 2001), as well as improved anxiety, depression, social resilience, and immune function in patients seeking mental health services (Fancourt et al., 2016). Group drumming has also been found to decrease PTSD symptoms and improve mood in combat veterans (Bensimon, Amir, & Wolf, 2008), and music therapy significantly improved PTSD symptoms among patients for whom previous cognitive behavior therapy was unsuccessful (Carr et al., 2012). For adults with childhood histories of adversity, music-based programs may be another avenue for improved physical and mental health.

Martial Arts Training

A small but growing body of research indicates that martial arts training may benefit physical and mental health. Martial arts, as practiced by many Eastern cultures for millennia, incorporate elements of physical activity and mind-fulness, functioning as both sport and therapy (D. T. Burke, Al-Adawi, Lee, & Audette, 2007). A recent review of 28 studies assessing the effects of martial arts training found it beneficial for balance, cognitive function, muscular-skeletal strength, cardiovascular fitness, metabolic functioning, mood, and perceived quality of life (Origua Rios, Marks, Estevan, & Barnett, 2018). Rewards outweighed risk of injury, which tended to be minor, and benefits were evident across all adult age ranges. Numerous studies with both adults and children showed training increased self-esteem and self-confidence (Weiser, Kutz, Kutz, & Weiser, 1995). Moreover, martial arts training is usually done in group settings, providing multiple compensatory benefits: social connection, mastery and self-confidence, self-awareness, and physical activity.

Cognitive, Socioemotional, and Behavioral Interventions

Adverse childhood experiences affect more than the body's programmed response to stress. Exposure to cumulative and related types of abuse, neglect, and family dysfunction during childhood may also negatively affect the concept of self, the ability to trust and form relationships with others, and behavioral coping mechanisms. Therapeutic approaches that directly address these issues are also an important part of recovery and posttraumatic growth.

Expressive Writing

In the 1980s, psychology professor Dr. Jamie Pennebaker conducted a survey to identify predictors of health symptoms and sensations among under-graduates. The approximately 15% who reported a traumatic sexual experience before age 17 also reported having more health symptoms and more trips to the doctor. Interviews and subsequent research revealed that the source of the health problems was not the trauma itself but the act of keeping it a secret. Those who had any kind of trauma but had not talked about it were most likely to have health problems (Pennebaker, 1989, 2018). He hypothesized that keeping traumatic events secret required *active inhibition*, itself a source of physiological stress (Selye, 1956). Pennebaker then developed the *expressive writing* paradigm as a therapeutic process for disclosing the secret and creating a coherent narrative to put the adversity into context. By the 1990s, dozens of randomized trials in a variety of populations yielded consistent findings: Individuals who wrote about an emotionally traumatic event exhibited improved health, as evidenced by improved measures of immune function and fewer illnesses, compared with individuals who wrote about superficial topics. In the research protocol for expressive writing, participants are asked to set aside a special time and place every day for 4 days to write continuously about an upsetting or traumatic experience without concern for grammar or spelling but focused on their deepest thoughts and feelings about the experience. Participants are allowed to choose any experience but encouraged to identify the most upsetting and least discussed event in their lives. They are encouraged to delve as deeply as possible into their emotions and are warned that many people find the process quite upsetting (Pennebaker, 1989).

The first decade of research on this process has been cited more than 2,500 times (Pennebaker, 1997), and research using this basic protocol continues (Pennebaker, 2018) unabated, with improvements and adaptations for use with special populations. For example, several studies show that writing from the first-person confers more perceived value (Seih, Chung, & Pennebaker, 2011) and activates more relevant emotions (McIsaac & Eich, 2004). Sayer and colleagues (2015) randomly assigned U.S. Afghanistan and Iraq war veterans with self-reported difficulty adjusting back into civilian life to expressive writing, factual control writing, or no-writing groups. Veterans in the expressive writing group, compared with both controls, experienced greater reductions in physical complaints, anger, and distress. Compared with the no-writing control, they had greater reductions in PTSD symptoms and reintegration difficulties and greater improvement in social support. In a study of college students with depression, expressive writing on 3 consecutive days resulted in reduced rumination and depressive symptoms (Gortner, Rude, & Pennebaker, 2006). Given the evidence for its effectiveness and the accessibility of the protocol, expressive writing is recommended for adults trying to recover from the effects of childhood adversity (Korotana et al., 2016; Smyth & Helm, 2003; van der Kolk, 2015).

Expressive writing improves well-being because it is an opportunity to create a coherent narrative of one's life, integrating trauma and stressful experiences within the larger story. Like hero stories in mythology and folktales, the hero encounters adversity or traumatic events, survives, initiates recovery, and eventually triumphs. Often, writers find that their stories contain elements of resilience and heroism, lessons learned, opportunities created, and feelings of gratitude that accompany memories of fear, shame, and loss. Research on the positive psychological changes resulting from childhood adversity reveals that posttraumatic growth is indeed possible and can also be cultivated through supportive relationships and environments (Tedeschi & Calhoun, 2004). These relationships are often forged in individual and group therapy.

Trauma-Informed Cognitive Behavior Therapy

Recovering from childhood trauma often requires help from others. Individuals do not always have the tools needed to begin and maintain a practice in mindfulness, reach out and trust others, join a yoga class, set and maintain healthy eating and sleep habits, and establish other PACEs in their lives. Professional counselling and therapy from a trauma-informed and skilled therapist is often exactly what is needed to get started in recovering from ACEs and to maintain the growth and development that can be lifelong.

Cognitive behavior therapy (CBT) is a highly researched and well-supported therapeutic approach that focuses on restructuring self-defeating thoughts and creating new patterns of behavior (A. Beck, 1979; J. Beck, 2011; Burns, 1999). CBT is goal-oriented, with a focus on breaking challenging and daunting problems into a series of smaller and more manageable action steps. Its focus on negative automatic thoughts make it a good option to address depression, anxiety, and other forms of psychological distress that may result from childhood adversity because it helps individuals address as adults the negative thoughts that were internalized from abusive interactions or conclusions drawn from childhood experiences of neglect. In CBT, clients learn to recognize these automatic thoughts (sometimes co-occurring with physical pains or sensations), bring them to conscious awareness, test them for accuracy, and replace them with more constructive and accurate statements. A variety of techniques may be used in CBT, including relaxation training, cognitive restructuring, behavioral activation, and exposure therapy. Mindfulness-based therapy has long been integrated into CBT programs and has been found to reduce relapse following treatment for depression (Segal, Gemar, & Williams, 1999).

Posttraumatic Growth

Recognizing the multifaceted, negative outcomes of childhood adversity does not preclude recognizing positive qualities and capacities that adversity can create. In her book *The Deepest Well*, Dr. Nadine Burke Harris talks about growing up with a wonderful mother who suffered from untreated paranoid schizophrenia. Although her home was full of love, there were also some very bad days. She and her brothers never knew whether they would come home from school to "happy Mom or scary Mom." To adapt to this stressful environment, Harris developed the ability to read cues quickly and function well in high-adrenaline situations:

> I would never want to repeat the distressing or unpredictable moments of my childhood, but I wouldn't wish them away either. They are a big part of what has made me who I am. Sometimes I like to think of this ability to tune in to people as my own little superpower. As a doctor it allows me to gently ask my patients the right follow-up questions and get to the heart of the matter quickly. (Harris, 2018, p. 216)

This is a powerful example of integrating adverse childhood experiences into a coherent story of resilience and gratitude. Holding on to the positive outcomes of adversities is not always easy because the negative consequences can be overwhelming. That is why an adult version of PACEs can aid ongoing recovery and growth from adversity to resilience.

PACEs FOR ADULTS

Neurobiological reprogramming, cognitive restructuring, and therapeutic social and emotional experiences are important elements of recovery from childhood adversity. However, sustained adult development and healing is also aided by the "ordinary magic" of common, everyday resilience-promoting relationships and environments. The experiences and environments that help adults overcome the negative physical and psychological effects of early life adversity are similar to the PACEs we describe for children and youth in Chapter 2 and are listed in Table 5.1 earlier in the chapter. They can be categorized as relationship-focused or resource- and environment-focused. They appear to be simple and self-evident. In fact, to our knowledge, few have been subjected to clinical trials to demonstrate their efficacy for promoting recovery from childhood adversity or for supporting posttraumatic growth. Each of them, however, has been found to promote physical and mental health and well-being in adults, prevent cognitive decline, and reduce social isolation in aging.

Relationship PACEs

One of the most important elements for healing and recovering from childhood adversity is having the experience of being loved and loving in return. Unconditional love is the ultimate antidote for fear and suffering. The source of this unconditional love may be a romantic or marital partner, a childhood friend, or a sibling. (We are even inclined to think it could be a particularly intelligent and loyal pet.) We do not earn that love; it is just there for us, like a spring bubbling forth in the desert. But we can and should value it for the life-giving force that it is and pay it forward when we have the opportunity.

Even separation does not separate us from the benefits of unconditional love. In his memoir of surviving Nazi concentration camps, Victor Frankl described his remarkable psychological triumph over terror and despair, and the realizations that launched the branch of humanistic psychology. It was his personal epiphany about the indestructibility of love, however, that has helped thousands of others suffering from trauma and loss. It happened on an icy predawn march to a work site. As he and his fellow prisoners struggled over stones and puddles, prodded by rifle butts and shivering in an icy wind, the man marching next to him whispered: "If our wives could see us now! I do hope they are better off in their camps." This brought thoughts of his own wife to mind, thoughts that he clung to as they marched on for miles and the sky began to turn pink. He imagined her face in vivid detail, her smile, her encouraging look, and heard her voice. He wrote:

> Real or not, her look was then more luminous than the sun which was beginning to rise.
>   A thought transfixed me: for the first time in my life I saw the truth as it is set into song by so many poets, proclaimed as the final wisdom by so many thinkers. The truth—that love is the ultimate and the highest goal to which man can aspire. Then I grasped the meaning of the greatest secret that human poetry and human thought and belief have to impart: *The salvation of man is through love and in love.* (Frankl, 1985, p. 57, italics in original)

Frankl was able to transcend the camps' unspeakable miseries and degradations by invoking the memory of love. Many of us can remember occasions when we were so challenged and stressed that we questioned whether we would survive intact. We can usually identify supportive and loving friends and family members who made that stress tolerable. Many people derive comfort during adverse experiences from their belief that they are loved and valued by a higher power (Cameron, Carroll, & Hamilton, 2018).

Supportive and loving relationships are essential for human development and well-being. These relationships often take time and energy to develop. One pathway to these opportunities is through community involvement. Daily life and routines have changed dramatically in the past hundred years (a nanosecond in evolutionary time), wreaking havoc on our social patterns. Our grandparents did not have the Internet, hundreds of cable channels, social media, or smartphones. In their day, people came home from work or school and talked to each other. They sat on front porches or stoops and visited with their neighbors. They went to lectures at the local library from someone who had recently been abroad, they joined bowling teams, went to the union hall, or just hung out at the general store or malt shop to escape boredom and isolation.

Avoiding Social Isolation

Social isolation has been identified as one of the leading causes of premature mortality in the industrialized world, on par with smoking (Holt-Lunstad, Smith, & Layton, 2010). Few of us know the names of our mail carrier, the barista at our favorite cafe, or anything about their lives. Holt-Lunstad (2018) and her colleagues (Holt-Lunstad, Robles, & Sbarra, 2017) found that social connectedness involves being socially engaged with a wide range of people in one's community in addition to having good-quality relationships with friends and family. Clearly, it is in our best interest to overcome the forces that prevent us from conversing and connecting with people we meet, getting involved in social groups for fun or a purpose, and spending time and energy making sure our relationships are mutually rewarding.

Having and being a mentor to others is also a valuable source of social connections that can deepen and expand individuals' knowledge of themselves as they seek more authentic ways to engage with others as they recover from traumatic childhood relationships. This may be especially valuable for adults in careers where seeking mental health support is perceived as career-ending or shameful, such as the military or law enforcement, or in environments with limited access to professional counselling (Keller et al., 2005). Mentoring relationships, whether through informally occurring or more structured programs at school, work, or other community groups, ideally foster mutual trust and reciprocal perspective-taking. Likewise, serving as a mentor and being a volunteer helper is a powerful promoter of resilience and mental health. Giving of one's time and resources is not only an act of generosity but an act of confidence, putting into action the belief that "I have plenty; I have enough time, energy, and resources that I can share with others who have less."

Resource PACEs

Creating enriching environments is essential for shifting from one way of being into another. We saw in the animal research discussed in Chapters 3 and 4 that enriched environments can repair the epigenetic and behavioral effects of early life adversity. Much less research exists with humans, but population studies of positive aging provide conclusive evidence that environments rich in supportive social connections, healthy routines and habits, and opportunities for meaningful work and play promote mental and physical health and overall quality of life (Holt-Lunstad et al., 2010; Sowa, Tobiasz-Adamczyk, Topór-Madry, Poscia, & la Milia, 2016; Woods et al., 2016). Because successful aging is dependent on being healthy throughout adulthood, researchers have investigated the attitudes, behaviors, and environments of individuals who have aged well (Kuh, 2019; Lafortune et al., 2016). In a sense, healthy aging is a window into healthy living.

Creating Healthy Routines and Lifestyles

Thousands of studies document the beneficial effects of a healthy diet, regular physical activity, and adequate sleep for maintaining good health across the life span. Activities that stimulate thinking, learning, and social connectivity promote both mental and physical health. In a longitudinal study of thousands of women enrolled in the Women's Health Initiative, positive emotional functioning and healthy habits were independently related to healthy aging, suggesting that addressing mental health issues such as depression and anxiety are important targets for improving health across the life span (Zaslavsky et al., 2014). In this study, women who maintained high levels of physical health were more physically active, had fewer general or depressive symptoms, had more optimism, and had less pain than women who did not maintain good physical health over time.

Studies in Western Europe have found similar results: A comprehensive survey of more than 11,000 individuals from six European countries aimed to identify the lifestyle and psychosocial predictors of health from midlife to old age (Sowa et al., 2016). Results showed that good health across the life span could be predicted by three categories of indicators: lifestyle, psychosocial, and sociodemographic. The most important lifestyle behaviors predicting long-term health were not smoking, getting moderate physical activity daily, engaging in more vigorous sport more than once a week, eating fruits and vegetables daily, consuming adequate healthy liquids daily, and eating regular meals. Psychosocial determinants included employment, participating in organized social activities (volunteering, learning, sports, clubs, religious, and community organizations), regular leisure activities (reading, playing games or chess, hobbies), satisfaction from the social network, and life satisfaction (Sowa et al., 2016). The importance of education, income, and location are well-recognized predictors of life span health in the United States and in Europe (Lafortune et al., 2016; Marmot & Allen, 2014). Given the effects of ACEs on cognitive development, school performance, and subsequent economic success, in addition to lifestyle behaviors and psychosocial indicators, there is good reason to include ACEs and PACEs in our efforts to address community health inequities and "social determinants of health" (Adler et al., 2016; Braveman & Gottlieb, 2014). This is a topic we discuss in Chapter 7.

CONCLUSIONS AND ACTIVITY: CREATING AN ADULT PACEs PLAN

In summary, recovering from childhood adversity, trauma, and the debilitating consequences of toxic stress is facilitated by developing relationships that provide emotional satisfaction and practical support, feeling connected and giving back to the community, and developing and maintaining regular healthy lifestyle habits. These factors are included in the adult PACEs scale. Although the basic elements of healthy living do not seem as integral to ACEs recovery as methods that more directly address the effects of trauma, we believe they are essential for supporting continued recovery and growth for several reasons.

First, childhood adversity affects the stress response system, increasing inflammatory and other systems that damage health and reduce the production of neurotransmitters and hormones associated with health and longevity. Diets high in refined carbohydrates (sugar and flour), inadequate sleep, and lack of physical activity exacerbate inflammatory responses, piling injury upon injury. Loving relationships, satisfying social connections, and meaningful work, learning, and recreational activities increase the positive hormones and neurotransmitters associated with well-being.

Second, as outlined in Chapter 1, adults with high ACEs are at risk for using health-harming behaviors as solutions or adaptations to adversity. Decreasing and eliminating unhealthy avoidant behaviors becomes habitual and are more likely to be sustained when substituted with more positive behaviors and routines. Establishing healthy habits and routines supports long-term recovery and growth by creating a new "normal," setting in place the relationships and environments that support continued development over many lifetimes.

Third, establishing supportive relationships and healthy routines is an effective way to maintain the benefits from cognitive behavior therapy, MBSR, and other trauma-informed approaches. When adults with a history of ACEs maintain the chaotic lifestyles and unhealthy habits learned in childhood, they unwittingly undermine their potential for continued growth and healing. Setting goals to establish habits and daily routines that support and strengthen relationships, positive physiological and behavioral responses to stress, and creating more enriched environments can be accomplished using the PACEs framework.

Adult PACEs Plan

Creating visual reminders of specific goals within a PACEs plan can help individuals establish and maintain these new behaviors and lifestyles. Visual records can help people stay on track and provide a springboard to launch more intentional patterns of healthy living, experiment with new patterns, and document what works and what does not. A PACEs plan can be used with CBT and other forms of trauma-informed therapies to support goal setting, cognitive restructuring, and flexible problem-solving. They also provide a way to track successes and observe progress over time. We believe it provides a useful source of support for adults as they seek to overcome childhood trauma by providing a blueprint for the creation and maintenance of more enriching and nurturing relationships and environments.

Figure 5.2 provides a PACEs plan template that may be helpful when working with adults seeking to establish environments that support recovery from childhood trauma and adversity.

FIGURE 5.2. Adult Protective and Compensatory Experiences (PACEs) Plan

Month _____

Relationship PACEs

Love. I know that I am loved and I love someone unconditionally. I do not doubt that I am cared for.

Current status: *Actions taken:*

Goal:

Friendship. I have at least one best friend, someone I can count on and have fun with.

Current status: *Actions taken:*

Goal:

Volunteer. I do something regularly to benefit others and/or participate in community helping projects.

Current status: *Actions taken:*

Goal:

Mentor. I have someone I can turn to for advice, information, or support.

Current status: *Actions taken:*

Goal:

FIGURE 5.2. Adult Protective and Compensatory Experiences (PACEs) Plan (*Continued*)

Community connection. I am an active member of at least one civic, social, or faith-based group.

Current status: *Actions taken:*

Goal:

Environment and Resources PACES

Home. I live in a home that is clean, uncluttered, and safe with healthy food.

Current status: *Actions taken:*

Goal:

Learning. I make opportunities for lifelong learning and have the resources I need to learn and grow in my work and as a person.

Current status: *Actions taken:*

Goal:

Physical activity. I get some type of physical exercise every day, either alone or with others.

Current status: *Actions taken:*

Goal:

(continues)

FIGURE 5.2. Adult Protective and Compensatory Experiences (PACEs) Plan (*Continued*)

Hobby. I have a hobby that gives me pleasure and allows me to be creative and productive and feel proud of my accomplishments.

Current status: *Actions taken:*

Goal:

Routines and rituals. I make a point to get enough sleep, eat regular meals with family and friends, and have other opportunities to spend time with others.

Current status: *Actions taken:*

Goal:

Notes:

6

Promoting Positive Development in Children With ACEs

It is easier to build strong children than to repair broken men.

—FREDERICK DOUGLASS

In 1946, Dr. Emmi Pikler founded a residential nursery in Budapest to care for babies and young children orphaned during World War II. Pikler was trained as a pediatrician in Vienna in the 1920s and had a thriving pediatrics practice before the war. She wrote several parenting books, one of which is charmingly titled *Peaceful Babies, Contented Mothers*, and she was known as an expert on infant motor development (Gonzalez-Mena & Briley, 2011). What differentiated Loczy, named for the street it was on, from other orphanages was that it was a peaceful, respectful caregiving environment where children had freedom of movement and time for play. They were never in their cribs except for sleeping. Pikler's goal was to promote attachment and individual identity, with a focus on respect (Chahin, 2008; Tardos, 2011).

What else made the Pikler home unique? First, caregivers had extensive training on caregiving methods and principles of attachment and individual respect. A caregiver was also responsible for only two or three children, keeping copious records on their progress. Basic caregiving (e.g., dressing, diapering) was conducted individually, and babies received undivided attention and continual verbal interaction during these activities. Babies could look the caregiver in the eye because she was at the foot of the changing table, not at the side. Caregivers encouraged children to dress themselves, providing support but not interfering unless necessary. Children played in groups, with a focus

http://dx.doi.org/10.1037/0000177-006
Adverse and Protective Childhood Experiences: A Developmental Perspective, by J. Hays-Grudo and A. S. Morris

on learning, not teaching. "Free movement," where children developed on their own in a safe, unrestricted space, was encouraged.

In a study reported by Gonzalez-Mena (2004), Hungarian researcher Margit Hirsch observed 30 children who had lived at Loczy during their infancy and found no emotional or cognitive delays in the children when placed with families. This suggests that Pikler's methods protected children from some of the adverse outcomes typically observed with parental separation. The Loczy children provide a stark contrast to the children raised in Romanian orphanages discussed in Chapter 3, who exhibited profound developmental delays in social and cognitive functioning. This suggests it is possible to facilitate positive development under even the most potentially adverse circumstances. Dr. Pikler was something of a visionary; her methods are in accord with developmental research and theory emphasizing attachment and autonomy, and they are still used today. In fact, scholars and educators from around the world visit Loczy each year to learn the Pikler Method and observe caregiving interactions (https://pikler.org).

In this chapter, we provide a framework for how to help children who have had adverse early life experiences. Information is based on empirically supported interventions and studies of child development that illustrate how caregivers (parents, teachers, grandparents) can help children and adolescents with a history of adverse childhood experiences (ACEs). This framework is based on the Intergenerational and Cumulative Adverse and Resilience Experiences (ICARE) model presented in Chapter 3. We have adapted the model to focus on ways to promote resilience and teach caregivers how to foster positive developmental outcomes in children with ACEs (see Table 6.1). First, we start with a discussion of promoting protective and compensatory experiences (PACEs) as a universal strategy to facilitate positive development in children and adolescents. Second, we discuss specific ways that caregivers and children can improve neurobiological and self-regulation. Next, we discuss ways to promote positive parent/caregiver–child relationships. We end with a discussion of system-level strategies aimed at fostering positive development and resilience at a broad, public health level. Throughout the chapter, we present examples of specific interventions and research studies to support our framework. This chapter is not an exhaustive review of positive parenting programs; rather, it is a more targeted review focused specifically on ways to help children who have experienced early life adversity. It is important to note that ACEs caused by caregivers require immediate intervention and assistance from other adults. Some of the programs discussed in this chapter are targeted for caregivers with a history of ACEs or who are at risk for maltreatment or have a history of maltreatment, and we note when this is the case.

PACEs FOR CHILDREN

Developmental scientists generally agree on what constitutes good parenting (Steinberg, 2001). As discussed in Chapter 2, this volume, caregivers should be nurturing and responsive, as well as firm and consistent. When caring for

TABLE 6.1. ICARE Framework for Promoting Resilience in Children and Adolescents With Adverse Early Life Experiences

Promoting PACEs		Enhancing neurobiological regulation	Fostering nurturing behaviors and positive relationships	Create system-level programs
0–5 years	6–18 years			
1. Nurturance	1. Love	*Caregiver activities:*	• Responsive/sensitive caregiving	*Examples:*
2. Playmate	2. Best friend	• Calm caregiving	• Delighting in the child and encouraging positive behavior	• Support caregivers (health, well-being)
3. Foster empathy	3. Volunteering	• Mindful parenting	• Following the child's lead and listening actively	• Disseminate positive parenting information
4. Play group	4. Part of social group	• Emotion coaching	• Encouraging exploration and autonomy	• Provide universal parenting classes and groups
5. Other caregiver	5. Mentor	*Child activities:*	• Avoiding harsh and frightening behavior (e.g., yelling, spanking)	• Make mental health resources available and accessible
6. Safe and child-friendly home	6. Safe home	• Mindfulness	• Setting limits	• Fund quality early childcare programs and schools
7. Learning opportunities	7. Good school	• Yoga	• Monitoring behavior	• Provide community-wide access to youth programs (sports, music, theater, job skills)
8. Family outings	8. A hobby	• Martial arts	• Involvement	
9. Physical activity	9. Physical activity	• Executive function games and activities		
10. Rules and routines	10. Rules and routines	• Music		
		• Sports		

children with ACEs, the same principles apply, but everything is more difficult. Caregivers need more patience and support, and children need more consistency and nurturance. In Table 6.1, we start by listing the PACEs that set the foundation for positive development. We also include separate PACEs for children aged 0 to 5 years because some of the original PACEs are more relevant as children grow older (see also the activity at the end of this chapter in Figure 6.3). In the next sections, we focus primarily on the routines and resources portion of PACEs because relationships are discussed in the section "Fostering Caregiver–Child Relationships."

Meeting Basic Needs

During childhood, in addition to secure, supportive relationships, children need a safe place to play and to engage in cognitively stimulating environments (Sciaraffa, Zeanah, & Zeanah, 2018). They also need regular routines to help them feel safe and know what to expect in the world. Again, this constancy is particularly important for children with ACEs. Establishing regular bedtimes, providing healthy meals, limiting screen time, and incorporating daily physical activity helps children grow and thrive. The U.S. Department of Health and Human Services (2019) recommended 1 hour of moderate to vigorous physical activity daily for children aged 6 to 17, through outdoor play or organized activities, and that younger children should be physically active throughout the day. Screen time should also be limited and supervised (see Table 6.2), and a number of studies suggest that early and excessive exposure to screen time impairs normative social and cognitive development (e.g., Maras et al., 2015). Another critical need for children is sleep, and many children do not get the recommended amount of sleep (see Table 6.3) causing problems in mood, self-regulation, and difficulties learning (Shochat et al., 2014; Smaldone, Honig,

TABLE 6.2. Screen Time Guidelines

Age	Recommendations
1–18 months	Avoid use of screen media other than video chatting. Parents of children 18 to 24 months of age who want to introduce digital media should choose high-quality programming and watch it with their children to help them understand what they are seeing.
2–5 years	Limit screen use to 1 hour per day of high-quality programs. Parents should coview media with children to help them understand what they are seeing and apply it to the world around them.
6 and older	Place consistent limits on the time spent using media and the types of media; make sure media does not take the place of adequate sleep, physical activity, and other behaviors essential to health.
All ages	Designate media-free times together, such as dinner or driving, as well as media-free locations at home, such as bedrooms.
All ages	Have ongoing communication about online citizenship and safety, including treating others with respect online and offline.

Note. Data from the American Academy of Pediatrics (2019).

TABLE 6.3. Sleep Recommendations by Age

Age	Recommended hours of sleep
Newborns 0–3 months	14–17
Infants 4–11 months	12–15
Toddlers 1–2 years	11–14
Preschoolers 3–5 years	10–13
School-age children 6–13 years	9–11
Teenagers 14–17 years	8–10

Note. From "National Sleep Foundation's Sleep Time Duration Recommendations: Methodology and Results Summary," by M. Hirshkowitz, K. Whiton, S. M. Albert, C. Alessi, O. Bruni, L. DonCarlos, . . . P. J. Adams Hillard, 2015, *Sleep Health*, *1*, p. 41. Copyright 2015 by Elsevier. Reprinted with permission.

& Byrne, 2007). Caregivers can see quick improvements in child behavior simply by increasing the amount of sleep children get, and when children go to bed early, parents have more time for themselves too. More specific recommendations on supporting children's healthy development follows.

Enriched Learning Opportunities

In the early 1990s, Hart and Risley (1995) conducted a highly influential study examining the number of words spoken in the homes of young children across various socioeconomic statuses. They recorded conversations in the homes of 42 families for 1 hour a month over 2.5 years. High-income families spoke an average of 300 more words per hour than low-income families. In 1 year, this difference is 11 million versus 3 million words. This is often referred to as the *30-million-word gap*—the difference in the number of words spoken to children among low- and high-income families before age 3. Why is this so important? Hart and Risley (2003) found that the number of words spoken was related to child outcomes in school, language production, and IQ. Moreover, children from low-income families were often discouraged from talking and were exposed to a simpler vocabulary. Researchers believe this negatively affects language development (Hart & Risley, 2003; Walker, Greenwood, Hart, & Carta, 1994), which is one of the best predictors of children's school success. More recent research emphasizes the importance of the quality of the interaction with children (talking back and forth, descriptive language, turn-taking), not just the number of words. However, the importance of conversing with children to improve overall development cannot be overstated (Golinkoff, Hoff, Rowe, Tamis-LeMonda, & Hirsh-Pasek, 2019).

Research also indicates that children who are read to do better in school and have better reading skills (Hargrave & Sénéchal, 2000; Whitehurst et al., 1994). Reading at bedtime reinforces the nighttime routine and is a great way to wind down and snuggle. It is never too early to start (and as children get older, they can take turns reading to their parents). As mentioned in Chapter 4, babies can hear their parents talking in the womb, know their parent's voice, and remember stories heard before birth (DeCasper & Fifer, 1980). The national *Talking Is Teaching* campaign encourages parents to talk, read, and sing to their babies and children. In Tulsa, we have been involved in this campaign with the George Kaiser Family Foundation. In the program, new parents are given tote bags and information on the importance of talking, reading, and singing to young children in the hospital after birth. Our evaluation of this and related programs found that these interactions promote positive parenting and language-building activities (Singh, Zapata, & Morris, 2018). (See http://talkingisteaching.org/.)

Children also benefit from simple outings such as going to the park or zoo. Even grocery shopping can be fun and a bonding experience, especially if caregivers engage children in dialogue regarding the activities and experiences. Among children with ACEs, quality early child care programs may be particularly helpful (Beckmann, 2017). The learning experiences and social interactions in early childhood programs can be especially beneficial to children in the child welfare system and in foster care (Pecora et al., 2017), as well as to their parents who get a break for their own work and activities and have more time for self-care.

A recent study of children aged 0 to 5 from the National Survey of Children's Health found that the positive parenting (i.e., reading stories, singing, eating meals together, playing with peers, engaging in family outings, limiting screen time) demonstrated robust protective effects independent of the number of ACEs (Yamaoka & Bard, 2019), underscoring the importance of these activities. Evidence from this study also indicated that the absence of these positive parenting practices could be viewed as another early life adversity.

Establishing Routines

Routines help children know what to expect and to feel safe. Research indicates that children living in an organized, uncluttered home fare better than those living in chaotic environments (Evans & English, 2002). As mentioned previously, young children with regular bedtimes and routines do better because their lives are less chaotic. To illustrate the importance of routines, a recent study examining structured daily activities found that elementary school children had accelerated weight gain during the summer compared with the school year (Brazendale et al., 2017). The study investigators believe that it is the structured day of the school year, daily routines, and adult supervision that prevent negative behaviors and outcomes such as excessive weight gain.

PACEs FOR ADOLESCENTS

Much of what we have discussed about children also applies to adolescents with ACEs. Routines and relationships are essential, but with this developmental period comes unique challenges and opportunities. The teenage brain is primed to experience heightened reward, but it does not have the control to consistently manage reward seeking and risk-taking behavior (Steinberg, 2014). Adults need to serve as children's prefrontal cortex, setting limits and encouraging responsibility. Adolescents who have experienced the effects of ACEs on brain development and stress reactivity are at increased risk for behaving in ways that satisfy immediate needs but have negative consequences in the future. This makes caring for teens with ACEs particularly challenging and explains why adolescents who have experienced adversity and maltreatment are at greater risk for teen pregnancy (Francisco et al., 2008), drug use (Somaini et al., 2011), and stress-related health problems (Evans, Kim, Ting, Tesher, & Shannis, 2007).

Like young children, teens also need enriching experiences to develop to their full potential, in and outside of the family. Attending a good school, having friends and being part of a positive group, having an engaging hobby, volunteering, and learning new skills all help adolescents transition to adulthood and develop a strong sense of self (see Chapter 2).

Involvement

As children develop and grow, they need greater autonomy and opportunities to interact with others outside of the family, but parents are still important. Caregivers must balance adolescents' need for autonomy with the importance of maintaining a close parent–child relationship (Steinberg, 1990). As children mature into teens, parents can strengthen their relationships through shared activities and being involved in teens' lives by attending their activities (e.g., school plays, sporting events). Not only does this strengthen family bonds, it actually makes it easier for parents to know where their children are, who they are with, and what they are doing with their time (behavioral monitoring, discussed in Chapter 2). Research indicates that parents' involvement predicts youth's academic success and serves as a protective factor against negative influences of peers (Borawski, Ievers-Landis, Lovegreen, & Trapl, 2003; Crosnoe, Erickson, & Dornbusch, 2002; Laird, Criss, Pettit, Dodge, & Bates, 2008; Rai et al., 2003). At the same time, parents need to avoid being overly intrusive (e.g., "helicopter parents") so that children can develop independence and needed life skills on their own. Nevertheless, family trips, game and movie nights, and volunteering in the community together are great ways for families to share common experiences and spend time together.

Research also indicates families should eat meals together. As mentioned in Chapter 2, numerous studies demonstrate the positive benefits of families eating meals together. Studies find that shared meals result in reduced rates of depression, drug and alcohol use, and suicide attempts, as well as better school grades, eating habits, and mental health (Eisenberg, Olson, Neumark-Sztainer, Story, & Bearinger, 2004; Videon & Manning, 2003). Particularly during adolescence, family meals can be a time for sharing ideas and experiences, as well as discussing daily activities and interests. Family rituals also help teens stay connected, and family dinners and celebrating events with the larger family facilitate positive experiences and socioemotional development (Harrist, Henry, Liu, & Morris, 2019).

Setting Limits

Parents need to continue to set limits and maintain regular communication with their adolescents. Within the context of nonjudgmental, two-way communication and active listening, parents and caregivers can set clear rules, limits, and consequences for breaking rules to keep teens safe. Indeed, having clear rules and limits and being involved in teens' lives can potentially prevent future ACEs. This is particularly important for adolescents with a history of ACEs because they are at greater risk for deviant behaviors (Somaini et al., 2011). Nevertheless, when problems do arise, caregivers must avoid power struggles by remaining calm, discussing options, and circling back to the discussion if anyone gets overly emotional.

One reason for such emotional swings during adolescence is puberty. Boys typically start puberty between ages 12 and 16, and girls start between 10 and 14 (Stoppler, 2018). With puberty comes hormonal changes and increased emotionality (Dahl, 2004). Before puberty starts, parents need to have open, repeated discussions with children about sexual health and pubertal development. There are many good online resources and books on how to have these conversations (e.g., https://www.todaysparent.com/family/parenting/age-by-age-guide-to-talking-to-kids-about-sex/). One interesting fact about puberty that parents may not know is that puberty triggers changes in sleep. Melatonin levels rise later at night, and teenagers naturally want to go to bed later because their biological clock has changed. This makes it more difficult to get enough hours and quality of sleep, so parents need to minimize screen time (e.g., have a phone curfew) and encourage regular bedtimes as much as possible.

ENHANCING NEUROBIOLOGICAL REGULATION

Numerous studies have demonstrated the importance of self-regulation in healing from ACEs and trauma. To help children with a history of ACEs, caregivers must stay calm in their interactions with children and regulate their own emotions and responses. Children who have a history of adversity can benefit from participating in activities that help facilitate their own neurobiological regulation, such as martial arts, executive function games, and yoga (see Table 6.1). Other ways caregivers can increase self-regulation is through mindful parenting interactions, caring for themselves (described subsequently), and engaging in adult PACEs as described in the previous chapter.

Mindful Caregiving

Pikler was one of the first to practice mindful caregiving. In the Pikler method, interactions are not rushed, and caregivers are calm and fully present. In Chapter 5, we discussed how mindfulness can help heal the brain. Mindfulness can also help caregivers regulate their own emotions and move interactions from brain-stem types of behaviors (flight, fight, freeze) to intentional, self-regulated interactions (Snyder, Shapiro, & Treleaven, 2012). Dimensions of mindful caregiving typically include (a) listening with full attention, (b) non-judgmental acceptance of self and child, (c) emotional awareness of the self and child, (d) self-regulation in the caregiving relationship, and (e) compassion for the self and child (L. G. Duncan, Coatsworth, & Greenberg, 2009).

Mindfulness-Enhanced Strengthening Families Program

Several parenting programs include mindfulness with standardized curricula and have found promising results. One example is the Mindfulness-Enhanced Strengthening Families Program (MSFP), which adapted an existing evidence-based parent management and behavioral training intervention for parents of children aged 10 to 14 to include training on mindful parenting. Mindfulness activities, discussion, and instructions were added (e.g., deep breathing, breath awareness, loving-kindness meditations; L. G. Duncan et al., 2009) to the seven-session group-based program. Evidence from randomized controlled trials suggests that adding mindfulness increased parent–youth relationship quality and mindful parenting, with participants maintaining gains in positive discipline and monitoring found in the original program (Coatsworth, Duncan, Greenberg, & Nix, 2010; Coatsworth et al., 2015). Importantly, this program focuses on early adolescence, an often difficult time of conflict and negativity in parent–youth relationships. This and other studies suggest that mindful parenting may be particularly valuable during this tumultuous phase (L. G. Duncan et al., 2009).

First Five Years

Another intervention that added mindfulness to an existing parenting program is Active Parenting's First Five Years (FFY). Our team in Tulsa piloted the addition of mindfulness activities in the Tulsa Children's Project and then added the activities to the Active Parenting 1,2,3,4! program. We next worked with Dr. Michael Popkin to add the piloted mindfulness activities to a new edition of *Active Parenting: First Five Years*. Importantly, activities were ones that parents could do with their young children, such as fun breathing exercises (e.g., balloon breaths, butterfly breaths; Popkin, 2017). Initial results of parents' pre- and post-FFY surveys indicate gains in parents' mindfulness and parenting efficacy, as well as decreases in children's behavior problems (Jespersen et al., 2019; Slocum, Hays-Grudo, Morris, & Bosler, 2016). Data collection is ongoing, but this is certainly a promising tool in our growing repertoire to eliminate ACEs.

We also added games and activities to FFY to increase parents' and children's executive functioning (e.g., matching games, freeze dance) because increasing executive function and mindfulness are both ways to heal the brain from adversity (Bethell, Gombojav, Solloway, & Wissow, 2016; Bethell, Solloway, et al., 2017; Deater-Deckard, 2014). Several programs for children have focused specifically on building executive functioning skills and have encouraging results (see Diamond & Lee, 2011; Neville et al., 2013); these programs include martial arts, yoga, executive function games, computerized training, and mindfulness, (Flook, Goldberg, Pinger, & Davidson, 2015; Razza, Bergen-Cico, & Raymond, 2015; Thierry, Bryant, Nobles, & Norris, 2016; Waechter & Wekerle, 2015). As with any newly learned behavior, engaging in these activities are most successful when they involve repeated practice and challenge (Diamond & Lee, 2011).

Caring for the Caregiver

In Chapter 5, we discussed some ways that caregivers and other adults can heal from their own ACEs. Healing may be particularly challenging for parents who also have children with ACEs because interactions can trigger behaviors and physiological responses from the past. A perfect illustration of the importance of caring for the caregiver is the oxygen mask on an airplane. Instructions for in-flight emergencies always advise parents to secure their own masks first before helping children secure theirs. More than just a face-mask or a yoga class (although those can help!), active self-care is encouraged in several parenting programs discussed in this chapter, including Triple P (described later) and Active Parenting FFY, as well as Legacy for Children.

Legacy for Children

Another program that does an excellent job of supporting parents is the Centers for Disease Control and Prevention's Legacy for Children, a group-based parenting program that is designed to nurture sensitive and responsive mother–child relationships, build self-efficacy, and foster peer support networks among mothers living in poverty. Groups start during pregnancy or infancy, and children are very close in age. Mothers can attend the groups until children are 3 or 5 years old, depending on the specific curricula (Robinson et al., 2018). Results of randomized controlled trials indicate positive gains in children's cognitive and socioemotional development 3 to 6 years post-intervention (Perou et al., 2012). One important component of Legacy is social support for caregivers through ongoing parenting group interactions and group leader support. We saw this firsthand when we implemented Legacy in several communities in Tulsa. The moms reported that the connections they made with each other and the group leaders were life-changing (Beasley, Bigfoot, & Curren, 2019).

Social Support

The importance of social support is illustrated in a model we proposed in a special issue of *Child Development* on programs to help at-risk children (Luthar & Eisenberg, 2017). We posited that parenting interventions that promote nurturing relationships (with children, among caregivers, and with group leaders) are especially promising for affecting parent and child outcomes because they increase positive parent–child interactions and strengthen social support (Morris, Robinson, Hays-Grudo, et al., 2017). In the article, Legacy, Nurse–Family Partnership (Olds, 2006), and Triple-P are cited as programs that achieve nurturing interaction and support goals. The social support element of the model is key. Parents need other parents to help and support their caregiving (Luthar & Ciciolla, 2015; Luthar, Curlee, Tye, Engelman, & Stonnington, 2017). Parents can be role models for good parenting and sound-boards for advice, and they can help one another with basic needs such as babysitting when parents need a break. This is particularly important for parents caring for children with ACEs (Woods-Jaeger, Cho, Sexton, Slagel, & Goggin, 2018). The need for peer support explains the proliferation of informal moms' groups that are based on neighborhood, preschool, work, or other settings. Although these mothers may or may not have children with ACEs, the desire to connect with and learn from each other is evident.

Emotion Coaching

Many parenting programs emphasize the importance of parents' emotion regulation during interactions with their children and of parents' facilitation of children's emotion management (or *coregulation* as it is called in ABC, described subsequently). In a number of studies, Amanda's lab examined the role of emotion regulation in children's development and how parents socialize, or teach, children to regulate emotions successfully. Studies using a variety of methods (observation, psychophysiological, parent and youth report) have demonstrated that parents who are warm, supportive, and involved have children with better emotion regulation and emotional competence. In turn, children's emotion regulation is associated with less depression, anxiety, and aggressive behavior and with more prosocial behavior (Morris, Criss, Silk, & Houltberg, 2017). This research supports the tripartite model of emotion regulation in which children learn about emotion management in three primary ways (Morris, Silk, Steinberg, Myers, & Robinson, 2007). First, children learn about emotion regulation by observing their parents and caregivers' emotional displays and regulation patterns. Second, children learn through parenting practices in response to children's emotions. Third, children's emotion regulation is influenced by the emotional climate of the family as indicated by parent–child attachment, parenting styles, and emotional expressivity and interactions among family members. In line with caregiver behaviors previously discussed, parents must work to sustain positive, nurturing relationships and regulate their own emotions during interactions with their children and other family members.

Caregiver Emotion-Coaching

Because caregiver in-the-moment responses to emotions are important, multiple studies support the idea of caregiver emotion coaching. Emotion coaching involves labeling and accepting children's emotions (as well as one's own emotions), problem-solving, and calmly discussing potential ways to manage a highly charged situation (Gottman, Katz, & Hooven, 1996). In addition, emotion coaches avoid magnification (getting upset when the child is distressed) and giving in to emotional demands. Emotion coaches also separate behavior from emotions (e.g., it is okay to be angry but not okay to hit your brother). In contrast to emotion coaching, emotion dismissing behavior occurs when caregivers minimize or deny children's feelings. Caregivers also may punish children for emotional displays, which sends a message that emotions are not valid or important. Emotion regulation may be more difficult for some individuals depending on their past (parents who have had ACEs) or their temperament (children who are naturally more emotionally reactive). In such cases, pointing out and discussing these challenges with caregivers and encouraging emotion coaching may provide validity and relief.

Tuning Into Teens

Several parenting programs have focused on teaching parents' emotion coaching skills. Tuning Into Teens (TINT; also see Tuning Into Kids for younger children and Dads Tuning Into Kids) is based on parental support of youth's emotion regulation. The program teaches parents to build emotional connections with their children by being emotion coaches. Specifically, in the teen version, the program helps parents be emotionally supportive and empathic during the adolescent years. TINT is a group-based parenting program with six to eight 2-hour sessions led by trained facilitators. Content includes role-play, DVD examples, and teaching emotion coaching principles. Analyses of multiple TINT studies using randomized controlled trials demonstrated improvement in parenting behavior, the parent–child relationship, and children's emotional competence postintervention (Havighurst, Kehoe, & Harley, 2015; Havighurst et al., 2013; Kehoe, Havighurst, & Harley, 2014). Although the program does not specifically target adolescents with ACEs, it has been successful among children at risk for behavior problems and is a promising approach for helping children and teens with ACEs.

FOSTERING POSITIVE CAREGIVER–CHILD RELATIONSHIPS

Because early relationships set the foundation for social, emotional, and cognitive development, one of the most important things caregivers can do to help a child with ACEs is to nurture attachment and increase responsive caregiving behaviors (see Table 6.1). This may be difficult: Children who have experienced adversity often have impaired attachment; they may have difficulty trusting or may be overly clingy. Moreover, children with ACEs often miscue caregivers. They whine and pull away when they need help. They get angry and throw a tantrum when they need support. These behaviors usually stem from fear because they do not know if or how a caregiver will respond to their needs or because of past experiences of abuse. Unfortunately, these behaviors sometimes trigger caregivers' own past experiences with adversity and related physiological stress responses, causing them to react in frightening, controlling, or withdrawn ways. This sends mixed messages to children and can undermine attachment. Sometimes caregivers think a child's behavior means they do not want help or that they are beyond help, which makes sensitive and appropriate caregiving even more difficult than it already is. In the next section, we discuss several programs that are designed to teach parents and caregivers nurturing responses to their children's cues and behaviors, "reinterpreting their cues and over-riding their own parents' voices from the past" (Costello, Roben, & Dozier, 2018).

Nurturing Attachment

There is evidence that short-term, prevention-focused attachment programs may be an effective intervention that changes caregiver behavior (i.e., increasing sensitivity) and can act as a catalyst for improving infant attachment (van IJzendoorn, Juffer, & Duyvesteyn, 1995). Supportive and sensitive caregiving behaviors reduce stress and can ameliorate the effects of early adversity on children's health (Chen, Brody, & Miller, 2017; Fisher, Frenkel, Noll, Berry, & Yockelson, 2016). Research indicates that maltreated children can form secure attachments (Stovall-McClough & Dozier, 2004), and there are several model programs that are designed to strengthen caregiver–child attachment among young children who have experienced adversity. The following two programs have documented efficacy and are examples of such programs.

Attachment Biobehavioral Catch-Up
Attachment Biobehavioral Catch-Up (ABC) was created by Dr. Mary Dozier at the University of Delaware and has been used across the country and internationally. It is rated at the highest level by the California Evidence-Based Clearing House for Child Welfare, which reviews evidence-based treatments for children in the child welfare system. ABC consists of 10 one-hour home sessions, facilitated by a trained coach. It is a manualized intervention with video feedback, but its primary method is in-the-moment commenting. The purpose of this commenting is to increase sensitive parenting by encouraging specific behaviors during parent–child interactions. Caregivers are encouraged to (a) delight in the child—display joy and affection (smile, laugh); (b) provide nurturing care when the child is distressed (respond with comfort and reassurance); (c) follow the child's lead when the child is not distressed (describe what

the child is doing, imitate the child's play; reduce overwhelming behavior such as tickling and rough housing); (d) avoid frightening behaviors such as intrusiveness, yelling, threats of harm (don't put a toy in a child's face or use scary voices); and (e) stay calm and provide support when the child is dysregulated (label feelings, stay close to the child; avoid saying things like "be a big girl, don't cry, don't act like a baby"). Coaches start with positive comments in the first few sessions and label the target behavior (e.g., following the lead) while also noting how the behavior is linked to research supporting optimal child development (e.g., "You took the teacup from her and pretended to drink the tea. That's a nice example of following the lead and shows how her actions influence others"). In later sessions, coaches talk with parents about their caregiving histories and why they may respond in certain ways based on their past experiences. ABC was originally designed for children aged 6 months to 24 months, but now there is a toddler program that includes strengthening coregulation of caregivers and children through calming behaviors (Costello et al., 2018) and a version for opioid-using pregnant mothers (Dozier & Bernard, 2019).

ABC is grounded in attachment theory and neurobiology. A number of randomized controlled trials have demonstrated the program's effectiveness at the end of the intervention and several years later across socioemotional, biological, and relational indices (Costello et al., 2018). Importantly, ABC has been effective with children in foster care and with families at risk for abuse. In several studies, Dr. Mary Dozier and colleagues examined diurnal patterns of the stress hormone cortisol. Cortisol levels are typically high in the morning and decrease throughout the day, nearing almost zero at night. However, children in foster care typically have flat patterns of cortisol, indicating physiological dysregulation. Post-ABC intervention research has indicated more normal diurnal patterns of cortisol, with effects maintained several years after program participation (Bernard, Dozier, Bick, & Gordon, 2015; Bernard, Hostinar, & Dozier, 2015). Among the control group, the pattern of cortisol remained blunted, suggesting ABC altered neurobiological stress pathways to be more normative.

In randomized clinical trials, ABC also demonstrated increases in several other domains including parental sensitivity, child executive function, and secure patterns of attachment (Bernard et al., 2012; Costello et al., 2018; Lewis-Morrarty, Dozier, Bernard, Terracciano, & Moore, 2012). In one study, Dozier and colleagues used encephalography to document changes in brain activity. Specifically, after the ABC program, mothers at risk for potential child abuse processed emotional cues similar to parents not at risk, suggesting alterations in parents' brain activity related to responsiveness (Bernard, Simons, & Dozier, 2015). Studies have also found lower scores on parenting stress and child abuse potential scales after ABC compared with scores of control participants (Sprang, 2009). Most of the research on the effectiveness of ABC has been conducted with mothers but the program has also been used with fathers and other family members, and anecdotal evidence suggests similar success (Costello et al., 2018).

ABC's results are in part due to its manualized training and supervision focus. Intervention sites are screened for agency buy-in, and coaches are selected on the basis of established research criteria that strengthen their success. As part of the training, coaches meet weekly with a fidelity supervisor, who codes a 5-minute segment of a session to ensure appropriate and significant rates of commenting. Coaches code sections of their sessions as well and meet regularly with a clinical supervisor. After a set number of sessions, coaches can be certified and are recertified every 2 years.

Circle of Security

Circle of Security (COS) is another attachment-based intervention. It has multiple formats, including a 20-week psychoeducational and therapeutic group program, an 8-week DVD psychoeducational group, and a four-session home intervention (Topham, 2018). COS was developed by Glen Cooper, Kent Hoffman, Bert Powell, and Bob Marvin. Like ABC, it is based on the concepts of attachment and was designed to help children with problematic attachment histories. COS uses simple illustrations and metaphors to teach the concepts of attachment, and it uses videos and self-reflection to help caregivers observe and understand their own attachment-related behaviors. The COS model, presented in Figure 6.1, illustrates the relationship needs of children and appropriate caregiver responses (Topham, 2018).

Children naturally seek proximity to caregivers and reassurance when distressed. This ensures safety and survival and can be reflected in different developmental systems. COS targets three specific systems: (a) attachment, which keeps the child close to the caregiver for comfort and survival; (b) exploration, which refers to children's need for discovery; and (c) caregiving, which reflects parental instinct to respond to children's needs and to act as a secure base (Ainsworth, Blehar, Waters, & Wall, 1978; Bowlby, 1988). COS's primary goal is for parents to develop the capacity to act as a secure base for children's exploration and to respond to their needs consistently and appropriately (Powell, Cooper, Hoffman, & Marvin, 2013).

In the COS figure, the top half of the circle reflects children's exploration system, their need to explore, and the need for parents to be a secure base to support exploration. Parents are encouraged to reflect on and utilize four behaviors that encourage exploration: watching over children, delighting in them, helping them when needed, and enjoying exploration with them (Cooper, Hoffman, Powell, & Marvin, 2011). The bottom half of the circle represents children's attachment system and their need for parents to welcome them in and respond to their needs. When children's attachment system "turns on," their exploratory system "turns off," signaling parents to protect, comfort, and help organize children's feelings while still showing delight in response to the child. This system can be activated when children are hurt, fearful, or upset (Zanetti, Powell, Cooper, & Hoffman, 2011). The adult hands on the circle represent the caregiving system. Parents are encouraged to always be bigger, stronger, wiser, and kind. Whenever possible, parents should follow

FIGURE 6.1. Circle of Security Model

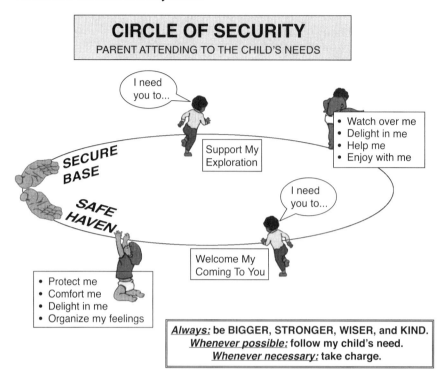

From "The Circle of Security Project: Attachment-Based Intervention With Caregiver-Pre-School Child Dyads," by R. Marvin, G. Cooper, K. Hoffman, and B. Powell, 2002, *Attachment & Human Development*, *4*, p. 109. Copyright 2000 by Cooper, Hoffman, Marvin, and Powell. Reprinted with permission.

their children's needs. Whenever necessary, parents should take charge (Marvin, Cooper, Hoffman, & Powell, 2002, p. 109). Children's sense of security and safety is dependent on parents being kind and on knowing that their parents are in control and in charge of their safety. If parents are kind but do not take charge when needed, they are weak; this is similar to permissive parenting (discussed in Chapter 2). If parents take charge but are not kind, they may come across as mean (authoritarian parenting). If they are not kind or in charge, they are "gone" and may be considered neglectful.

The COS program uses "shark music" as a sensory example for parents. Caregivers are shown a video clip from a first-person view of someone walking along a wooded path that opens onto a beautiful beach. The first time the video is shown, parents hear soft serene music playing in the background. The second time the video is shown, parents hear the music from the movie *Jaws* in the background—da dun, da dun, da dun. The scene changes from calm to danger. Parents see that the background music changes the tone of the film even though the film clip is identical. This experience is then linked to how parents' past experiences play in the caregiving background and can change the tone of an interaction from something pleasant to something scary and dangerous (and vice versa). Parents are encouraged to think about where their feelings of distress during interactions with their child come from and how their feelings shape their interactions. Relationship histories are considered as not part of a caregiver's awareness (this is usually subconscious), and it is pointed out that such experiences may trigger feelings of distress and "shark music." COS helps parents understand their feelings and develop a more objective, calm state of mind during interactions with their children (Powell et al., 2013; Topham, 2018). It also helps parents build empathy and emotion regulation skills, while engaging in reflective dialogue with the group facilitator who acts as a source of support.

There is less research on COS than ABC, but there is evidence that disorganized attachment and attachment insecurity decreases after the program (Hoffman, Marvin, Cooper, & Powell, 2006) and that parents display fewer unsupportive responses to children's distress postintervention. There is also evidence that children display greater self-regulation (i.e., inhibitory control) compared with children in a waitlist control group (Cassidy et al., 2017). There are now more than 15,000 trained providers, conducting the program in 11 languages (Topham, 2018), and COS provides a promising framework to help children, and even adolescents, with a history of ACEs.

Balancing Autonomy and Connectedness

As mentioned previously, children need clear rules and limits and thrive when parents have high, yet reasonable, expectations (Morris et al., 2013). As children grow, there is a constant need to balance exploration and autonomy with connectedness and involvement, as is illustrated in the Circle of Security model. Children want to make decisions and be independent, but they also need to feel safe and protected. Securely attached children know what to expect, and adolescents who have clear limits set by parents fare better than those who do not (Morris et al., 2013). Nevertheless, with freedom comes responsibility, and parents should encourage autonomy when children and adolescents make good choices and display responsible behavior. In the Active Parenting program, they call this *freedom within limits*, and boundaries widen as children grow and mature (Popkin, 2014). This idea is also reflected in authoritative parenting, discussed in Chapter 2, where parents balance warmth and control while encouraging autonomy.

Harsh Discipline and Corporal Punishment

We cannot emphasize enough how important it is to avoid harsh discipline with children who have ACEs. Harsh discipline is passed from generation to generation, and eliminating this behavior is one way to stop the intergenerational cycle of ACEs (Chung et al., 2009; Herrenkohl, Klika, Brown, Herrenkohl, & Leeb, 2013). Moreover, yelling, hitting, and threatening can trigger past adverse experiences psychologically and physiologically, retraumatizing children and hurting the development of attachment relationships.

As parents, caregivers, and service providers, we need to discuss the difference between discipline and punishment and talk about alternatives to physical punishment. What is the difference between discipline and punishment? In the fourth edition of *Active Parenting: A Parent's Guide to Raising Happy and Successful Children*, Popkin (2014) talked about the origins of the word *discipline*. It is similar to the word *disciple* from the Bible and means *to teach*. The goal of discipline, then, is to teach children right from wrong, not to punish them. Punishment often results in sneaky behavior and fear, rather than learning to do the right thing. Caregivers can teach children by explaining how behaviors affect others, helping them learn to calm down (maybe using "time-in" instead of "time-out"), using logical consequence (the toy goes away because it's not being shared), and praising children for positive social interactions (reinforcing good behavior). Families can agree on simple rules and logical consequences together, even when children are young. This helps children know what to expect.

There is a growing body of evidence indicating that spanking, specifically, has detrimental outcomes for children. Numerous studies find that spanking is linked with child aggression. Although not all children who are spanked become aggressive, research indicates that most of the effects of spanking are negative, including more aggression and less internalization of right and wrong. In an extensive review of studies on corporal punishment, Gershoff and colleagues concluded that

> the strength and consistency of the links between physical punishment and detrimental child outcomes lead the authors to recommend that parents should avoid physical punishment, psychologists should advise and advocate against it, and policymakers should develop means of educating the public about the harms of and alternatives. (Gershoff et al., 2018, p. 626; see also Gershoff, 2013)

In addition to negative psychological effects, research also indicates physiological effects of spanking. In a recent study of harsh parenting, researchers examined structural brain differences in participants with extensive histories of corporal punishment and found that they had lower gray matter volume in regions of the prefrontal cortex associated with social cognition and behavioral regulation (Tomoda et al., 2009). Although this study is correlational, it does support other research suggesting negative effects of corporal punishment.

Indeed, typically children are not allowed to hit others, and adults are not allowed to hit other adults. Moreover, spanking is currently banned in 53 countries across the world (https://brilliantmaps.com/corporal-punishment/). It is time to consider the role of corporal punishment in the high rate of ACEs and violence in the United States (Elgar et al., 2018) and in some specific cultural groups with a history of physical punishment. There are many other ways for parents to discipline and guide children, and as researchers and clinicians, we should provide and teach parents alternatives.

SYSTEMS-LEVEL PROGRAMS

The fourth column in Table 6.1 represents system-level change, and lists programs and policies that can be implemented at a large scale. More information on these types of programs and policies is presented in Chapter 7, but here we focus on several specific programs designed to help children and adolescents by increasing caregiver–child relationships and enriching resources for youth with ACEs. In addition to the activities described next (i.e., universal parenting classes, dissemination of positive parenting information, provision of resources for children's activities), we also argue that high-quality mental health resources must be available for all children and families with a history of ACEs and that all children should have enriching learning environments and quality schooling available regardless of socioeconomic status.

Triple P (Positive Parenting Program)

Triple P is an example of a system-level program. It is a multilevel public health program using a five-level approach to increase positive parenting. Triple P is designed to help parents of infants to adolescents through Tip Sheets, group presentations, educational DVDs, and workbooks. Triple P helps parents learn strategies to promote children and adolescents' self-regulation. Participants develop a parenting plan and learn parenting skills and ways to reduce parenting stress and increase parenting confidence (Sanders, 2008). Importantly, Triple P is tiered so that communities can adopt the program at different levels. Level 1 involves a media campaign to disseminate positive parenting information. Level 2 includes a single session focused on positive parenting skills. Level 3 has brief sessions (one–four sessions) focused on resolving children's behavior problems. Level 4 includes eight to 10 group or individual sessions on comprehensive strategies for improving the parent–child relationship. Finally, Level 5 is the same as Level 4 but with a focus on high-risk families (with group or individual formats; see https://www.triplep.net/glo-en/home/). Numerous studies of Triple P indicate postintervention decreases in children's emotional and behavioral problems, as well as increases in parenting confidence and positive parenting behaviors (Sanders, Kirby, Tellegen, & Day, 2014). In a study examining the Triple P multilevel system, 18 counties in the United States were randomly assigned to Triple P or services as usual. Results showed significant decreases in indicators of substantiated child maltreatment, out-of-home child placements, and child maltreatment injuries in the counties that implemented Triple P (Prinz, Sanders, Shapiro, Whitaker, & Lutzker, 2009; Sanders, 2008; Sanders et al., 2014). This indicates that Triple P may be an ideal program to prevent ACEs at the population level.

Youth in Iceland

Several of the PACEs (volunteering, being part of a group) reflect the importance of keeping children active and busy, so that they use their time wisely and avoid unhealthy activities such as drug and alcohol use. An impressive example of the benefits of keeping youth busy and engaged in challenging activities is a nationwide youth program in Iceland. Before implementing this program in the 1990s, Iceland had one of the largest teen drug problems in Europe. Almost 25% of teens smoked every day, and more than 40% reported getting drunk in the past month. Research indicated that youth who did not engage in these behaviors were participating in organized activities, especially sports, three or four times a week. These youth were also not staying out late at night unsupervised. In response, Iceland created Youth in Iceland. This social movement for teens encouraged after school activities, such as clubs for music and art, hip-hop dancing, and martial arts. The goal was to replace negative thrill-seeking and boredom-reduction activities (e.g., drug and alcohol use and criminal activity) with positive and socially acceptable activities. In addition, adolescents received life-skills training, and parents could attend classes on positive parenting and discipline. Laws were changed to establish new norms and consequences: Teens between the ages of 13 and 16 were prohibited from being out after 10:00 PM: tobacco and alcohol advertising was banned; and parents were encouraged to sign a pledge not to allow their adolescents to attend unsupervised parties and not to buy alcohol for minors. State funding was increased for sports, music, art, dance, and other activities. The impact of this program is impressive. Results of youth surveys pre- and post-program indicate plummeting rates of cigarette smoking, drinking, and marijuana use. Adolescents also reported spending much more time with parents and significantly more time in sports activities (Milkman, 2017; E. Young, 2017). Not only did this program change teen and parent attitudes and behavior, it changed the national culture, policies, initiatives, and funding.

CONCLUSIONS AND ACTIVITY: CREATING A CHILD PACEs PLAN

It is beyond the scope of this chapter to discuss all the parenting and caregiver programs beneficial to children suffering from ACEs. Programs not mentioned previously that have also been scientifically validated as restorative for children and families who experienced trauma include Nurse Family Partnership (Olds, 2006), Child–Parent Psychotherapy (Lieberman, Ghosh Ippen, & Van Horn, 2006), Parent–Child Interaction Therapy (Hembree-Kigin & McNeil, 2013), and the Incredible Years parenting program (Webster-Stratton & Reid, 2010). Along with these exemplary PACEs-aligned programs, we provide resources on other recommended programs and therapies at the end of this book.

It is essential to realize that working with children who have a history of ACEs may involve the need for intensive treatment and therapy. Caregivers need to be aware of the symptoms of reactive attachment disorder (RAD) and disinhibited social engagement disorder, which are often caused by gross neglect during early childhood, typically before age 5. Symptoms of these disorders include rarely seeking comfort from a caregiver, limited positive emotions, dysregulated emotional outbursts, or overly familiar behavior with adults. These disorders often cooccur with other mental health problems such as attention-deficit/hyperactivity disorder (American Psychiatric Association, 2013) and likely need treatment from professionals trained in working with children who have a history of ACEs.

To conclude this chapter, we present a new model of ACEs that also includes a model of PACEs. As you may recall, in Chapter 3 we introduced the ACEs pyramid, which illustrates the pathways through which ACEs affect health and development: through disrupted neurological development; social, emotional, and cognitive impairment, leading to health-risk behaviors; and disease and early death. In our new PACEs heart model (see Figure 6.2), we place an iconic symbol of love next to the ACEs pyramid. The heart model starts at the top with PACEs, relationships and resources. PACEs lead to optimal neurological development; social, emotional, and cognitive functioning; healthy behaviors and development; and health and longevity. The PACEs heart counteracts the stress effects of ACEs and provides an alternative way to think about development. A number of studies support the PACEs heart model, affirming that in the face of adversity, positive relationships and childhood experiences lead to resilience, emotion regulation, and neurological functioning (Hanson et al., 2019; Hillis et al., 2010; Poole, Dobson, & Pusch, 2018; Skodol et al., 2007). As researchers, clinicians, and individuals studying and helping people with ACEs, we encourage you to think about ways to bring more love, richness, and heart into the lives of those with a history of

FIGURE 6.2. Heart Model: Mechanisms Through Which Protective and Compensatory Experiences Influence Health and Well-Being

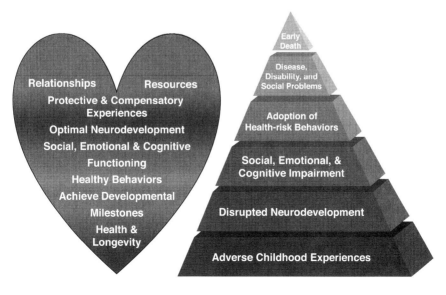

adversity and to create communities that are healing and hopeful rather than hurtful and in despair.

As in Chapter 5, at the end of this chapter we provide a PACEs plan, but this one is for children (Figure 6.3). It can be used with clients in therapy, families in intervention programs, or even with your own family. In the plan, we have separate PACEs for children aged 0 to 5 and 6 to 18, as we did in Table 6.1. Similar to the PACEs plan for adults, completing the plan can help to create and sustain important habits and behaviors and can encourage new experiences to promote resilience. Boxes include a place for current PACEs status, future goals, and actions taken throughout the month to meet the goals. When completing the activity, we encourage individuals to note current strengths with new strategies, building on positive experiences and relationships already in place.

FIGURE 6.3. Protective and Compensatory Experiences (PACEs) Plan for Children

Child PACEs Plan Month _____

Relationship PACEs

Unconditional love. A caregiver who loves them unconditionally. They do not doubt that they are cared about, no matter what.

0–5: Nurturing care. Caregivers respond in sensitive ways to soothe and support children's needs, particularly in times of distress.

Current status: *Actions taken:*

Goal:

Best friend. At least one best friend. Someone they can trust and have fun with.

0–5: Opportunity for play with another child. Individual play and interaction with a child the same age or a sibling close in age.

Current status: *Actions taken:*

Goal:

**FIGURE 6.3. Protective and Compensatory Experiences (PACEs) Plan
for Children (*Continued*)**

Volunteering. Regular opportunities to help others (e.g., volunteer at a hospital,
nursing home, church) or participate in special projects in the community to help
others (food drives, Habitat for Humanity).

0–5. Fostering empathy, perspective-taking, and sharing. Encouraging prosocial,
helping behaviors with peers, siblings, adults, and/or pets.

Current status: *Actions taken:*

Goal:

Being part of a group. Active membership in at least one civic group or a nonsport
social group, such as scouts, faith-based, or a youth group.

0–5: Play groups. Being part of a play group of children similar ages with free time
for play and exploration, child-directed play.

Current status: *Actions taken:*

Goal:

A mentor. An adult (not a parent) they can trust and can count on when they need
help or advice (e.g., coach, teacher, minister, neighbor, relative).

0–5: Other adult caregiver. Having a relationship with another caring adult such as a
grandparent, baby-sitter, or teacher.

Current status: *Actions taken:*

Goal:

(continues)

FIGURE 6.3. Protective and Compensatory Experiences (PACEs) Plan for Children (*Continued*)

Month _____

Environment and Resource PACES

Safe home. A home that is typically clean AND safe with enough food to eat.

0–5: Safe and child friendly home. A home where children can explore and play safely with limited screen time to encourage play and social interaction. Dietary needs are met with healthy options.

Current status: *Actions taken:*

Goal:

A good school. A school, or educational environment, that provides the resources and academic experiences children need to learn.

0–5: Opportunities for learning and daily reading. Adult interactions that promote language and socioemotional development, including daily reading and storytelling, talking about activities and experiences, singing and interactive games, and quality early childcare programs.

Current status: *Actions taken:*

Goal:

A hobby. An engaging hobby—an artistic or intellectual pastime either alone or in a group (e.g., chess club, debate team, musical instrument or vocal group, theater, spelling bee, or reading a lot).

0–5: Family outings and exposure to art and music. Outings to parks, zoos, libraries; regular time for drawing, painting, music and other artistic activities.

Current status: *Actions taken:*

Goal:

FIGURE 6.3. Protective and Compensatory Experiences (PACEs) Plan for Children (*Continued*)

Physical activity. Regular involvement in organized sports groups (e.g., soccer, basketball, track) or other physical activity (e.g., competitive cheer, gymnastics, dance, marching band, martial arts).

0-5: Physical activity and play. Unstructured play time outdoors. Active group play.

Current status: *Actions taken:*

Goal:

Rules and routines. A home where rules are clear and fairly administered. Family meals.

0–5: Daily routines and limit setting. Daily routines including bedtime, bath time, mealtime, nap time, and play time. Clear limits as children get older.

Current status: *Actions taken:*

Goal:

Notes:

7

ACEs and PACEs and Communities

Safety and security don't just happen, they are the result of collective consensus and public investment. We owe our children, the most vulnerable citizens in our society, a life free of violence and fear.

—NELSON MANDELA

We began this book with the story of friends whose riverside picnic was interrupted by an urgent need to rescue children being swept out to sea. You will recall that one of the party breaks away from the rescue effort to run upstream, to find the "hole in the bridge," the circumstances that caused the children to fall into the river. The research we reviewed, the models we discussed, and the prevention and intervention results we presented reflect our search for the hole in the bridge. In fact, we believe we have found the hole in the bridge. We stand by it, gazing at the terrifying drop to the waters below. We cannot turn our heads and ignore the danger it poses—not just to individual children and families, but to our communities, to all of us as a society. We look around and we see that we are not alone. Others have joined us—neighbors, friends, mothers, fathers, teachers, doctors, nurses, lawyers, police officers, researchers, and therapists. We stand shoulder to shoulder and realize that together we can repair this breach.

In Chapters 5 and 6, we described ways to help adults recover from adverse childhood experiences (ACEs) and the ways that parents and caregivers can build resilience in children who have experienced adversity and trauma.

http://dx.doi.org/10.1037/0000177-007
Adverse and Protective Childhood Experiences: A Developmental Perspective, by J. Hays-Grudo and A. S. Morris

We described the programs and approaches that have solid evidence to support their use with individuals and families. But therapeutic and preventive interventions that target individual children and families are not a feasible response to the widespread prevalence of ACEs in our society. We do not have a sufficient mental health workforce or resources to provide individual-level treatment for the millions of children and adults living with the enduring effects of ACEs.

Thus, we turn our attention in this chapter to the strategies and policies that can foster healing, recovery, and resilience within systems and communities. This discussion must include an acknowledgment of the legacy of adversity resulting from the historical and geopolitical events that profoundly affect families and children. War, population removals, mass migrations and immigration, poverty, and institutional racism and discrimination are the context in which childhood adversity flourishes, with little opposition from protective or resilience-building experiences. Designing and implementing environment and contextual responses to ACEs requires frank assessment of the continued effects of historical and contemporaneous traumatic events, comprehensive efforts to implement trauma-informed practices within the systems that provide services to children and adolescence, and development of community-wide programs and policies to address the continuing barriers to optimal development and health in all children.

THE HISTORICAL AND SOCIAL CONTEXT OF ACEs

We described in Chapter 4 how ACEs may be passed from generation to generation. Behavior patterns are learned and repeated, and epigenetic changes resulting from early life stress may also be transmitted, making future generations more reactive to stress and less able to provide safe and nurturing homes. We learned that infant rats experience something akin to ACEs when exposed to mothers who were stressed by being placed in an unfamiliar environment without enough bedding material. The mothers dropped them, stepped on them, and spent less time nursing, licking, and grooming than mothers in a familiar environment with enough bedding and wood chips. Multiple studies show that such treatment produces offspring who are fearful, reluctant to explore new environments, have increased methylation of the *BDNF* gene (which reduces the production of the protein associated with brain plasticity and cognitive function), and are likely to expose their own offspring to similarly abusive and neglectful behavior (Blaze & Roth, 2013; Roth et al., 2009; Roth & Sweatt, 2011). Similar epigenetic changes have also been found in offspring of Holocaust survivors (Yehuda et al., 2016).

We are only beginning to understand the link between historical trauma and current childhood adversity, but we can be certain that the trauma experienced by previous generations lives on in memories, behavioral responses, and, perhaps, in the epigenome. It may be one of the reasons for recent news articles asserting that "zip code is more important than genetic code" in determining your health and longevity. This is not entirely true, of course, because many factors are involved, but there is an element of truth. For example, according to the interactive website maintained by the Robert Wood Johnson Foundation (see Resources), Jennifer lives in a zip code in Tulsa where residents' average life expectancy is 82.9 years, 6 years more than the average person in Tulsa County (76.7 years), and 7 years more than the average person in Oklahoma (75.7). Amanda also lives in Tulsa but in a different neighborhood, where life expectancy is 80.6 years. Jennifer lives in a fairly homogeneous middle-class neighborhood, and Amanda lives in a trendier neighborhood with more diverse socioeconomic levels. Both are above the national average of 78.6 years. Neither lives in a Tulsa neighborhood where life expectancies are dismally lower than the national average. For example, if we enter in our work address on North Greenwood Avenue, we (statistically) take 12 to 14 years from our lives because the life expectancy in north Tulsa is only 68.3 years, 10 years less than the national average. There are undoubtedly many reasons for these disparities, but two of the major factors are historical trauma and continued adversity in the community.

Historical Trauma: The 1921 Tulsa Race Massacre

On May 31, 1921, Greenwood was a thriving community of approximately 8,000 people on the north side of Tulsa, Oklahoma. Greenwood was populated by the sons and daughters of freed slaves who went to Indian Territory after the Civil War, "repeating a pattern begun by runaway slaves and by the Negroes who accompanied the Indian tribes along the death march which took so many lives that it became known as 'The Trail of Tears'" (Ellison, 2003, p. 8). There were also the more recent arrivals, Blacks from other parts of the country looking to prosper from the oil boom that was making many Tulsans rich. In fact, Greenwood was prosperous—its main thoroughfare was called the "Black Wall Street." It was largely self-sufficient, with its own hospital, high school, hotels, stores, banks, two newspapers, and two movie theaters.

Everything changed on May 30, when Sarah Page, a 17-year-old White elevator operator, accused Dick Rowland, a 19-year-old Black delivery man, of attacking her in the elevator of a downtown building. A sensational account was published in the *Tulsa Tribune* ("Nab Negro for Attacking Girl in Elevator"), stating that he scratched her face and tore her clothes. Attempted rape was rumored, and he was arrested the next day. What happened during the next 2 days has been studied extensively, although many facts will never be known, and much was done to cover up crimes committed (Messer, Shriver, & Beamon, 2017). Fearing a lynching—which was not uncommon during this time and which, historians believe, was called for in a newspaper editorial—a group of armed Black men went to the police station to protect him, encountering a much larger group of armed White men and women. Shots were fired, and at least one person was killed. Like a spark to dry kindling, tempers exploded, triggering 2 days of mob violence. Thousands of Whites rampaged through the Greenwood community, looting, burning, and killing. Police arrested any Black person on the street, leaving houses and buildings unprotected. Tulsa Fire Department trucks were turned away at gunpoint when they tried to put out the flames. It has been estimated that hundreds of Black residents were killed, although precise numbers are unknown. Most were left homeless, as 35 city blocks were burned to the ground.

Within a week, the state attorney impaneled a grand jury, but the all-White jury placed the cause of the riot on Black "mobs." No one was ever tried for the deaths, injuries, or property damage. Not all Whites were complicit. Many were appalled and raised funds to aid in the rebuilding, but most of Greenwood was rebuilt by Black Tulsans themselves. Active efforts were made to erase the event from history (Brophy, 2003). Seventy-five years later, the Oklahoma state legislature authorized a commission to study the "Tulsa Race Riot of 1921." The commission's report documented that the city had conspired with the mob of White Tulsans. They recommended a program of monetary reparations to survivors and their descendants, a scholarship fund for Greenwood descendants, a memorial park, and the creation of an economic development zone for the neighborhood. In response, the state legislature passed the 1921 Tulsa Race Riot Reconciliation Act, which established the recommended provisions for scholarships, a memorial park (the John Hope Franklin Reconciliation Park was dedicated in 2010), and initiated economic development in the community. But no direct reparations were made (Brophy, 2003).

History is replete with examples of injustice, cruelty, hardships, and deprivations imposed by one group on another. The land on which the devastating events of 1921 occurred had already seen its share of hardship and betrayal. This land was Indian Territory before Oklahoma statehood in 1907, the destination of thousands of Native Americans who were forced from their lands across the southern United States by the Indian Removal Act of 1830. Examples of mass migrations are not limited to the past. Our news feeds are filled with stories of Central Americans seeking safety in the United States and of the 12 million Syrians who have been displaced and an estimated half a million killed in the ongoing conflict in their country. These are instances of historical trauma in the making. They require an honest look at what we can do as a society to support families with children or step in when the enormity of disaster makes it difficult or impossible for parents and caregivers to serve as a shield for their children.

Contemporaneous Trauma: Promoting Resilience in Bosnia

Few studies have been done to evaluate ways to promote resilience in children exposed to traumatic events on such a scale that they would be thought of as historical trauma. One of the earliest of these was conducted during the year after the end of the violence and civil war in the former Yugoslavia (Dybdahl, 2001). Similar to the more recent conflict in Syria, nearly half of the residents of Bosnia and Herzegovina had been displaced from their homes, and severe atrocities were common. With funding from UNICEF, European researchers designed and evaluated a psychosocial support and education intervention for displaced mothers and their young children following exposure to wartime trauma. At the time of the intervention, the displaced mothers and children had fled their homes and were living in either refugee settlements or private homes under conditions of poverty, crowdedness, and proximity to war threats. At 5 and 6 years old, children were young enough to have memories only of war or refugee life, and most had direct traumatic experiences of war, for example, shelling, seeing the dead and wounded, and separation from and the death of relatives. Indirect effects included the traumas suffered by their parents, loss of their homes and neighborhoods, and lack of basic needs—water, electricity, fuel, medical care.

The intervention was based on observations that children are more likely to be resilient after political violence if they have access to family or maternal support (Cairns & Dawes, 1996). Thus, the intervention was designed to promote child well-being and development by providing mothers with support and guidance, emphasizing the importance of the mother–child interaction for the child's growth and healing. Mothers randomized to the control group attended scheduled evaluations and received medical care. Mothers in the intervention group attended semistructured group sessions weekly for 5 months. The intervention content was based on the International Child Development Program (Hundeide, 1991; Sherr, Skar, Clucas, von Tetzchner, & Hundeide, 2014) and was informed by discussion and therapy groups with women before the intervention. The group sessions were designed to support the mothers and to increase their own well-being, self-confidence, and ability to care for their children and "be their children's best healer" (Dybdahl, 2001). Group leaders began each meeting by speaking about one of the program topics, such as "the importance of love and ways of showing affection, or typical traumatic stress reactions and the importance of helping children rather than punishing them for their problems (e.g., for repetitive play or bedwetting"; Dybdahl, 2001, p. 1218). Mothers then shared their own feelings and experiences about the topic, discussed suggestions proposed by the group leader, and shared their own coping strategies.

Not surprisingly, baseline data revealed significant negative consequences of the early life trauma experienced by the children, with dramatic lags in physical growth and cognitive development relative to normative peers, and both mothers and children exhibited symptoms of depression and anxiety. However, the intervention had significant positive effects on children's growth, their cognitive development, and reduced problem behaviors as evaluated by blind observers. Mothers also reported increases in perceived social support, life satisfaction, and overall positive descriptions of their children, despite reporting that conditions actually worsened during the course of the study.

The author concluded that a "probable explanation for the positive effects of the intervention on the children is that through their mothers' symptom reduction, the mothers became more able to help their children" (Dybdahl, 2001, p. 1228). As previously described in Chapter 6, engaging with and supporting caregivers—many of whom have experienced trauma themselves—is an important element of interventions that effectively buffers the effects of trauma in children (National Academies of Sciences, Engineering, and Medicine, 2019b). Extending these findings into the systems that support children and their families, trauma-informed practices support not only parents but also other types of caregivers who interact with children.

TRAUMA-INFORMED PRACTICES

Implementing trauma-informed approaches in response to the enduring effects of childhood adversity is increasingly prevalent among individual practitioners and a variety of systems providing services to at-risk children and youth (Ko et al., 2008). Although trauma-informed care (TIC) is still a relatively new paradigm, there is growing evidence supporting its effectiveness in promoting resilience and minimizing retraumatization in trauma-exposed children (Frydman & Mayor, 2017; Holmes, Levy, Smith, Pinne, & Neese, 2015). As defined by the U.S. Substance Abuse and Mental Health Services Administration (SAMHSA), the trauma-informed approach has four key elements, sometimes referred to as the four Rs: (a) Realizing the widespread impact of trauma; (b) Recognizing how trauma may affect individual clients, staff, or others in the program; (c) Responding by applying knowledge about trauma into practice; and (d) preventing Retraumatization (SAMHSA, 2014). They also recommend six key principles that can be adapted for a variety of settings: (a) safety; (b) trustworthiness and transparency; (c) peer support; (d) collaboration and mutuality; (e) empowerment; and (f) addressing cultural, historical, and gender issues. The trauma-informed approach was originally designed to improve therapeutic clinical practice and social services (M. Harris & Fallot, 2001a) but has been adapted for use in other settings, primarily schools, health care, and the juvenile justice system. A basic description of trauma-informed approaches in each of these systems is provided in the following subsections, and additional resources for trauma-informed practices are provided in the Resource section.

Mental Health and Social Services

To reflect these trauma-informed principles and practices, a mental health care facility or social service agency typically undergoes an organizational change process that prioritizes healing and reduces the risk of retraumatization of vulnerable clients or others involved in the process (M. Harris & Fallot, 2001b). One of the hallmarks of this paradigm change is shifting the mind-set from *What is wrong with you?* to *What happened to you?* Helping children (or adults) exposed to trauma requires not only screening by trauma-trained service providers but having continuity of care across services provided to children and their families. Practitioners within mental health care settings and social service agencies are well aware of the relationship between childhood trauma and subsequent psychological distress and related functional difficulties. Nonetheless, a trauma-informed approach at the system level ensures that the role of trauma is understood and acknowledged. This involves seeing through a trauma lens, recognizing the way that childhood adversity can influence emotions, patterns of thought, and therefore behavior. What are often seen as problematic or health-harming behavior are thus reframed as coping strategies that had, or may continue to have, short-term utility despite their long-term negative consequences.

The effects of the invisible traumas that may result from historical, cultural, and social adversities (i.e., racism, disability, homophobia, sexism, colonialism) are also acknowledged. Trauma-informed systems ensure that all staff within the system are trained in the "Four Rs" and are especially aware of maintaining policies and interactions that prevent inadvertent retraumatization, focusing on the building of trust through openness and respect, striving for collaboration, mutuality, and empowerment, avoiding coercion, force, and accompanying triggers. Importantly, trauma-informed direct service systems recognize the importance of creating safety for staff members and clients, with both groups defining and negotiating this relationally (Sweeney, Filson, Kennedy, Collinson, & Gillard, 2018). Evidence is mounting that trauma-informed treatment is an effective strategy for improving the developmental trajectories for children exposed to trauma and adversity (Bartlett et al., 2018).

Health Care

Pediatricians are taking major strides in integrating ACEs research into health care. After a 2013 survey of American Academy of Pediatrics (AAP) members revealed that only 4% of respondents were familiar with childhood trauma and most did not ask parents about ACEs, the AAP implemented a national education program, Pediatric Approach to Trauma, Treatment, and Resilience (PATTeR). In collaboration with university partners and funding from SAMHSA (https://www.samhsa.gov/), PATTeR educates pediatricians and pediatric health care professionals about trauma screening, care, and management through primary care.

Pediatricians' reasons for not screening for ACEs included lack of knowledge about them, lack of confidence or skills in asking uncomfortable questions, lack of time and reimbursement, and lack of resources or referrals for parents who have experienced significant ACEs (Kerker et al., 2016; Szilagyi et al., 2016). Parents, in contrast, report that they welcome a conversation about ACEs with their pediatricians (Conn et al., 2018). Screening approaches and guidelines help ensure that screening is more widely used (Bethell, Carle, et al., 2017; N. J. Burke, Hellman, Scott, Weems, & Carrion, 2011; N. B. Harris, 2018).

In addition to the importance of ACEs screening for increasing the efficacy of care (Dube, 2018), pediatricians are also encouraged to develop partnerships with social service providers to leverage modifiable resilience factors for children exposed to ACEs (Talmi et al., 2016), to implement trauma-informed care approaches (Oral et al., 2016), and to incorporate behavioral consultation and support services within the pediatric medical home (Buchholz & Talmi, 2012; Talmi et al., 2016). For example, the Healthy Steps program pairs a developmental specialist with pediatricians during well-child visits to extend primary care services and follow up on psychosocial and developmental issues (Buchholz & Talmi, 2012). Screening for ACEs and trauma-informed approaches are also beginning to be implemented during obstetric visits (Flanagan et al., 2018) and in emergency departments (Corbin et al., 2011). Following the National Child Traumatic Stress Network's (2003) inclusion of *medical traumatic stress* as "psychological and physiological responses of children and their families to pain, injury, serious illness, medical procedures, and invasive or frightening treatment experiences" (see https://www.nctsn. org/what-is-child-trauma/trauma-types/medical-trauma), trauma-informed practices have been implemented in a number of pediatric health care networks (Marsac et al., 2016) and neonatal intensive care units (Sanders & Hall, 2018).

School Programs

Trauma-informed schools are an increasingly common approach for addressing ACEs and increasing children's resilience (Overstreet & Chafouleas, 2016). Schools are an especially appropriate avenue for promoting resilience in children because they touch more children's lives than any other public or private institution, and (along with health care) are the primary portal of entry to mental health services for children who exhibit early signs of trauma and adversity. Although the goals of education in childhood and adolescence have historically focused on academic achievement, there is increasing recognition that social, emotional, and behavioral outcomes are also essential for success in school and later in adulthood. These outcomes are particularly relevant in early childhood education, where the objectives are to promote school readiness and the development of foundational executive function skills, including the ability to focus attention, regulate emotions, and form positive relationships with peers and teachers.

Helping children living in poverty develop these competencies has been the focus of Head Start and Early Head Start for decades. Initially established to reduce the gap in school readiness between children living in poverty and their more affluent peers, both have been found to be a cost-effective investment (Heckman, 2006). More recently, Head Start programs have also focused on addressing the effects of maternal depression (Beardslee, Ayoub, Avery, Watts, & O'Carroll, 2010) and other types of trauma that may cooccur with poverty (Kinniburgh, Blaustein, Spinazzola, & van der Kolk, 2017).

Head Start Trauma Smart (HSTS) is an integrated set of interventions to identify and address the effects of trauma in Head Start and elementary school programs. Funded by the Robert Wood Johnson Foundation, HSTS is currently being implemented and evaluated in several states. Its goals are to decrease the impact of toxic stress and support preschoolers' social and cognitive development by creating a trauma-informed networks and culture (Holmes et al., 2015). The intervention integrates three existing evidenced-based modalities: (a) Attachment, Self-Regulation, and Competency Model (Kinniburgh et al., 2017) training for school personnel; (b) Trauma-Focused Cognitive Behavioral Therapy (TF-CBT) for trauma-exposed children (Cohen, Mannarino, & Deblinger, 2006; Silverman et al., 2008); and (c) classroom consultation by Early Childhood Mental Health consultants (Brennan, Bradley, Allen, & Perry, 2008). Although not designed as a research study, preliminary evaluations indicate that HSTS reduced teacher-reported child externalizing behavior and parent-reported child externalizing and internalizing behavior, with high levels of program satisfaction from parents, teachers, and administrators. Other school-based programs with preliminary evidence of effectiveness include the Supportive Trauma Interventions for Educators program for preschoolers (McConnico, Boynton-Jarrett, Bailey, & Nandi, 2016); the University of San Francisco's HEARTS (Healthy Environments and Response to Trauma in Schools) program for trauma-exposed kindergarten and elementary school children (Dorado, Martinez, McArthur, & Leibovitz, 2016); the Cognitive Behavioral Intervention for Trauma in Schools program for Grades 4 and higher (McConnico et al., 2016); Multimodal Trauma Treatment (Amaya-Jackson et al., 2003); and the RAP Club for seventh and eighth graders, which provides trauma-informed programming facilitated by a mental health counselor to improve self-regulation and decision making (Mendelson, Tandon, O'Brennan, Leaf, & Ialongo, 2015).

Home Visiting Programs

Programs developed from public health models that provide support for new mothers and young children have been effective for improving outcomes in children at risk because of poverty and adversity (Beckmann, 2017). The perinatal period is a critical transition for mothers and fathers with a history of childhood adversity (see Chapter 4) and a unique opportunity to conduct trauma screening and trauma-sensitive interventions (Atzl, Narayan, Rivera, & Lieberman, 2019; Chamberlain et al., 2019; Hudziak, 2018; Racine et al., 2018). Most of the research on the effectiveness of these programs has come from evaluations of federally funded programs. The U.S. Health Resources and Services Administration (2019) provides grants to states, territories, and tribal entities to fund home visiting programs for high-risk mothers and children through the Maternal, Infant, and Early Childhood Home Visiting Program. Program goals are consistent with promoting resilience and breaking the intergenerational cycle of adversity (a) to improve maternal and child health, (b) prevent child abuse and neglect, (c) encourage positive parenting, and (d) promote child development and school readiness.

One of the most widely studied home visiting programs is the Nurse–Family Partnership (NFP) program (Olds et al., 2004). Starting during pregnancy, nurses support first-time mothers by providing instrumental and emotional support to improve pregnancy outcomes, help mothers become knowledgeable and responsible parents, and improve children's health and development. Research showed NFP reduced all-cause maternal and preventable child mortality (Olds et al., 2014) and child internalizing problems, and it increased academic achievement at age 12 (Kitzman et al., 2010). NFP costs approximately $5,000 per family per year and is estimated to yield an estimated $2.37 in benefit for every dollar spent (S. Lee et al., 2012).

The Lemonade for Life program was developed by researchers and clinicians with expertise in home visiting, child abuse and neglect prevention, early childhood, and resilience. It includes concrete tools and training for home visitors on using ACEs research to foster resilience. Preliminary results indicate it is effective in helping already-skilled home visitors increase their comfort and ability to talk with clients struggling with ACEs and refer families for ACEs-related help (Counts, Gillam, Perico, & Eggers, 2017). Home visitors reported that after receiving Lemonade for Life training, despite their already strong and trusting relationships with families, their connections and engagement with families improved. One of the most important benefits of Lemonade for Life is likely the significant increase in home visiting professionals' understanding of how their own early life experiences, adverse and otherwise, affect their lives and their work (Counts et al., 2017). Social workers, child development professionals, and other social service employees may have higher ACEs than average (Esaki & Larkin, 2013). A 2011 survey of clinicians, milieu therapists, child care workers, home visitors, and teachers, more than half (53%) reported two or more ACEs, significantly higher than the 38% reported in the original Kaiser-Permanente sample (Esaki & Larkin, 2013). Although this is only one study, the findings suggest that social service agencies and training programs should incorporate trauma-informed practices within their own cultures, helping professionals assess the impact of ACEs in their own lives and teaching them to use their experiences mindfully and nonreactively when working with clients.

Juvenile Justice and Law Enforcement

Trauma-informed initiatives have also been implemented to train police officers, other first responders, and the judicial system in ACEs and trauma-informed care (Ko et al., 2008). First responders encounter trauma-exposed children on a daily basis and are often the first to interact with children in cases of family violence, so they are in a unique position to help mitigate the effects of stress in these situations. Many national organizations support the implementation of trauma-informed policing, including the U.S. Department of Justice and the International Association of Chiefs of Police. The Yale Child Study Center and New Haven Department of Police developed the Child Development Community Police (CD-CP) program, which has been widely adopted by many other communities (Marans, Berkowitz, & Cohen, 1998). CD-CP places mental health professionals in the community with police to intervene early when children are exposed to violence or other trauma.

Nationally, a number of organizations have advocated for trauma-informed perspectives in the juvenile justice system, recognizing the frequency of trauma and violence in the histories of court-involved youth, many of whom have previously been involved in family courts (Garbarino, 2017). Childhood trauma is not only a major factor for youth involvement in the criminal justice system, but is also a predictor of rehabilitation success (Baglivio, Wolff, Piquero, & Epps, 2015; B. H. Fox, Perez, Cass, Baglivio, & Epps, 2015), spurring interest in trauma-informed juvenile justice systems. A recent systematic review of this research indicated that there is general consensus on recommendations for staff training and trauma-specific treatment, but a lack of agreement on other policies or practices that would define trauma-informed juvenile justice systems (Branson, Baetz, Horwitz, & Hoagwood, 2017).

Zero to Three (2019) launched the Safe Babies Court Teams Project to improve outcomes and prevent future court involvement in neglected or maltreated infants and toddlers. This program creates teams that include professionals from mental health, law enforcement, child welfare, and other agencies involved in protecting children using an infant mental health framework. Families are supported and given targeted and timely services. For example, rather than police officers, prosecutors, and Child Protective Services designating parents identified as abusive as "perps" and focusing on appropriate criminal charges and punishment, the trauma-informed approach focuses on valuing the parent–child relationship, supporting the parent in changing behaviors, and supporting foster parents. In 2014, the U.S. Administration on Children, Youth and Families, Children's Bureau funded Zero to Three to develop a quality improvement center to share information, build knowledge, and provide technical assistance to community sites implementing Safe Babies Courts. More information is available at the Zero to Three website (https://www.zerotothree.org).

Each of the trauma-informed approaches described thus far have focused on one set of systems that touch the at-risk child. Creating systems of care and policies that support trauma recovery and healing systemwide are important steps. However, one of the recommendations made by the recent National Academies of Sciences, Engineering, and Medicine (2019a, 2019b) to improve health equity and opportunities for children and adolescents is to create *coordinated systems of care*. Imagine, for example, that a trauma-informed teacher of a 5-year-old boy whose father is in prison and whose mother is depressed, recognizes that his inability to sit still and listen during circle time is not because he has a bad attitude or even attention-deficit/hyperactivity disorder, but more likely the effects of the stress and trauma. She notes worsening conditions during the semester and begins to suspect that the mother has a substance use disorder. If her school system has adopted a trauma-informed practice, she is able to connect with others in the system to access school-based services and resources for him. If other social and governmental agencies in her community are also trauma informed, the school system is able to coordinate appropriate responses with other agencies, to provide appropriate interventions that will ensure both the child's well-being and the mother's return to healthy functioning. This simple example illustrates the importance of creating trauma-informed cultures within communities. It is almost impossible for one teacher to create a trauma-informed classroom when the school, the school system, indeed the entire community, adheres to the "sink-or-swim" attitude that pervades much of our culture.

When we create trauma-informed communities, we ensure that the institutions and organizations providing services and care for children, particularly the more seriously traumatized children, are supported throughout the community. We ensure that when services are provided, whether in doctors' offices, schools, social services, or law enforcement and judicial systems, they are coordinated and build on existing and accessible strengths without children falling into the cracks or being revictimized. We are a long way from reaching that goal in most cities, counties, and states, but we have started.

COMMUNITY COALITIONS FOCUSED ON ACES AND RESILIENCE

Current conditions across the world and in local communities can overwhelm parents' abilities to protect their children. When the parents themselves have a history of childhood adversity, it is difficult to respond mindfully rather than reflexively or to find a rational response rather than an emotional reaction. We find remarkable parallels between the maternal support and parenting goals in the wartime Bosnian intervention and the programs described in Chapter 6 for at-risk mothers in the United States (e.g., Circle of Security and ABC). If mothers and other caregivers are overwhelmed and unable to shield their children from violence and trauma—whether it comes from an ethnic-political civil war, gangs in the neighborhood, or within the family itself—the most logical and cost-effective strategy is to make available to those caregivers the relatively simple and inexpensive psychosocial intervention programs described in previous chapters. We believe it is unreasonable and unproductive to blame parents who grew up in high-ACE homes without adequate protection from their own parents and, at the same time, to hope that they somehow figure out how to get right with their own children. To help interrupt this cycle of intergenerational trauma and dysfunction in families, many communities have recognized that coordinated efforts are required to address ACEs at the level of policies and social systems.

Payne County Resilience Coalition

In spring 2017, one of our colleagues at Oklahoma State University (OSU) in Stillwater cosponsored with the Stillwater Child Advocacy Center a public showing of the film *Resilience,* a documentary about the ACEs study and programs to promote resilience (Pritzker & Redford, 2016). Afterward, Dr. Carolynn Macallister, a board member of the center and a recently retired OSU faculty member, contacted Jennifer for more information. Later, she told Jennifer that hearing about ACEs was like a light bulb switching on. They began meeting regularly to delve more deeply into the research on ACEs, on protective and compensatory experiences (PACEs) and resilience, and potential steps they could take to address the high prevalence rates of ACEs in Oklahoma and the local community. Carolynn sent invitations to friends and colleagues in this small university town to come together to "do something about ACEs in Stillwater" and nearly 100 people showed up on a hot June morning at the local hospital auditorium to create the Stillwater Resilience Coalition. After Jennifer gave a brief presentation about ACEs and PACEs, and local pediatrician Dr. Dwight Sublett confirmed that ACEs were indeed the biggest problem he sees in clinic every day, the group divided into four working groups: (a) education (schools and professional development), (b) health care (pediatricians, behavioral health), (c) law enforcement and the justice system (police, lawyers, judges), and (d) policy and legislation (lawmakers, city government). A. J. Griffin, a state senator from Oklahoma City, attended that first meeting and began planning a legislative response. The energy and the enthusiasm at that meeting was inspiring and motivating. Each working group embarked on a summer of meetings, gathering information and input from others in the community. When we met again in the fall, action steps were already underway, and other groups from surrounding communities joined, changing our name from Stillwater to Payne County Resilience Coalition.

After 2 years, coalition accomplishments are truly remarkable. The local school board conducted an interim study, school principals began holding training sessions on trauma-sensitive practices and implementing new programs adapted from other communities, and Jennifer presented results and recommendations of the Task Force at the 2018 Zero to Three annual conference (Hays-Grudo, Welch, & Shellhammer, 2018). The law enforcement group identified an evidence-based trauma-sensitive training program for police officers and OSU faculty, staff, and local therapists collaborated in conducting the trainings. The pediatric health care group began screening parents in the pediatric clinic for ACEs and using ACEs in its diagnostic and referral system following guidelines recommended by the AAP (2019). Physicians and therapists continue to work together to provide support and resources for children and families. On the legislative front, our group worked closely with the Potts Family Foundation in Oklahoma City and other organizations to prepare a bill that State Senator Griffin and cosponsors shepherded through committees and both legislative houses. In 2018, OK Senate Bill 1517 was signed into law, creating a task force to recommend and guide implementation of trauma-informed programs in every state government service sector. More than 20 communities across the state have active resilience coalitions in development and met as a group in fall 2019 to learn best practices from experts and colleagues. State agencies are embarking on trauma-informed training programs in collaboration with communities and experts from across the nation. The Oklahoma Resilience Initiative is underway.

The Stillwater story is an example of what can be done when people learn about the repercussions of adversity and join forces to help communities prevent, protect, and recover from trauma. Other communities around the country have also begun this effort, serving as models and resources for others to follow.

Washington State

Washington State was one of the first states to develop coalitions to address the effects of ACEs in communities across the state. The Adverse Childhood Experiences Public-Private Initiative (APPI), a consortium of public agencies, private foundations, and local networks, was formed to study ways to mitigate and prevent ACEs throughout the state (Hargreaves, Pecora, & Williamson, 2017). APPI has developed the ACEs and Resilience Collective Community Capacity (ARC³) to measure collective community capacity to achieve their ACEs goals. The ARC³ assesses capacity across four domains: coalition leadership and infrastructure, network capacity, community-based solutions, and community-wide impact. Pilot testing in non-APPI communities and testing in the five APPI communities reveal that the measure has good reliability and validity and is capable of identifying the range of effective community networks and goals. Several public–private partnerships with national networks of communities have also been established to address the effects of ACEs on children's development. Progress has been documented, with significant reductions in birth to teen mothers, infant mortality, youth suicide, youth arrests for violent crime, and high school dropout rates (Porter, Martin, & Anda, 2017). Several essential capacities for creating community change were also identified, including recruiting and training new leaders, conceptualizing problems using a systems perspective and thinking strategically, and emphasizing learning, bringing in outside consultants and using iterative cycles of action and reflection (Porter et al., 2017).

National and International Coalitions

The Change in Mind coalition is a partnership that includes both U.S. and Canadian sites to integrate brain science research into nonprofit human service agencies to create systems and policy changes (Jones, Reidy, Hargreaves, & Rog, 2017). Another partnership, Mobilizing Action for Resilient Communities, is coordinated by the Health Federation of Philadelphia, with additional funding from the California Endowment, and supports the efforts of 14 communities with networks already in place to reduce ACEs and promote resilience. Members, which include a variety of agency-based service providers and community members, pledge to practice trauma sensitivity, serve actively on committees, and participate in peer-to-peer learning collaboratives, sharing knowledge and best practices (Jones et al., 2017).

Philadelphia ACE Task Force

This coalition was organized in 2012 when a local nonprofit organization, the Institute for Safe Families, brought together several child health leaders in Philadelphia to develop an initiative to prevent family violence and child abuse by strengthening and nurturing families. It initially focused on integrating ACEs screening into pediatric primary care but has expanded, on the basis of the needs identified by data collected from the community (presented in Chapter 1), to a broader vision of creating a citywide service system aligned with an ACEs and resilience framework. The coalition includes a wide range of individuals who have experience or interest in developing trauma-informed approaches to psychosocial stress and adversity, representing health care, behavioral health, social services, a public service sectors, school systems, the child welfare system, juvenile court, affordable housing advocates, parks and recreation, and neighboring communities. As the goals and membership expanded, workgroups were formed in three areas—community education, professional development, and practical interventions—two of which have received funding to support their work. This coalition sponsored the first national ACEs summit in May 2013, which Amanda and Jennifer attended, partnering with ACEs Connection, the online community education and support network, and the Robert Wood Johnson Foundation.

ACEs Connection

One of the most useful resources for community coalition-building, as well as general networking and resource identification related to ACEs and resilience, is the website ACEs Connection (https://www.acesconnection.com/). This online network, supported by several foundations, is managed by Jane Stevens, a social journalist committed to supporting the ACEs and resilience movement through journalism and social media. ACEs Connection provides guidance and tools for hundreds of communities across the United States that are developing trauma-informed and resilience-promoting practices and policies in community agencies and institutions. It also provides a safe place for members to request and share information and access training programs and other tools. A companion site (https://acestoohigh.com/) provides information for the public. In addition, members who join ACEs Connection can opt to receive weekly or daily updates, find ACEs-based programs by area, post blogs and comments, and access a resource center. The support provided for community members committed to developing resilient communities is integral in creating and developing community-based ACEs responses, such as the Payne County Resilience Coalition described previously.

POLICY CHANGE AND LEGISLATION

For nearly 2 decades, there have been strong calls to overhaul systems and policies to reflect the scientific evidence that childhood adversity and trauma have devastating effects on health and development, creating intractable social and public health problems (Phillips & Shonkoff, 2000). As evidence mounts, so does the number and intensity of appeals from researchers, clinicians, and policy makers to change systems focused on treating the observable problems and chronic conditions above the waterline (see the ACEs Iceberg in Chapter 5) to address the hidden neurobiological and developmental deficits below the surface (Anda, Butchart, Felitti, & Brown, 2010; Perry, 2009; Shonkoff, 2012; van der Kolk, 2016). Encouragingly, in the past several years, several states have launched trauma-informed initiatives.

In 2012, Wisconsin established the statewide Wisconsin State Trauma Project (Wisconsin Department of Children and Families, n.d.). To date, 43 counties and three tribes have participated in one or more of its three components: (a) training for caregivers in trauma-informed parenting workshops, (b) training for mental health professionals in TF-CBT, and (c) training and technical assistance in trauma-informed county/tribal organizational systems change.

In Oklahoma, the legislature passed SB1517, which created a governor-appointed Task Force on Trauma Informed Care. The Task Force represents state departments of health, mental health and substance abuse, human services, and education; state physician associations; the University of Oklahoma Pediatrics Department; the Oklahoma Health Care Authority; Indian Health Services; the law enforcement and justice system (attorney general's office, state law enforcement); child advocacy (Oklahoma Institute for Child Advocacy); and researchers with expertise in early childhood (OSU Institute for Building Early Relationships [IBEaR]) and childhood adversity (OSU's Center for Integrative Research in Childhood Adversity [CIRCA]). Jennifer and Amanda are founding members of IBEaR, and Jennifer is the director of CIRCA, a National Institutes of Health (NIH)–funded research center supporting projects to better elucidate the relationship between adversity and protective factors of development. One of the arguments that proved most persuasive in talking with legislators about the need for this bill and this initiative was the documentation that children in Oklahoma have among the highest rates of ACEs in the United States, due at least in part to the historical traumas endured by the people in this state. We were also able to point to research going on in the state (e.g., the Lemonade for Life program led by the University of Oklahoma's Department of Pediatrics, CIRCA's NIH-funded center), CIRCA research, and other resources involved in moving Oklahoma from having high levels of problems resulting from ACEs (e.g., poor health, high rates of incarceration, school dropout, teen pregnancy) to becoming more trauma-informed and resilient.

Following the lead of Oklahoma and other ACEs-progressive states, in February 2018, the U.S. House of Representatives unanimously approved HR443 recognizing the importance of trauma-informed care within federal programs and agencies. HR443 includes designation of a national trauma awareness month and day to increase public knowledge of the impact of ACEs. Trauma-informed practices have been inserted into other legislative proposals at the federal level.

Reviewing the bills passed between December 22, 2009, when the first trauma-informed bill was introduced, and December 31, 2015, Purtle and Lewis (2017) observed a dramatic increase in legislative initiatives that included language referring to trauma-informed practices. There are several reasons to be optimistic about continued support for legislation promoting systems change that reflect neuroscience and ACEs research. First, concern about the effects of ACEs is a bipartisan issue, as evidenced by its support from Republican governors and legislators as well as Democratic officials. Second, although the health care debate in the United States is a deeply divided issue, there is bipartisan support for treatment and research on mental health and substance abuse, the focus of many of the trauma-informed initiatives (Purtle & Lewis, 2017).

In summary, there has been a groundswell of support for addressing the effects of ACEs in communities and organizations. As this initiative gains momentum, we believe it is important to maintain the commitment to listening to the many perspectives that can inform the movement, from the many academic disciplines that study adversity and resilience, the many professionals working with children and families to ameliorate the effects of ACEs, and the many individuals who have experienced adverse and resilience-building experiences.

ADVERSE COMMUNITY ENVIRONMENTS AND ADVERSE CHILDHOOD EXPERIENCES: A PAIR OF ACES

A useful framework for integrating the effects of context on children's adverse and protective experiences is found in the Pair of ACEs Tree depicted in Figure 7.1 (W. R. Ellis & Dietz, 2017).

The tree is rooted in *Adverse Community Environments*, reflecting the hostile conditions created by poverty, discrimination, and lack of opportunity. The branches and leaves of the tree, *Adverse Childhood Experiences*, seem almost inevitable when depicted growing from this soil. How could these negative outcomes not result from being rooted in this environment? Interviewing leaders from health care, behavioral health, and community- and school-based agencies, W. R. Ellis and Dietz (2017), who created this model, advocate for redesigning and aligning health and social service delivery systems to serve children better, to support parents in shielding children from adversity and

FIGURE 7.1. A Pair of ACEs

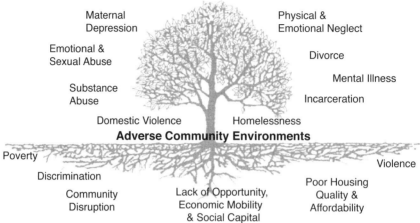

The "Pair of ACEs" concept was first discussed in W. R. Ellis and Dietz (2017). Reprinted from "*Introducing the 'Pair of ACEs' Tree,*" by W. R. Ellis and W. H. Dietz, 2018 (https://publichealth.gwu.edu/sites/default/files/downloads/Redstone-Center/BCR%20Pair%20of%20ACEs%20Webinar%20Slides.pdf). CC BY-NC-SA 4.0.

stress, and to engage better with related professions. They also found strong support among interviewed health professionals for a new model of health care delivery that incorporates psychosocial and behavioral stressors and policies that address ACEs and social determinants of health to improve health outcomes.

Although ACEs occur in families of all socioeconomic conditions and racial/ethnic groups, poverty and other sources of stress make adversity more likely and minimize opportunities for resilience. The resources available to parents—both internal and external—are likely to be more limited in families living with low incomes, in neighborhoods or rural areas with limited access to resources, and in socially marginalized and historically traumatized groups. The poorest census tracts in the United States tend to be highly racially segregated; they are the "richest" in the proportion of their population that is young children but the "poorest" in publicly available supports for those children (i.e., parks, playgrounds, and libraries; Bruner, 2017). We are hopeful that the recognition that current conditions in many communities have the effect of promoting adversity within individuals and families rather than protecting children, promoting resilience, and supporting their caregivers will continue to motivate researchers, funders, and community organizations to identify opportunities to implement the systems and community-level changes to reverse these conditions.

8

Putting It All Together

Summary and Solutions

Trauma is now our most urgent public health issue, and we have the knowledge necessary to respond effectively. The choice is ours to act on what we know.

—BESSEL VAN DER KOLK, 2015, p. 356

My politics are children.

—EDWARD ZIGLER

A few days after Jennifer's 42nd birthday, she realized she had lived longer than her mother, who died of breast cancer 2 days after her own 42nd birthday. She also realized she had never imagined a future beyond that point and felt completely adrift. The next week she began seeing a therapist, and she dreamt about a flood. In this dream, she was standing with colleagues in an office on the 20th floor of a building in the Texas Medical Center, watching the rising floodwaters below. As the waters rose higher and higher, the building began to creak and sway. She said to her coworkers, "We should jump out— if we stay here, we may die." One of them replied, "But I'm the architect— I designed the building to withstand this stress" and thus set up the dilemma: If she jumped, she might hurt someone's feelings; if she didn't jump, she might die. She jumped into the water—down, down, down, until her foot touched a rooftop, which she pushed off of to springboard back up to the surface. As she got to the surface and took a big gulp of air, she saw floating in front of her a big yellow life raft, and she woke up. When she reported this dream in

http://dx.doi.org/10.1037/0000177-008
Adverse and Protective Childhood Experiences: A Developmental Perspective, by J. Hays-Grudo and A. S. Morris

therapy the next week, her therapist smiled widely, and said, "I never worry about a client who puts a big yellow life raft into her dreams."

Although Jennifer acquired some adverse childhood experiences (ACEs) in adolescence after her mother died, her early childhood was full of protective and compensatory experiences (PACEs). Those PACEs gave her the life raft that she needed to navigate safely into and through adulthood. We believe the key to solving the legacy of problems caused by ACEs is to create a legacy of PACEs.

WHAT WE HAVE LEARNED

During the past 2 decades, interest in ACEs has proliferated. Dozens of studies with thousands of children, adolescents, and adults have confirmed and expanded on the initial findings that early life adversity creates a cascade of negative developmental and health outcomes. Researchers have identified many of the neurobiological mechanisms and behavioral processes under-lying what is increasingly recognized as having a causal relationship (Anda, Butchart, et al., 2010; Nemeroff, 2016) between ACEs and undesirable out-comes (Danese & Lewis, 2017). Intergenerational transmission of epigenetic responses to early life stress are being identified, providing biological as well as behavioral explanations for the cycles of abuse, neglect, and trauma that play out in families and communities across the globe.

Equally important is the burgeoning research on resilience and recovery. Building on earlier findings focused on the characteristics of resilient individ-uals, the scope of recent research has broadened to identify the characteristics of neighborhoods, schools, programs, and everyday experiences that protect and buffer children from the full consequences of adversity, and help children, youth, and adults recover from trauma. Concerned professionals in schools, courts, law enforcement, health care, and other organizations are increasingly seeking the knowledge, skills, and evidence-based prevention and treatment programs to respond to the ACEs epidemic with trauma-sensitive and effective practices.

We began writing this book because we had many questions about the effects of adverse and protective childhood experiences. We wanted to synthe-size models and results from many scientific disciplines and perspectives to form a more complete and coherent picture and discuss how this knowledge could be applied to create more nurturing and positive environments for children and adults who have experienced childhood adversity. During this process, we discovered many answers to these questions and summarize what we have learned about childhood adversity and protective experiences in what follows.

Adverse Childhood Experiences

- ACEs are common (a majority of people have at least one), co-occur (if you have one, you are likely to have others), and have cumulative impact in a dose–response effect (as the number of ACE categories increase, so does the risk for health problems, risky health behaviors, and cognitive, social, and emotional problems).

- ACEs are global and ancient, affecting millions of children around the world today and throughout history.

- ACEs have such strong and enduring effects on physical health and mental abilities (learning, remembering, planning, problem-solving, taking others' perspectives) because of the physiological effects of stress during sensitive periods of development.

- Many biological systems adapt to survive in an adverse environment: The brain, the immune system, hormones, and epigenetics all respond to meet the challenge of childhood maltreatment, poverty, and other forms of adversity. These short-term adaptive responses often have long-term negative consequences.

- Behavior and psychosocial systems adapt to survive in an adverse environment as well. Like physiological responses to stress, these adaptive behaviors promote survival in the moment but are maladaptive in the long run.

- Childhood adversity is often intergenerational. Biology and behavior contribute to patterns of family dysfunction and poor parenting in adults with ACEs, increasing the likelihood of creating ACEs for the next generation. Human and animal models show epigenetic changes linked with early life stress and deficits in development that are transferred generationally.

- Historical trauma lives in the cells of individuals and communities, sustaining patterns of violence, neglect, and despair in families and neighborhoods.

- Fear, mistrust, and hypervigilance—of verbal and physical mistreatment and of physical and emotional needs going unmet—are logical and adaptive childhood responses to ACEs. Fear may take different forms—*fight, flight,* or *freeze*—but it blocks positive, trusting, and open approaches to others and to the world.

Protective and Compensatory Experiences

- PACEs combine the many relationship-based and resource-dependent experiences that decades of developmental research have identified as protective in adverse childhood conditions.

- PACEs can mitigate the effects of ACEs by providing opportunities to experience love, safety, and trust; develop cognitive, social, and emotional competencies; and acquire behaviors and habits that protect and promote continued development.

- The ratio of ACEs to PACEs is critical in determining both immediate- and long-term effects of stress.

- We are wired to connect. All mammals are biologically driven to have social interaction, and human babies absolutely will not survive or thrive without it. Parents are also biologically programmed to respond to babies unless their own childhoods get in the way.

- Emotion regulation is key for discerning between real and assumed sources of fear. Being aware of negative responses—fear, anger, shame—and observing emotions in the moment allows one to choose a response. If we can stay calm, or regain a sense of calm, we can problem solve. We can shift perspective—put ourselves in other's shoes and see ourselves in the larger situation. We can avoid responding out of fear or anger, saying things that can never be unsaid, reacting in ways that hurt others or ourselves.

- There are many ways to develop emotion regulation. These include "top-down" (i.e., therapy with trauma-informed therapists) and "bottom-up" (i.e., activities that allow the body to have experiences that viscerally contradict the helplessness that results from trauma, observing ourselves and our responses). These avenues include mindfulness-based stress reduction, yoga, martial arts, music, dance, drama, and other programs that emphasize self-awareness and control over emotional and physical responses.

- Parents are children's primary protectors and source of love. Positive discipline is teaching—right from wrong, how to express feelings and needs, and how to empathize and respond to others.

- If parents are the ones causing ACEs, children need other caregivers to intervene, but most parents can recover from their own childhood traumas and learn more positive ways to care for their children.

- Parenting programs such as ABC, Circle of Security, Legacy for Children, and other infant mental health programs are effective in helping parents of babies and young children heal and learn to parent in ways that break the intergenerational cycle of ACEs.

- Research on brain plasticity confirms that although "practice makes perfect" may be an exaggeration, it is an adage for good reason. As we create safe, nurturing, supportive relationships and environments for ourselves and others around us, we create neural connections that allow new patterns of thinking, emotional responses, and habits and behaviors.

- The ACEs movement has been launched, and it is time to build PACEs. There are policy changes, legislation, and community initiatives happening throughout the United States and around the world that reflect a growing commitment to supporting healthy development for children exposed to adversity.

- PACEs provide a blueprint for creating enriching environments to promote continued development and recovery for adults with a history of ACEs. They create the pathway to maintain the gains in cognitive restructuring, flexible thinking, and emotion regulation brought about by cognitive behavior therapy and other trauma-informed interventions. PACEs are the antidote to ACEs for adults as well as children.

SOLUTIONS—WHAT TO DO NEXT

In Chapter 3, we proposed the Intergenerational and Cumulative Adverse and Resilience Experiences (ICARE) model to integrate and consolidate models and theories from the many disciplines that contribute to our knowledge about the effects of childhood experiences on health and development. We believe this is an essential step for moving the field forward and to support more interdisciplinary research, new scientific outlets for this work such as journals and conferences, community partnerships and training, and policies and systems that prevent ACEs and promote PACEs.

Forge Interdisciplinary Research Initiatives

We are calling for researchers from many disciplines to come together to answer big questions, such as the following:

- How does timing of adversity affect immediate- and long-term outcomes? We know from research and clinical work that critical functions occur during different stages of brain development, with implications for therapeutic interventions (Perry, 2006). How should interventions vary on the basis of the timing of ACEs?

- Resilience can be considered a product of the environment and broader social system, facilitating the capacity for growth (Ungar, 2013, 2018). How can culture and context promote resilience and healing from trauma? Are there cultures that are more resilient? If so, what can we learn from them?

- Is there a dose–response effect of PACEs? Of other protective factors? How do PACEs interact with timing of ACEs to predict developmental and health outcomes?

- Many interventions focus on children. What about adolescents? Which interventions are the best for adolescents with ACEs? The National Academies of Sciences, Engineering, and Medicine's (2019a) recent recommendations to improve developmental outcomes for adolescents acknowledges that brain development (and thus adolescence) effectively continues through the mid-20s. What programs help adolescents with a history of trauma best transition to young adulthood?

- How can we change biology to facilitate recovery from ACEs? There is some indication in research with rodents that cross-fostering, chemical interventions, and enriched environments can reverse epigenetic changes brought about by early life stress. Is this possible in humans?

- Is it ever too late to recover from ACEs? What are the limitations on ACEs recovery? How can PACEs in adulthood promote well-being and post-traumatic growth?

- How do we integrate positive psychology theories and methods, for example, the research on hope and optimism, with the research on ACEs and PACEs?

- How do we ensure that there is public support and political will for addressing ACEs and promoting PACEs? The National Academies of Sciences, Engineering, and Medicine (2019b) recently recommended "routinely tracking children's risk for adversity, transforming perinatal and pediatric care to address the root causes of poor health and well-being—the social, economic, environmental, and cultural determinants of health and early adversity—and to align with the work of other sectors addressing these issues" (p. S11). How can we translate ACEs findings to garner public and private support for funding to support such initiatives?

- How do we balance the need for additional research on brain development with the need for immediate interventions to apply current knowledge and programming to all children and families in need? This is a careful balancing act, and we believe as scientists that we must advocate for funding programs that have sufficient scientific support to help children now (see Luthar & Eisenberg, 2017). We also need funding to support interdisciplinary science on ACEs and PACEs with an eye toward prevention and treatment.

One example of financially supported interdisciplinary research on ACEs/PACEs is the National Institutes of Health–funded Center for Integrative Research on Childhood Adversity (CIRCA; P20) at OSU (http://circaok.com/index.html). Jennifer is the director of CIRCA; its aims are to investigate the effects of childhood adversity using a variety of methods, to develop effective interventions for children and families facing adversity, and to create a research infrastructure that supports interdisciplinary cross-training and collaboration. Other academic institutions are starting similar initiatives, such as the University of Texas's Dell Medical School's Institute for Early Life Adversity Research. Public and private universities are primed to do this work because they bring together interdisciplinary researchers and students eager to be trained in multiple disciplines, with joint missions to improve the health and well-being of those who provide our support.

Launch Interdisciplinary Journals and Conferences

The scientific study of childhood adverse and protective experiences, their interaction, and the processes and mechanisms involved in resulting outcomes requires a host of disciplinary approaches and perspectives, including but not limited to basic and applied developmental psychology, pediatrics, child and adult psychiatry and clinical psychology, epidemiology, epigenetics, neuroscience, immunology, and public health. We need more interdisciplinary and integrative research that investigates basic processes as well as intervention and policy studies. In March 2020, the first issue of a new journal, *Adversity and Resilience Science: Journal of Research and Practice*, is being launched with Springer Nature. A diverse and international group of scholars and practitioners have committed to support this initiative by submitting, reviewing, and guiding the journal as members of the editorial board (see journal website at http://www.springer.com/42844). As Editor-in-Chief and Associate Editor, respectively, Jennifer and Amanda, along with co-Associate Editor Hiram Fitzgerald, have been amazed and gratified by the enthusiastic and generous offers to develop and promote this new collaborative endeavor. A series of annual conferences is also being initiated and our hope is that the journal and its associated conference will provide a platform from which to accelerate research and the translation of findings into practice and policy.

Create Research–Community Partnerships

Academic–community partnerships are paramount if research is to be both meaningful and rigorous. Community-based participatory research guidelines (CBPR) are a good starting point for these collaborations (Minkler & Wallerstein, 2011). These include enhancing community capacity, ensuring that the community is an equal partner in the research and benefits from the research, and creating sustainable programs that reach the partnering communities (e.g., minority populations, health disparate populations). Research funding exists to promote these initiatives (National Institute on Minority Health and Health Disparities, 2018), to accelerate the translation of research using culturally appropriate methods and strategies to improve health outcomes in health disparate populations. Privately and foundation-funded research–community partnerships can help communities evaluate their results and provide researchers with opportunities to work in "living laboratories" using CBPR and culturally appropriate methods (Hargreaves, Pecora, & Williamson, 2017).

Research focused on ACEs and protective factors in underserved populations is becoming more prevalent, but this is also an area in desperate need of research on effective methods to address trauma that cooccurs with ACEs when children and their families are exposed to additional traumas imposed by economic conditions, racial, ethnic and other forms of discrimination, and other adverse events and conditions. In Chapter 1, we described studies documenting horrific rates of adversity among juveniles in the justice system (Fox, Perez, Cass, Baglivio, & Epps, 2015; Perez, Jennings, & Baglivio, 2018) and the displacements and trauma of war (Dybdahl, 2001). Other disproportionately affected groups include military families (Oshri et al., 2015), children from homeless families (Narayan et al., 2017), children experiencing racism and discrimination (Thurston, Bell, & Induni, 2018), and children separated from their parents because of immigration policies (Muñiz de la Peña, Pineda, & Punsky, 2019).

Partnerships between universities, schools, and faith-based communities are well suited to developing and evaluating interventions to increase PACEs and reduce ACEs. Schools and faith-based institutions can be sources of PACEs themselves. We have partnered with early childhood education centers, including Tulsa Educare and Community Action Project—Tulsa (Head Start and Early Head Start; Hays-Grudo, Slocum, Root, Bosler, & Morris, 2019). We partnered with Educare and Catholic Charities to implement and evaluate the CDC's Legacy for Children program (Morris, Robinson, et al., 2017). The benefits of these partnerships are many and mutual. Funding to implement and evaluate these programs on a much wider basis is essential to shifting the ACEs/PACEs ratio in our youth.

Create Trauma-Informed Communities and Training Programs

We described the importance of forging public–private partnerships and alliances among organizations in Chapter 7. To do this, we need a culture that shifts from shame and blame to healing and recovery. This requires training and practice. An excellent example of an initiative at the community level is coming out of the Child and Adolescent Health Measurement Initiative (https://www.cahmi.org). It emphasizes the importance of translating the science of ACEs and resilience, cultivating cross-sector collaborations, and training across systems. Implementing trauma-informed care into a range of health and social service systems is an integral part of shifting the culture (Bowen & Murshid, 2016).

The success of community transformations that reduce ACEs depends on strategic partnering with other sectors in society to educate, influence, and implement policy changes. Social journalism can be an important partner in this effort by translating research findings to the larger community, as is evidenced by the impact of publications and books by ACEs-informed journalists and authors (Nakazawa, 2015; Stevens, 2017). Disseminating accurate information on the enormity of ACEs and sharing viable solutions (PACEs) will "accelerate the movement by moving information from people who have successfully implemented practices on the basis of ACEs science to people who want to do so" (Stevens, 2017, p. S26). Screenings for ACEs are becoming increasingly common. Although there is some concern regarding the potential for retraumatization if screening is not sensitively conducted and with adequate resources for follow-up (Finkelhor, 2018), there is increasing awareness that ACEs pose a public health crisis (Dube, 2018) requiring that our policies and programs incorporate trauma-informed approaches in the systems capable of recognizing and addressing childhood adversity (Murphey & Bartlett, 2019).

Support for education and training in trauma-informed practices, particularly with young children and their families, is essential and can be facilitated by connecting with mental health professionals who have expertise in this work. Unfortunately, current models in mental health do not always provide training in trauma, nor is that training itself always trauma-informed (Carello & Butler, 2014). Many effective training resources are available through the National Child Trauma Stress Network (https://www.nctsn.org) and Zero to Three (https://www.zerotothree.org). Other segments of community providers are also on the front lines of ACEs consequences, including police, firefighters, and social service workers (Ko et al., 2008). These providers must be given the tools to understand ACEs if their communities are to thrive. There is growing support for preprofessional training in trauma-informed practices at the graduate level for teachers and educational administrators (Chafouleas, Johnson, Overstreet, & Santos, 2016), in undergraduate medicine (Goldstein, Murray-García, Sciolla, & Topitzes, 2018), and for other preprofessionals in mental health, public health, and social and health sciences (Ford, 2017).

Implement PACEs Policies With a Focus on Prevention

We discussed the Youth in Iceland program in Chapter 6. Many communities need just such a movement. Obviously, this initiative requires a great deal of coordination, commitment, agreement—not to mention funding—and seems beyond our reach at the moment. However, more attainable goals are being realized at the community level, such as trauma-informed preschools and therapeutic classrooms, where classrooms and staff are equipped to address the needs of children who have experienced maltreatment and trauma. One example is the Children's Center in Salt Lake City, Utah. This preschool program brings together psychiatrists, psychologists, child development specialists, social workers, and educators in an education environment, with support for families and ongoing training for staff and students (https://childrenscenter utah.org). Therapeutic classrooms are urgently needed nationwide, but they are few and far between. Our teachers are currently handling behavior and emotional problems that stem from ACEs with minimal information, resources, training, or support.

As one of the Rockefeller Foundation's 100 Resilient Cities (100RC) network, Tulsa has been able to hire a chief resilience officer to operate within the mayor's office, supporting initiatives to heal the wounds inflicted by decades of historical trauma. The work is far from over, but the 100RC network is one way that foundation–community partnerships are helping cities around the world become more resilient in response to the social, economic, and physical challenges resulting from violence, natural disasters, economic disparities, and racial discrimination. This program has used strategies such as deliberative dialogue and partnerships to create plans for improving racial and other disparities in Tulsa (Stout, 2015). The 100RC is a powerful example of public–private partnerships providing training, information, and support for communities addressing the need to build resilience and recover from adversity.

FINDING A LIFE RAFT

We started this book by talking about the hole in the bridge, the slippery chasm through which children fall into the river below. We believe that we found the hole in the bridge when we learned about ACEs. Others across the globe have joined us in this conviction and are working to make the bridge safer, but we know that many more children will fall through before that can be accomplished. It also is not possible to reach all those who are struggling in the current of the river before they are swept out to sea. However, we can make sure that there is a life raft for each of them to grab and hold on to for safety. Each of the protective experiences we described functions as a life raft. Most of us have had more life rafts in our lives than we may have realized: the love and support of family and friends, an education, a talent or ability that we had the opportunity to develop, opportunities to connect with others. We invite you to think about the life rafts that have given you buoyancy when life was pulling you down and to recognize the ways that you have been and could be a life raft for others.

We know that children with ACEs need supportive relationships and enriched environments if they are to develop into adults capable of loving and healthy relationships, good parenting, meaningful work, and good citizenship. We also know the essential elements that make up these enriched and caring environments. The question is whether we have the will to invest in all our children, especially those who need our help the most. We also wonder whether we have the will to invest in their parents—those whose life trajectories may have been disrupted years ago by their own ACEs and who did not receive the interventions that would have righted their course. We believe that all the research we have presented brings us closer to being able to advocate effectively for the families wrecked by cycles of trauma. Although many research questions continue to beckon and need answering, we know enough to change policies, create trauma-informed systems of care, and heal ourselves. It's time to act.

Questions for Reflection

In spring 2018 Dr. Robert Anda came to Oklahoma to talk with our research team at the Center for Integrative Research on Childhood Adversity and to speak to business and community leaders from across the state. At a meeting of more 500 teachers, counselors, physicians, and law enforcement and government officials, he shared his considered opinion that communities can become "self-healing" if those of us who study adverse childhood experiences (ACEs) and those of us who have experienced ACEs talk with and listen to each other. To facilitate these reflections and conversations, he shared a list of questions that ask each of us to find the meaning in both the scientific study of experience and in our lived experiences. In Questions for Reflection, we include some of his questions and some of our own for reflection, inviting you to use them as you apply ACEs science to your work and to create deeper understandings of your own and others' lived experiences.

CHAPTER 1

1. The ACEs Study and subsequent research have consistently found that ACEs are common, interrelated, and have a cumulative effect on human development. What examples of this can you find in our society or in your community?

2. How might ACEs affect your neighbors, clients, family, or friends?

3. How might knowing about the effects of ACEs change the way you think about and relate to someone else? Consider someone you have difficulty relating to or working with or the child who throws tantrums at school.

4. Do the ACEs Study findings suggest new or better approaches to dealing with health and social problems in your family, work, or community?

5. What are four research questions that need to be addressed to better understand the enduring, interrelated, and cumulative effects of ACEs on health and development?

CHAPTER 2

1. How did learning about protective and compensatory experiences (PACEs) affect your perception of ACEs? Can you use PACEs in your own family or in your work with children and families? How?

2. What PACE had the most measurable effect on your life? Why?

3. Did you list any additional PACEs that have had a significant impact? Are these PACEs relationship-based, resources, or both?

4. What PACEs are in your life today, and how committed are you to maintaining those PACEs? How do you nurture PACEs?

5. How can you build PACEs in the lives of children, adolescents, and families with whom you work?

CHAPTER 3

1. Do you recall stressful experiences as a child? Now that you know the depth and breadth of the physiological consequences of childhood stress, do you think you have any long-term repercussions?

2. What common sources of stress do children experience today? Consider the types of adversity covered so far, such as family relationships, poverty, and the like. How about technology? Peer pressure?

3. The human brain takes a long time to develop compared with other mammals. What are the implications that parts of the brain are still developing into young adulthood? For example, teenagers tend to feel invincible, which can lead to reckless behaviors, such as driving, unprotected sex, and so on. What are the risks and benefits of this developmental timing?

4. Think about the paradox of stress, not only how it triggers the fight–flight responses ensuring survival during a crisis but also results in serious damage to the body and brain when it is toxic and prolonged. What advice would you give someone dealing with chronic stressors to prevent their damaging effects?

5. What surprised you about epigenetic research with animals? With humans? Were you surprised that much of our behavior and development appears to be biologically programmed in response to early experience? How does this change the way you view others' behavior?

CHAPTER 4

1. Do you have "ghosts and angels" in your life? How have they influenced your parenting, caregiving, or intimate relationships?

2. How do you think early attachment experiences influence adult romantic relationships or friendships? Can these patterns be changed? How?

3. Have you had relationships that helped you understand how your early experiences influenced your adult patterns of relating to others? Have you had relationships that helped you "work through" issues rooted in negative early influences?

4. Have you experienced a jolt of oxytocin? Can you think of a time when you had a physical urge to nurture or care for someone or something?

5. Did you find patterns of adversity and resilience in your family histories? Did you gain insight into some of your family dynamics? Are there sources of concern? Of inspiration? How does knowing about intergenerational patterns influence your thoughts and plans for your future?

CHAPTER 5

1. What has been your own experience with mindfulness-based programs? If you have tried it, what changes did you notice as a result? If you have not yet tried it, what are your thoughts about trying it?

2. What research questions do you have about mindfulness-based programs? Are there situations in which mindfulness-based stress management may be more appropriate than others?

3. Have you tried any body-based interventions, such as yoga or martial arts? Do you have ideas about integrating these programs with more traditional talk therapies?

4. Have you ever journaled to deal with emotional upheavals or trauma? How do you think Pennebaker's expressive writing method could be used with other types of therapies?

5. What benefits do you expect from a PACEs plan? What difficulties or obstacles do you expect to encounter from changing your habits? Do you think PACEs items can help you overcome obstacles to change?

CHAPTER 6

1. What can you do to nurture attachment? Did any specific behaviors mentioned in this chapter resonate with you? Why? As a practitioner, how can you help parents nurture attachment?

2. Compare the story of the Pikler Institute with the story of the Romanian orphans. How did two types of "institutions" likely affect children's long-term development, and why?

3. What is your "shark music"? When do you feel panic and fear when everything is really okay? Do these feelings stem from your early experiences? Does being aware of feelings and subconscious triggers change how you will parent, or how you will work with families?

4. How do you feel about corporal punishment? Is spanking still an issue in your community? Why or why not? Spanking has been banned in a number of countries. Why do you believe it is still legal in the United States?

5. Many activities were suggested in this chapter (e.g., reading to children daily, volunteering, getting children involved in sports and clubs). What activities do you think are most important? Are there specific activities that helped you as a child? As an adolescent?

6. How can we be more mindful as parents and caregivers? As practitioners, what can be done to encourage mindful parenting and mindful interactions with children?

CHAPTERS 7 AND 8

1. Does your work relate to ACE prevention or mitigation in communities?

2. Do you have opportunities to work in partnership with other people or organizations to prevent ACEs and mitigate their effects?

3. What might a collective group be able to do that you cannot do alone?

4. What next steps can you identify to reduce ACEs and promote PACEs?

5. What values in our funding and programming systems influence the structures we build to respond to ACEs and promote PACEs? What other values might we tap into to make big changes with respect to ACE reduction and mitigation?

6. How might we create a "market force" for preventing ACEs and promoting trauma informed care/communities? Market forces are the effects of supply and demand—how can we generate demand for transformational improvements in ACEs and thereby create sustainable health, safety, and productivity for generations to come?

7. If the general public really understood ACEs Study findings and factors to promote PACEs, what might be possible?

8. What is in the way of transformational change using the ACE and resilience science? What are the barriers to networking, changing the way we work and collaborate, and halting the intergenerational transmission of ACEs?

What road, if we were walking it together, could break through those barriers?

9. Think about the story of the hole in the bridge at the beginning of the book and the story of the life rafts in Chapter 8. What life rafts have helped you in the past? What are current life rafts in your community, and what life rafts do we need to create to help children today?

RESOURCES

To follow Dr. Hays-Grudo's and Morris's research and see more information, visit the ACES and PACEs website (www.acesandpaces.com).

GENERAL INFORMATION

Centers for Disease Control and Prevention (CDC)
https://www.cdc.gov/violenceprevention/acestudy/
   Provides links to published studies on adverse childhood experiences (ACEs), useful information and graphics for presentations, and links to other relevant websites.

Administration for Children and Families (ACF)
https://www.acf.hhs.gov/trauma-toolkit
   A site for trauma-informed programs for children and families.

Substance Abuse and Mental Health Services Administration (SAMHSA)
https://www.samhsa.gov/capt/practicing-effective-prevention/prevention-
   behavioral-health/adverse-childhood-experiences
   Features information on ACEs as it relates to reducing the impact of substance abuse and mental illness on America's communities.

ACEs Connection
https://www.acesconnection.com/

We credit Jane Stevens and ACEs Connection, which she established, with doing more to publicize the ACEs study and related initiatives than any other source. On October 8, 2012, she published a series of articles in the *Huffington Post* on the ACEs study. It was a clarion call for action, and millions heeded it. She subsequently obtained resources for private foundations and launched a website that now connects thousands of individuals and hundreds of communities. ACEs Connection is a social network that supports communities to "accelerate the global ACEs science movement, to recognize the impact of adverse childhood experiences (ACEs) in shaping adult behavior and health, and to promote trauma-informed and resilience-building practices and policies in all communities and institutions—from schools to prisons to hospitals and churches—to help heal and to develop resilience instead of traumatizing already traumatized people." Daily or weekly news posts are available, as well as blogs, resources, events, activities, and the opportunity to connect with others on topics related to ACEs.

One of the communities within ACEs Connection is specifically for parents with a history of ACEs and parents of children with ACEs. Their goal is to be trauma-informed and "resilience-building parents and caregivers, honoring both lived and learned experience in applying their own knowledge and the knowledge from science and practitioners." Like ACEs Connection, members share information, encourage and support each other. https://www.acesconnection.com/g/Parenting-with-ACEs

National Child Traumatic Stress Network (NCTSN)
https://www.nctsn.org/
NCTSN has as its mission to raise the standard of care and improve access to services for traumatized children, their families, and communities throughout the United States. It provides training for professionals and information for parents, caregivers, and professionals on a variety of topics (e.g., coping after mass violence, helping a child after the death of a parent, responding to bullying). It also raises awareness of the importance of early identification and age-appropriate treatment for children who have experienced trauma.

National Council for Behavioral Health
https://www.thenationalcouncil.org
This website has information on suicide prevention, mental health first aid, and trauma-informed programming.

Center on the Developing Child at Harvard University
https://developingchild.harvard.edu/guide/a-guide-to-toxic-stress/
This multidisciplinary team is committed to driving science-based innovation in policy and practice. Their website is an excellent resource for information on toxic stress research and policy.

Robert Wood Johnson Foundation

https://www.rwjf.org/en/library/collections/aces.html

This website is dedicated to ACEs, with resources for communities working to address the impact of ACEs, links to other resources, and information on grant funding on ACEs and health disparities. https://www.rwjf.org/en/library/interactives/whereyouliveaffectshowlongyoulive.html

Nadine Burke Harris, MD, pediatrician and CEO of the Center for Youth Wellness in San Francisco. Her 2018 book, *The Deepest Well: Healing the Long-Term Effects of Childhood Adversity* (New York, NY: Houghton Mifflin Harcourt), is an engaging description of how she and her colleagues are using ACE-based science to help patients and families in pediatric practices serving a low-income neighborhood in the San Francisco Bay area. She also has an excellent TED talk (https://www.ted.com/talks/nadine_burke_harris_how_childhood_trauma_affects_health_across_a_lifetime?utm_campaign=tedspread&utm_medium=referral&utm_source=tedcomshare).

Maternal, Infant, and Early Childhood Home Visiting (MIECHV)

https://homvee.acf.hhs.gov/

Through regular, planned home visits from health, social service, and child development professionals, parents in the Maternal, Infant, and Early Childhood Home Visiting (MIECHV) programs learn how to improve their family's well-being and provide better opportunities for their children. Home visits may include the following:

- supporting healthy prenatal practices;
- assisting mothers breastfeeding and caring for their babies;
- helping parents understand child development milestones and behaviors;
- promoting parents' use of positive parenting techniques; and
- working with mothers to create goals for the future, continue their education, and find employment and child care solutions.

Adult Attachment Survey

http://www.web-research-design.net/cgi-bin/crq/crq.pl

You can learn more about your adult attachment style by taking this short survey created by psychologist Chris Fraley. Your score includes a report on your style, which you can then research more thoroughly.

PARENTING INFORMATION

Circle of Security: https://www.circleofsecurityinternational.com/
ABC Intervention: http://www.abcintervention.org/
Active Parenting: http://www.activeparenting.com/

Tuning Into Kids: http://www.tuningintokids.org.au/
PCIT: http://www.pcit.org/
Incredible Years: http://www.incredibleyears.com/
Talking Is Teaching: https://talkingisteaching.org/
Triple P: https://www.triplep.net/glo-en/home/

MENTAL HEALTH AND INFORMATION

Suicide Prevention Lifeline: https://suicidepreventionlifeline.org/
National Alliance on Mental Illness (NAMI): https://www.nami.org/Find-Support/NAMI-HelpLine#crisis
Child and Adolescent Health Measurement Initiative (CAHMI): https://www.cahmi.org/
Still face video: https://www.youtube.com/watch?v=apzXGEbZht0
KPJR Films: https://kpjrfilms.co/resilience/

BUILDING RESILIENCE: PROJECTS, INTERVENTIONS, AND EXERCISES

American Academy of Pediatrics has a website (https://www.aap.org/en-us/advocacy-and-policy/aap-health-initiatives/resilience/Pages/ACEs-and-Toxic-Stress.aspx) for its Resilience Project, with resources and guidelines to provide pediatricians and all medical home teams with the resources they need to modify practice operations to more effectively identify, treat, and refer children and youth who have been exposed to or victimized by violence or toxic stress.

Changing Minds®
https://changingMindsNow.org

Maternal, Infant, and Early Childhood Home Visiting Programs
https://mchb.hrsa.gov/maternal-child-health-initiatives/home-visiting-overview

Mindfulness
https://health.ucsd.edu/specialties/mindfulness/programs/mbsr/Pages/audio.aspx
  The University of California–San Diego Center for Mindfulness has prepared a number of practices that are available here in MP3 format. Please feel free to download and/or share these guided practices.

The Possibility Project
https://the-possibility-project.org/

Self-Healing Communities: A transformational process model for improving intergenerational health

https://www.rwjf.org/en/library/research/2016/06/self-healing-communities.html

Sesame Street in Communities

https://sesamestreetincommunities.org/topics/traumatic-experiences/

This website has dozens of resources for parents and caregivers to help children cope with trauma and build resilience.

Zero to Three

https://www.zerotothree.org/early-development/trauma-and-stress

This is an excellent source of information for parents and caregivers on babies and toddlers in general and also has a section with resources for caregivers providing love and support for children during times of trauma and stress.

TRAINING PROGRAMS

Pikler Institute

https://pikler.org/?v=f24485ae434a

EDUCARING

https://www.rie.org/educaring/ries-basic-principles/

Lemonade for Life

http://lemonadeforlife.com/what-is-lemonade-for-life/

The Center for Prevention & Early Intervention Policy

Florida State University

https://cpeip.fsu.edu/index.cfm

Children's Center for Resilience and Trauma Recovery (CCRTR)

Rutgers University

https://rukidsrresilient.org/

Trauma-Informed, Resilience-Oriented Approaches Learning Community

National Council for Behavioral Health

https://www.thenationalcouncil.org/consulting-best-practices/areas-of-expertise/trauma-informed-care-learning-community/

Threshold GlobalWorks

https://www.thresholdglobalworks.com/

What Works: A Manual for Designing Programs That Build Resilience

http://www.resilienceresearch.org/whatworks

RESEARCH CENTERS AND INITIATIVES

Center for Integrative Research on Childhood Adversity (CIRCA)

Oklahoma State University, Center for Health Sciences

https://www.circaok.com

Child and Adolescent Health Measurement Initiative (CAHMI)

Johns Hopkins, Bloomberg School of Public Health

https://www.jhsph.edu/departments/population-family-and-reproductive-
   health/child-adolescent-health-measurement-initiative/index.html

Institute for Early Life Adversity Research

University of Texas at Austin, Dell Medical School

https://dellmed.utexas.edu/units/department-of-psychiatry/institute-for-
   early-life-adversity-research

IN THE MEDIA

Recovery and Healing

"7 Ways Childhood Adversity Can Change Your Brain," *Psychology Today*
https://www.psychologytoday.com/us/blog/the-last-best-cure/201508/
   7-ways-childhood-adversity-can-change-your-brain

"8 Ways People Recover from Post Childhood Adversity Syndrome,"
   Psychology Today
https://www.psychologytoday.com/us/blog/the-last-best-cure/201508/
   8-ways-people-recover-post-childhood-adversity-syndrome

"Breaking the Cycle of Patient Trauma," *ACP Internist*
https://acpinternist.org/archives/2019/02/breaking-the-cycle-of-patient-
   trauma.htm

Even the Best Meditators Have Old Wounds to Heal, buddhanet
https://www.buddhanet.net/psymed1.htm

"Nurturing Resilience," *Psychology Today*
https://www.psychologytoday.com/us/blog/nurturing-resilience

"Rutgers University Behavioral Health Care Awarded $2 Million Grant to
   Create Children's Center for Resilience and Trauma Recovery," *Rutgers Today*
https://news.rutgers.edu/news-release/rutgers-university-behavioral-health-
   care-awarded-2-million-grant-create-childrens-center-resilience/20160927#.
   XVHUz-hKjb0

"Preventing, Healing Childhood Trauma Before it Damages Kids' Chances,"
  NJ Spotlight
https://www.njspotlight.com/stories/19/07/29/preventing-healing-
  childhood-trauma-before-it-damages-kids-chances/

"Treating the Lifelong Harm of Childhood Trauma," *The New York Times*
https://www.nytimes.com/2018/01/30/opinion/treating-the-lifelong-harm-
  of-childhood-trauma.html

TRAUMA-INFORMED CARE

Creating Trauma-Informed Systems
The National Child Traumatic Stress Network
https://www.nctsn.org/trauma-informed-care/creating-trauma-informed-
  systems

From Trauma to Resilience: One Doctor's Journey to Transform Trauma-Informed Care
National Council for Behavioral Health
https://www.thenationalcouncil.org/BH365/2019/04/08/from-trauma-to-
  resilience-one-doctors-journey-to-transform-trauma-informed-care/

Need for Trauma-Informed Care
National Council for Behavioral Health
https://www.thenationalcouncil.org/consulting-best-practices/trauma/

"Trauma-Informed Care Treats Injuries That Can Be Seen, Those That Can't,"
  NJ Spotlight
https://www.njspotlight.com/stories/17/02/02/trauma-informed-care-
  treats-injuries-that-can-be-seen-and-those-that-can-t-be/

Trauma-Informed Primary Care: Fostering Resilience and Recovery
National Council for Bchavioral Health
https://www.thenationalcouncil.org/consulting-areas-of-expertise/trauma-
  informed-primary-care/

JUDICIAL SYSTEM

Family Court Tool Kit: Trauma and Child Development
https://www.flcourts.org/Resources-Services/Court-Improvement/Family-
  Courts/Family-Court-Basics2/Family-Court-Tool-Kit-Trauma-and-Child-
  Development

In Safe Babies Courts, 99% of kids don't suffer more abuse—but less than 1%
of U.S. family courts are Safe Babies Courts
https://acestoohigh.com/2015/02/23/in-safe-babies-courts-99-of-kids-dont-suffer-
more-abuse-but-less-than-1-of-u-s-family-courts-are-safe-babies-courts/

STATE INITIATIVES

The Washington State ACEs Public–Private Initiative (APPI)
http://www.appi-wa.org/

Guidelines for statewide initiatives
https://www.futureswithoutviolence.org/wp-content/uploads/State-Policy-
Framework_FINAL3B.pdf

State profiles of ACEs initiatives (50 States and District of Columbia)
https://www.acesconnection.com/g/state-aces-action-group/blog/state-profiles-
list-of-50-states-and-district-of-columbia-with-links-to-individual-profiles

Florida's Early Childhood Court
https://www.flcourts.org/Resources-Services/Court-Improvement/Problem-
Solving-Courts/Early-Childhood-Courts

BOOKS

Altman, D. (2011). *One minute mindfulness*. Novato, CA: New World Library.
Ameli, R. (2014). *25 lessons in mindfulness*. Washington, DC: American Psychological
Association.
Blaustein, M. E., & Kinniburgh, K. M. (2019). *Treating traumatic stress in children and
adolescents: How to foster resilience through attachment, self-regulation, and competency*
(2nd ed.). New York, NY: Guilford Press.
Curran, L. A. (2013). *101 trauma-informed interventions*. Eau Claire, WI: PESI.
Dozier, M., & Bernard, K. (2019). *Coaching parents of vulnerable infants: The attachment
and biobehavioral catch-up approach*. New York, NY: Guilford Press.
Galinsky, E. (2010). *Mind in the making*. New York, NY: Harper Studio.
Gillihan, S. J. (2018). *Cognitive behavioral therapy made simple*. Emeryville, CA: Althea Press.
Halloran, J. (2018). *Coping skills for kids workbook*. Eau Claire, WI: PESI.
Harris, N. B. (2018). *The deepest well: Healing the long-term effects of childhood adversity*.
Boston, MA: Houghton Mifflin Harcourt.
Hoffman, K., Cooper, G., & Powell, B. (2017). *Raising a secure child: How circle of security
parenting can help you nurture your child's attachment, emotional resilience, and freedom to
explore*. New York, NY: Guilford Press.
Kabat-Zinn, J. (2005). *Coming to our senses: Healing ourselves and the world through
mindfulness*. London, England: Hachette UK.
Mate, G. (2003). *When the body says no*. New York, NY: Wiley.
Morris, A. S., & Williamson, A. C. (Eds.). (2019). *Building early social and emotional relationships with infants and toddlers: Integrating research and practice*. Cham, Switzerland: Springer.
Nakazawa, D. J. (2015). *Childhood disrupted: How your biography becomes your biology, and
how you can heal*. New York: Atria Books.

Nicholson, J., Perez, L., & Kurtz, J. (2019). *Trauma-informed practices for early childhood educators*. New York, NY: Routledge.

Pennebaker, J. W., & Smyth, J. M. (2016). *Opening up by writing it down: How expressive writing improves health and eases emotional pain*. New York, NY: Guilford Press.

Rubin, G. (2015). *The happiness project*. New York, NY: Harper Paperbacks.

Sapolsky, R. (2004). *Why zebras don't get ulcers*. New York, NY: Holt Paperbacks.

Siegel, D. (2014). *Parenting from the inside out*. New York, NY: Tarcher/Penguin.

Steele, W., & Malchiodi, C. A. (2012). *Trauma-informed practices with children and adolescents*. New York, NY: Routledge.

Steinberg, L. D. (2004). *The ten basic principles of good parenting*. New York, NY: Simon & Schuster.

Steinberg, L. D. (2011). *You and your adolescent: The essential guide for ages 10 to 25*. New York, NY: Simon & Schuster.

Steinberg, L. D. (2014). *Age of opportunity: Lessons from the new science of adolescence*. New York, NY: Simon & Schuster.

Tarrant, J. (2017). *Meditation interventions to rewire the brain: Integrating neuroscience strategies for ADHD, anxiety, depression, and PTSD*. Eau Claire, WI: PESI.

Ungar, M. (2019). *Change your world: The science of resilience and the true path to success*. Toronto, Canada: Southerland House.

van der Kolk, B. A. (1994). The body keeps the score: Memory and the evolving psycho-biology of posttraumatic stress. *Harvard Review of Psychiatry, 1*(5), 253–265.

BRIEFS AND FACT SHEETS

An Introduction to the Social Resilience Model
https://www.thresholdglobalworks.com/about/social-resilience/

Creating, Supporting, and Sustaining Trauma-Informed Schools: A System Framework
https://www.nctsn.org/resources/creating-supporting-and-sustaining-trauma-informed-schools-system-framework

How to Manage Trauma
https://www.thenationalcouncil.org/wp-content/uploads/2013/05/Trauma-infographic.pdf

The Missing Link: The Biology of Human Resilience
https://www.thresholdglobalworks.com/portfolio-items/the-missing-link-the-biology-of-human-resilience/

Trauma-Informed Schools for Children in K–12: A system framework
https://www.nctsn.org/resources/trauma-informed-schools-children-k-12-system-framework

What Is a Trauma-Informed Child and Family Service System?
https://www.nctsn.org/sites/default/files/resources//what_is_a_trauma_informed_child_family_service_system.pdf

REFERENCES

Abraham, E., Hendler, T., Shapira-Lichter, I., Kanat-Maymon, Y., Zagoory-Sharon, O., & Feldman, R. (2014). Father's brain is sensitive to childcare experiences. *Proceedings of the National Academy of Sciences.* 201402569.

Adams, R. E., Santo, J. B., & Bukowski, W. M. (2011). The presence of a best friend buffers the effects of negative experiences. *Developmental Psychology, 47,* 1786–1791. http://dx.doi.org/10.1037/a0025401

Adamson, L. B., & Frick, J. E. (2003). The still face: A history of a shared experimental paradigm. *Infancy, 4,* 451–473. http://dx.doi.org/10.1207/S15327078IN0404_01

Adler, N. E., Cutler, D. M., Jonathan, J., Galea, S., Glymour, M., Koh, H. K., & Satcher, D. (2016). *Addressing social determinants of health and health disparities: A vital direction for health and health care.* Washington, DC: National Academy of Medicine. Retrieved from https://nam.edu/addressing-social-determinants-of-health-and-health-disparities-a-vital-direction-for-health-and-health-care/

Ainsworth, M. D. (1989). Attachments beyond infancy. *American Psychologist, 44,* 709 716. http://dx.doi.org/10.1037/0003-066X.44.4.709

Ainsworth, M. D., & Bell, S. M. (1970). Attachment, exploration, and separation: Illustrated by the behavior of one-year-olds in a strange situation. *Child Development, 41,* 49–67. http://dx.doi.org/10.2307/1127388

Ainsworth, M. D., Blehar, M. C., Waters, E., & Wall, S. (1978). *Patterns of attachment: Assessed in the strange situation and at home.* Hillsdale, NJ: Erlbaum.

Allen, J. P., Porter, M., McFarland, C., McElhaney, K. B., & Marsh, P. (2007). The relation of attachment security to adolescents' paternal and peer relationships, depression, and externalizing behavior. *Child Development, 78,* 1222–1239. http://dx.doi.org/10.1111/j.1467-8624.2007.01062.x

Amaya-Jackson, L., Reynolds, V., Murray, M. C., McCarthy, G., Nelson, A., Cherney, M. S., & March, J. S. (2003). Cognitive behavioral treatment for pediatric post-traumatic stress disorder: Protocol and application in school and community setting. *Cognitive and Behavioral Practice, 10,* 204–213. http://dx.doi.org/10.1016/S1077-7229(03)80032-9

American Academy of Pediatrics. (2019). *The Resilience Project.* Retrieved from https://www.aap.org/en-us/advocacy-and-policy/aap-health-initiatives/resilience/Pages/Resilience-Project.aspx

American Psychiatric Association. (2013). *Diagnostic and statistical manual of mental disorders* (5th ed.). Washington, DC: Author.

Anda, R. F., Butchart, A., Felitti, V. J., & Brown, D. W. (2010). Building a framework for global surveillance of the public health implications of adverse childhood experiences. *American Journal of Preventive Medicine, 39,* 93–98. http://dx.doi.org/10.1016/j.amepre.2010.03.015

Anda, R. F., Dong, M., Brown, D. W., Felitti, V. J., Giles, W. H., Perry, G. S., . . . Dube, S. R. (2009). The relationship of adverse childhood experiences to a history of premature death of family members. *BMC Public Health, 9,* 106. http://dx.doi.org/10.1186/1471-2458-9-106

Anda, R. F., Felitti, V. J., Bremner, J. D., Walker, J. D., Whitfield, C., Perry, B. D., . . . Giles, W. H. (2006). The enduring effects of abuse and related adverse experiences in childhood: A convergence of evidence from neurobiology and epidemiology. *European Archives of Psychiatry and Clinical Neuroscience, 256,* 174–186. http://dx.doi.org/10.1007/s00406-005-0624-4

Anda, R. F., Tietjen, G., Schulman, E., Felitti, V., & Croft, J. (2010). Adverse childhood experiences and frequent headaches in adults. *Headache, 50,* 1473–1481. http://dx.doi.org/10.1111/j.1526-4610.2010.01756.x

Andersen, S. L., & Teicher, M. H. (2004). Delayed effects of early stress on hippocampal development. *Neuropsychopharmacology, 29,* 1988–1993. http://dx.doi.org/10.1038/sj.npp.1300528

Andersen, S. L., & Teicher, M. H. (2008). Stress, sensitive periods and maturational events in adolescent depression. *Trends in Neurosciences, 31,* 183–191. http://dx.doi.org/10.1016/j.tins.2008.01.004

Anthony, L. G., Anthony, B. J., Glanville, D. N., Naiman, D. Q., Waanders, C., & Shaffer, S. (2005). The relationships between parenting stress, parenting behaviour and preschoolers' social competence and behaviour problems in the classroom. *Infant and Child Development, 14,* 133–154. http://dx.doi.org/10.1002/icd.385

Arnone, D., McIntosh, A. M., Chandra, P., & Ebmeier, K. P. (2008). Meta-analysis of magnetic resonance imaging studies of the corpus callosum in bipolar disorder. *Acta Psychiatrica Scandinavica, 118,* 357–362. http://dx.doi.org/10.1111/j.1600-0447.2008.01229.x

Arthi, V. (2014). *"The dust was long in settling": Human capital and the lasting impact of the American dust bowl* (Oxford Economic and Social History Working Paper 129). University of Oxford, Department of Economics, Oxford, England.

Atzl, V. M., Narayan, A. J., Rivera, L. M., & Lieberman, A. F. (2019). Adverse childhood experiences and prenatal mental health: Type of ACEs and age of maltreatment onset. *Journal of Family Psychology, 33,* 304–314. http://dx.doi.org/10.1037/fam0000510

Austin, A., Herrick, H., & Proescholdbell, S. (2016). Adverse childhood experiences related to poor adult health among lesbian, gay, and bisexual individuals. *American Journal of Public Health, 106,* 314–320. http://dx.doi.org/10.2105/AJPH.2015.302904

Baglivio, M. T., Epps, N., Swartz, K., Huq, M. S., Sheer, A., & Hardt, N. S. (2014). The prevalence of adverse childhood experiences (ACE) in the lives of juvenile offenders. *Journal of Juvenile Justice, 3*, 1–17.

Baglivio, M. T., Wolff, K. T., Piquero, A. R., & Epps, N. (2015). The relationship between adverse childhood experiences (ACE) and juvenile offending trajectories in a juvenile offender sample. *Journal of Criminal Justice, 43*, 229–241. http://dx.doi.org/10.1016/j.jcrimjus.2015.04.012

Balistreri, K. S., & Alvira-Hammond, M. (2016). Adverse childhood experiences, family functioning and adolescent health and emotional well-being. *Public Health, 132*, 72–78. http://dx.doi.org/10.1016/j.puhe.2015.10.034

Bandura, A. (1997). *Self-efficacy: The exercise of self-control.* New York, NY: Freeman.

Barber, B. K. (2002). *Intrusive parenting: How psychological control affects children and adolescents.* Washington, DC: American Psychological Association. http://dx.doi.org/10.1037/10422-000

Barber, B. K., & Harmon, E. L. (2002). Violating the self: Parental psychological control of children and adolescents. In B. K. Barber (Ed.), *Intrusive parenting: How psychological control affects children and adolescents* (pp. 15–52). Washington, DC: American Psychological Association. http://dx.doi.org/10.1037/10422-002

Barch, D. M., Belden, A. C., Tillman, R., Whalen, D., & Luby, J. L. (2018). Early childhood adverse experiences, inferior frontal gyrus connectivity, and the trajectory of externalizing psychopathology. *Journal of the American Academy of Child & Adolescent Psychiatry, 57*, 183–190. http://dx.doi.org/10.1016/j.jaac.2017.12.011

Barch, D., Pagliaccio, D., Belden, A., Harms, M. P., Gaffrey, M., Sylvester, C. M., . . . Luby, J. (2016). Effect of hippocampal and amygdala connectivity on the relationship between preschool poverty and school-age depression. *The American Journal of Psychiatry, 173*, 625–634. http://dx.doi.org/10.1176/appi.ajp.2015.15081014

Barker, D. J., & Osmond, C. (1986). Infant mortality, childhood nutrition, and ischaemic heart disease in England and Wales. *The Lancet, 1*, 1077–1081. http://dx.doi.org/10.1016/S0140-6736(86)91340-1

Barnes, G. M., & Farrell, M. P. (1992). Parental support and control as predictors of adolescent drinking, delinquency, and related problem behaviors. *Journal of Marriage and the Family, 54*, 763–776. http://dx.doi.org/10.2307/353159

Bartlett, J. D., Griffin, J. L., Spinazzola, J., Fraser, J. G., Noroña, C. R., Bodian, R., . . . Barto, B. (2018). The impact of a statewide trauma-informed care initiative in child welfare on the well-being of children and youth with complex trauma. *Children and Youth Services Review, 84*, 110–117. http://dx.doi.org/10.1016/j.childyouth.2017.11.015

Baumrind, D. (1966). Effects of authoritative parental control on child behavior. *Child Development, 37*, 887–907. http://dx.doi.org/10.2307/1126611

Baumrind, D. (1971). Current patterns of parental authority. *Developmental Psychology, 4*(1, Pt. 2), 1–103. http://dx.doi.org/10.1037/h0030372

Baumrind, D., & Black, A. E. (1967). Socialization practices associated with dimensions of competence in preschool boys and girls. *Child Development, 38*, 291–327. http://dx.doi.org/10.2307/1127295

Beardslee, W. R., Ayoub, C., Avery, M. W., Watts, C. L., & O'Carroll, K. L. (2010). Family Connections: An approach for strengthening early care systems in facing depression and adversity. *American Journal of Orthopsychiatry, 80*, 482–495. http://dx.doi.org/10.1111/j.1939-0025.2010.01051.x

Beasley, L. O., Bigfoot, D. S., & Curren, H. K. (2019). Building early relationship programming across cultures. In A. S. Morris & A. C. Williamson (Eds.), *Building early social and emotional relationships with infants and toddlers* (pp. 305–324). Cham, Switzerland: Springer Nature.

Beck, A. T. (1979). *Cognitive therapy and the emotional disorders*. New York, NY: Penguin Books.

Beck, J. S. (2011). *Cognitive behavior therapy: Basics and beyond* (2nd ed.). New York, NY: Guilford Press.

Becker, D. R., McClelland, M. M., Loprinzi, P., & Trost, S. G. (2014). Physical activity, self-regulation, and early academic achievement in preschool children. *Early Education and Development, 25*, 56–70. http://dx.doi.org/10.1080/10409289.2013.780505

Beckmann, K. A. (2017). Mitigating adverse childhood experiences through investments in early childhood programs. *Academic Pediatrics, 17*(Suppl. 7), S28–S29. http://dx.doi.org/10.1016/j.acap.2016.09.004

Bellis, M. A., Lowey, H., Leckenby, N., Hughes, K., & Harrison, D. (2014). Adverse childhood experiences: Retrospective study to determine their impact on adult health behaviours and health outcomes in a UK population. *Journal of Public Health, 36*, 81–91. http://dx.doi.org/10.1093/pubmed/fdt038

Belsky, J., & de Haan, M. (2011). Annual Research Review: Parenting and children's brain development: The end of the beginning. *Journal of Child Psychology and Psychiatry, 52*, 409–428. http://dx.doi.org/10.1111/j.1469-7610.2010.02281.x

Belsky, J., Steinberg, L., & Draper, P. (1991). Childhood experience, interpersonal development, and reproductive strategy: And evolutionary theory of socialization. *Child Development, 62*, 647–670. http://dx.doi.org/10.2307/1131166

Benjet, C., Borges, G., Medina-Mora, M. E., Zambrano, J., Cruz, C., & Méndez, E. (2009). Descriptive epidemiology of chronic childhood adversity in Mexican adolescents. *Journal of Adolescent Health, 45*, 483–489. http://dx.doi.org/10.1016/j.jadohealth.2009.03.002

Bensimon, M., Amir, D., & Wolf, Y. (2008). Drumming through trauma: Music therapy with post-traumatic soldiers. *The Arts in Psychotherapy, 35*, 34–48. http://dx.doi.org/10.1016/j.aip.2007.09.002

Berens, A. E., Jensen, S. K. G., & Nelson, C. A., III. (2017). Biological embedding of childhood adversity: From physiological mechanisms to clinical implications. *BMC Medicine, 15*, 135. http://dx.doi.org/10.1186/s12916-017-0895-4

Bernard, K., Dozier, M., Bick, J., & Gordon, M. K. (2015). Intervening to enhance cortisol regulation among children at risk for neglect: Results of a randomized clinical trial. *Development and Psychopathology, 27*, 829–841. http://dx.doi.org/10.1017/S095457941400073X

Bernard, K., Dozier, M., Bick, J., Lewis-Morrarty, E., Lindhiem, O., & Carlson, E. (2012). Enhancing attachment organization among maltreated children: Results of a randomized clinical trial. *Child Development, 83*, 623–636. http://dx.doi.org/10.1111/j.1467-8624.2011.01712.x

Bernard, K., Hostinar, C. E., & Dozier, M. (2015). Intervention effects on diurnal cortisol rhythms of Child Protective Services–referred infants in early childhood: Preschool follow-up results of a randomized clinical trial. *JAMA Pediatrics, 169*, 112–119. http://dx.doi.org/10.1001/jamapediatrics.2014.2369

Bernard, K., Simons, R., & Dozier, M. (2015). Effects of an attachment-based intervention on child protective services–referred mothers' event-related potentials to children's emotions. *Child Development*, *86*, 1673–1684. http://dx.doi.org/10.1111/cdev.12418

Bernstein, D. P., Ahluvalia, T., Pogge, D., & Handelsman, L. (1997). Validity of the Childhood Trauma Questionnaire in an adolescent psychiatric population. *Journal of the American Academy of Child & Adolescent Psychiatry*, *36*, 340–348. http://dx.doi.org/10.1097/00004583-199703000-00012

Bernstein, D. P., Stein, J. A., Newcomb, M. D., Walker, E., Pogge, D., Ahluvalia, T., . . . Zule, W. (2003). Development and validation of a brief screening version of the Childhood Trauma Questionnaire. *Child Abuse & Neglect*, *27*, 169–190. http://dx.doi.org/10.1016/S0145-2134(02)00541-0

Berthelot, N., Ensink, K., Bernazzani, O., Normandin, L., Luyten, P., & Fonagy, P. (2015). Intergenerational transmission of attachment in abused and neglected mothers: The role of trauma-specific reflective functioning. *Infant Mental Health Journal*, *36*, 200–212. http://dx.doi.org/10.1002/imhj.21499

Bethell, C. D., Carle, A., Hudziak, J., Gombojav, N., Powers, K., Wade, R., & Braveman, P. (2017). Methods to assess adverse childhood experiences of children and families: Toward approaches to promote child well-being in policy and practice. *Academic Pediatrics*, *17*(Suppl. 7), S51–S69. http://dx.doi.org/10.1016/j.acap.2017.04.161

Bethell, C. D., Gombojav, N., Solloway, M., & Wissow, L. (2016). Adverse childhood experiences, resilience and mindfulness-based approaches: Common denominator issues for children with emotional, mental, or behavioral problems. *Child and Adolescent Psychiatric Clinics of North America*, *25*, 139–156. http://dx.doi.org/10.1016/j.chc.2015.12.001

Bethell, C. D., Newacheck, P., Hawes, E., & Halfon, N. (2014). Adverse childhood experiences: Assessing the impact on health and school engagement and the mitigating role of resilience. *Health Affairs*, *33*, 2106–2115. http://dx.doi.org/10.1377/hlthaff.2014.0914

Bethell, C. D., Solloway, M. R., Guinosso, S., Hassink, S., Srivastav, A., Ford, D., & Simpson, L. A. (2017). Prioritizing possibilities for child and family health: An agenda to address adverse childhood experiences and foster the social and emotional roots of well-being in pediatrics. *Academic Pediatrics*, *17*(Suppl. 7), S36–S50. http://dx.doi.org/10.1016/j.acap.2017.06.002

Bittman, B. B., Berk, L. S., Felten, D. L., Westengard, J., Simonton, O. C., Pappas, J., & Ninehouser, M. (2001). Composite effects of group drumming music therapy on modulation of neuroendocrine-immune parameters in normal subjects. *Alternative Therapies in Health and Medicine*, *7*, 38–47.

Blair, C., & Raver, C. C. (2012). Child development in the context of adversity: Experiential canalization of brain and behavior. *American Psychologist*, *67*, 309–318. http://dx.doi.org/10.1037/a0027493

Blaustein, M. E., & Kinniburgh, K. M. (2018). *Treating traumatic stress in children and adolescents: How to foster resilience through attachment, self-regulation, and competency*. New York, NY: Guilford Press.

Blaze, J., & Roth, T. L. (2013). Exposure to caregiver maltreatment alters expression levels of epigenetic regulators in the medial prefrontal cortex. *International Journal of Developmental Neuroscience*, *31*, 804–810. http://dx.doi.org/10.1016/j.ijdevneu.2013.10.001

Blaze, J., & Roth, T. L. (2015). Evidence from clinical and animal model studies of the long-term and transgenerational impact of stress on DNA methylation.

Seminars in Cell & Developmental Biology, 43, 76–84. http://dx.doi.org/10.1016/j.semcdb.2015.04.004

Blomfield, C. J., & Barber, B. L. (2009). Brief report: Performing on the stage, the field, or both? Australian adolescent extracurricular activity participation and self-concept. *Journal of Adolescence, 32,* 733–739. http://dx.doi.org/10.1016/j.adolescence.2009.01.003

Borawski, E. A., Ievers-Landis, C. E., Lovegreen, L. D., & Trapl, E. S. (2003). Parental monitoring, negotiated unsupervised time, and parental trust: The role of perceived parenting practices in adolescent health risk behaviors. *Journal of Adolescent Health, 33,* 60–70. http://dx.doi.org/10.1016/S1054-139X(03)00100-9

Bornstein, M. H., Putnick, D. L., Rigo, P., Esposito, G., Swain, J. E., Suwalsky, J. T. D., . . . Venuti, P. (2017). Neurobiology of culturally common maternal responses to infant cry. *Proceedings of the National Academy of Sciences of the United States of America, 114,* E9465–E9473. http://dx.doi.org/10.1073/pnas.1712022114

Bowen, E. A., & Murshid, N. S. (2016). Trauma-informed social policy: A conceptual framework for policy analysis and advocacy. *American Journal of Public Health, 106,* 223–229. http://dx.doi.org/10.2105/AJPH.2015.302970

Bowlby, J. (1953). *The roots of parenthood.* National Children's Home convocation lecture. London, England.

Bowlby, J. (1969). *Attachment* (Vol. 1). New York, NY: Basic Books.

Bowlby, J. (1988). *A secure base: Clinical applications of attachment.* London, England: Routledge.

Bowlby, J. (2008). *A secure base: Parent–child attachment and healthy human development* (reprint ed.). New York, NY: Basic Books.

Bradley, R. H., & Corwyn, R. F. (2002). Socioeconomic status and child development. *Annual Review of Psychology, 53,* 371–399. http://dx.doi.org/10.1146/annurev.psych.53.100901.135233

Braithwaite, E. C., Kundakovic, M., Ramchandani, P. G., Murphy, S. E., & Champagne, F. A. (2015). Maternal prenatal depressive symptoms predict infant NR3C1 1F and BDNF IV DNA methylation. *Epigenetics, 10,* 408–417. http://dx.doi.org/10.1080/15592294.2015.1039221

Branson, C. E., Baetz, C. L., Horwitz, S. M., & Hoagwood, K. E. (2017). Trauma-informed juvenile justice systems: A systematic review of definitions and core components. *Psychological Trauma: Theory, Research, Practice and Policy, 9,* 635–646. http://dx.doi.org/10.1037/tra0000255

Braveman, P., & Barclay, C. (2009). Health disparities beginning in childhood: A life-course perspective. *Pediatrics, 124*(Suppl. 3), S163–S175. http://dx.doi.org/10.1542/peds.2009-1100D

Braveman, P., & Gottlieb, L. (2014). The social determinants of health: It's time to consider the causes of the causes. *Public Health Reports, 129*(1, Suppl. 2), 19–31. http://dx.doi.org/10.1177/00333549141291S206

Brazendale, K., Beets, M. W., Weaver, R. G., Pate, R. R., Turner-McGrievy, G. M., Kaczynski, A. T., . . . von Hippel, P. T. (2017). Understanding differences between summer vs. school obesogenic behaviors of children: The structured days hypothesis. *The International Journal of Behavioral Nutrition and Physical Activity, 14,* 100. http://dx.doi.org/10.1186/s12966-017-0555-2

Brennan, E. M., Bradley, J. R., Allen, M. D., & Perry, D. F. (2008). The evidence base for mental health consultation in early childhood settings: Research synthesis addressing staff and program outcomes. *Early Education and Development, 19,* 982–1022. http://dx.doi.org/10.1080/10409280801975834

Bretherton, I. (1992). The origins of attachment theory: John Bowlby and Mary Ainsworth. *Developmental Psychology, 28,* 759–775. http://dx.doi.org/10.1037/0012-1649.28.5.759

Brett, E. I., Espeleta, H. C., Lopez, S. V., Leavens, E. L. S., & Leffingwell, T. R. (2018). Mindfulness as a mediator of the association between adverse childhood experiences and alcohol use and consequences. *Addictive Behaviors, 84,* 92–98. http://dx.doi.org/10.1016/j.addbeh.2018.04.002

Brito, N. H., & Noble, K. G. (2014). Socioeconomic status and structural brain development. *Frontiers in Neuroscience, 8,* 276. http://dx.doi.org/10.3389/fnins.2014.00276

Brooks-Gunn, J., & Duncan, G. J. (1997). The effects of poverty on children. *The Future of Children, 7,* 55–71. http://dx.doi.org/10.2307/1602387

Brophy, A. L. (2003). *Reconstructing the dreamland: The Tulsa Riot of 1921: Race, reparations, and reconciliation.* New York, NY: Oxford University Press.

Brown, B. B., & Klute, C. (2003). Friendships, cliques, and crowds. In G. R. Adams & M. D. Berzonsky (Eds.), *Blackwell handbook of adolescence* (pp. 330–348). Malden, MA: Blackwell.

Brown, D. W., Anda, R. F., Tiemeier, H., Felitti, V. J., Edwards, V. J., Croft, J. B., & Giles, W. H. (2009). Adverse childhood experiences and the risk of premature mortality. *American Journal of Preventive Medicine, 37,* 389–396. http://dx.doi.org/10.1016/j.amepre.2009.06.021

Brown, M. J., Masho, S. W., Perera, R. A., Mezuk, B., Pugsley, R. A., & Cohen, S. A. (2017). Sex disparities in adverse childhood experiences and HIV/STIS. Mediation of psychopathology and sexual behaviors. *AIDS and Behavior, 21,* 1550–1566. http://dx.doi.org/10.1007/s10461-016-1553-0

Bruce, J., Gunnar, M. R., Pears, K. C., & Fisher, P. A. (2013). Early adverse care, stress neurobiology, and prevention science: Lessons learned. *Prevention Science, 14,* 247–256. http://dx.doi.org/10.1007/s11121-012-0354-6

Brumariu, L. E., & Kerns, K. A. (2010). Parent–child attachment and internalizing symptoms in childhood and adolescence: A review of empirical findings and future directions. *Development and Psychopathology, 22,* 177–203. http://dx.doi.org/10.1017/S0954579409990344

Bruner, C. (2017). ACE, place, race, and poverty: Building hope for children. *Academic Pediatrics, 17*(Suppl. 7), S123–S129. http://dx.doi.org/10.1016/j.acap.2017.05.009

Buchholz, M., & Talmi, A. (2012). What we talked about at the pediatrician's office: Exploring differences between healthy steps and traditional pediatric primary care visits. *Infant Mental Health Journal, 33,* 430–436. http://dx.doi.org/10.1002/imhj.21319

Burke, D. T., Al-Adawi, S., Lee, Y. T., & Audette, J. (2007). Martial arts as sport and therapy. *The Journal of Sports Medicine and Physical Fitness, 47,* 96–102.

Burke, N. J., Hellman, J. L., Scott, B. G., Weems, C. F., & Carrion, V. G. (2011). The impact of adverse childhood experiences on an urban pediatric population. *Child Abuse & Neglect, 35,* 408–413. http://dx.doi.org/10.1016/j.chiabu.2011.02.006

Burns, D. D. (1999). *The feeling good handbook.* New York, NY: Plume/Penguin Books.

Buss, C., Entringer, S., Moog, N. K., Toepfer, P., Fair, D. A., Simhan, H. N., . . . Wadhwa, P. D. (2017). Intergenerational transmission of maternal childhood maltreatment exposure: Implications for fetal brain development. *Journal of the American Academy of Child & Adolescent Psychiatry, 56,* 373–382. http://dx.doi.org/10.1016/j.jaac.2017.03.001

Cairns, E., & Dawes, A. (1996). Children: Ethnic and political violence-a commentary. *Child Development, 67,* 129–139. http://dx.doi.org/10.2307/1131691

Cameron, L. D., Carroll, P., & Hamilton, W. K. (2018). Evaluation of an intervention promoting emotion regulation skills for adults with persisting distress due to adverse childhood experiences. *Child Abuse & Neglect, 79,* 423–433. http://dx.doi.org/10.1016/j.chiabu.2018.03.002

Campbell, J. A., Walker, R. J., & Egede, L. E. (2016). Associations between adverse childhood experiences, high-risk behaviors, and morbidity in adulthood. *American Journal of Preventive Medicine, 50,* 344–352. http://dx.doi.org/10.1016/j.amepre.2015.07.022

Cao-Lei, L., Massart, R., Suderman, M. J., Machnes, Z., Elgbeili, G., Laplante, D. P., . . . King, S. (2014). DNA methylation signatures triggered by prenatal maternal stress exposure to a natural disaster: Project Ice Storm. *PLoS ONE, 9,* e107653. http://dx.doi.org/10.1371/journal.pone.0107653

Carello, J., & Butler, L. D. (2014). Potentially perilous pedagogies: Teaching trauma is not the same as trauma-informed teaching. *Journal of Trauma & Dissociation, 15,* 153–168. http://dx.doi.org/10.1080/15299732.2014.867571

Carr, C., d'Ardenne, P., Sloboda, A., Scott, C., Wang, D., & Priebe, S. (2012). Group music therapy for patients with persistent post-traumatic stress disorder—An exploratory randomized controlled trial with mixed methods evaluation. *Psychology and Psychotherapy, 85,* 179–202. http://dx.doi.org/10.1111/j.2044-8341.2011.02026.x

Carter, C. S. (1998). Neuroendocrine perspectives on social attachment and love. *Psychoneuroendocrinology, 23,* 779–818. http://dx.doi.org/10.1016/S0306-4530(98)00055-9

Carter, C. S., Devries, A. C., & Getz, L. L. (1995). Physiological substrates of mammalian monogamy: The prairie vole model. *Neuroscience and Biobehavioral Reviews, 19,* 303–314. http://dx.doi.org/10.1016/0149-7634(94)00070-H

Cassidy, J., Brett, B. E., Gross, J. T., Stern, J. A., Martin, D. R., Mohr, J. J., & Woodhouse, S. S. (2017). Circle of Security-Parenting: A randomized controlled trial in Head Start. *Development and Psychopathology, 29,* 651–673. http://dx.doi.org/10.1017/S0954579417000244

Centers for Disease Control and Prevention. (2018). *Adverse childhood experiences presentation graphics.* Retrieved from https://www.cdc.gov/violenceprevention/childabuseandneglect/acestudy/ace-graphics.html

Chafouleas, S. M., Johnson, A. H., Overstreet, S., & Santos, N. M. (2016). Toward a blueprint for trauma-informed service delivery in schools. *School Mental Health, 8,* 144–162. http://dx.doi.org/10.1007/s12310-015-9166-8

Chahin, E. (2008, September/October). Caregiving with respect: Important lessons from the Pikler Institute. *Exchange, 30*(2), 40–42.

Chamberlain, C., Gee, G., Harfield, S., Campbell, S., Brennan, S., Clark, Y., . . . "Healing the Past by Nurturing the Future" Group. (2019). Parenting after a history of childhood maltreatment: A scoping review and map of evidence in the perinatal period. *PLoS ONE, 14,* 1–41. e0213460.

Champagne, F. A. (2008). Epigenetic mechanisms and the transgenerational effects of maternal care. *Frontiers in Neuroendocrinology, 29,* 386–397. http://dx.doi.org/10.1016/j.yfrne.2008.03.003

Chapman, D. P., Whitfield, C. L., Felitti, V. J., Dube, S. R., Edwards, V. J., & Anda, R. F. (2004). Adverse childhood experiences and the risk of depressive disorders in adulthood. *Journal of Affective Disorders, 82,* 217–225. http://dx.doi.org/10.1016/j.jad.2003.12.013

Chase-Lansdale, L., & Brooks-Gunn, J. (2014). Two-generation programs in the twenty-first century. *The Future of Children, 24,* 13–39. http://dx.doi.org/10.1353/foc.2014.0003

Chen, E., Brody, G. H., & Miller, G. E. (2017). Childhood close family relationships and health. *American Psychologist, 72,* 555–566. http://dx.doi.org/10.1037/amp0000067

Chen, E., Miller, G. E., Kobor, M. S., & Cole, S. W. (2011). Maternal warmth buffers the effects of low early-life socioeconomic status on pro-inflammatory signaling in adulthood. *Molecular Psychiatry, 16,* 729–737. http://dx.doi.org/10.1038/mp.2010.53

Chu, J. A., & Dill, D. L. (1990). Dissociative symptoms in relation to childhood physical and sexual abuse. *The American Journal of Psychiatry, 147,* 887–892. http://dx.doi.org/10.1176/ajp.147.7.887

Chung, E. K., Mathew, L., Rothkopf, A. C., Elo, I. T., Coyne, J. C., & Culhane, J. F. (2009). Parenting attitudes and infant spanking: The influence of childhood experiences. *Pediatrics, 124,* e278–e286. http://dx.doi.org/10.1542/peds.2008-3247

Cicchetti, D., & Schneider-Rosen, K. (1984). Toward a transactional model of childhood depression. *New Directions for Child and Adolescent Development, 1984,* 5–27. http://dx.doi.org/10.1002/cd.23219842604

Clarkson Freeman, P. A. (2014). Prevalence and relationship between adverse childhood experiences and child behavior among young children. *Infant Mental Health Journal, 35,* 544–554. http://dx.doi.org/10.1002/imhj.21460

Coatsworth, J. D., Duncan, L. G., Greenberg, M. T., & Nix, R. L. (2010). Changing parent's mindfulness, child management skills and relationship quality with their youth: Results from a randomized pilot intervention trial. *Journal of Child and Family Studies, 19,* 203–217. http://dx.doi.org/10.1007/s10826-009-9304-8

Coatsworth, J. D., Duncan, L. G., Nix, R. L., Greenberg, M. T., Gayles, J. G., Bamberger, K. T., . . . Demi, M. A. (2015). Integrating mindfulness with parent training: Effects of the Mindfulness-Enhanced Strengthening Families Program. *Developmental Psychology, 51,* 26–35. http://dx.doi.org/10.1037/a0038212

Cohen, J. A., Mannarino, A. P., & Deblinger, E. (2006). *Treating trauma and traumatic grief in children.* New York, NY: Guilford Press.

Cole, P. M., & Putnam, F. W. (1992). Effect of incest on self and social functioning: A developmental psychopathology perspective. *Journal of Consulting and Clinical Psychology, 60,* 174–184. http://dx.doi.org/10.1037/0022-006X.60.2.174

Conn, A. M., Szilagyi, M. A., Jee, S. H., Manly, J. T., Briggs, R., & Szilagyi, P. G. (2018). Parental perspectives of screening for adverse childhood experiences in pediatric primary care. *Families, Systems, & Health, 36,* 62–72. http://dx.doi.org/10.1037/fsh0000311

Conradt, E., Fei, M., LaGasse, L., Tronick, E., Guerin, D., Gorman, D., . . . Lester, B. M. (2015). Prenatal predictors of infant self-regulation: The contributions of placental DNA methylation of NR3C1 and neuroendocrine activity. *Frontiers in Behavioral Neuroscience, 9,* 130. http://dx.doi.org/10.3389/fnbeh.2015.00130

Conradt, E., Hawes, K., Guerin, D., Armstrong, D. A., Marsit, C. J., Tronick, E., & Lester, B. M. (2016). The contributions of maternal sensitivity and maternal depressive symptoms to epigenetic processes and neuroendocrine functioning. *Child Development, 87,* 73–85. http://dx.doi.org/10.1111/cdev.12483

Cook, A., Spinazzola, J., Ford, J., Lanktree, C., Blaustein, M., Cloitre, M., . . . van der Kolk, B. (2005). Complex trauma in children and adolescents. *Psychiatric Annals, 35,* 390–398. http://dx.doi.org/10.3928/00485713-20050501-05

Cooper, G., Hoffman, K., Powell, B., & Marvin, R. (2011). The circle of security intervention. In J. Solomon and C. George (Eds.), *Disorganized attachment and caregiving* (pp. 318–342). New York, NY: Guilford Press.

Corbin, T. J., Rich, J. A., Bloom, S. L., Delgado, D., Rich, L. J., & Wilson, A. S. (2011). Developing a trauma-informed, emergency department–based intervention for victims of urban violence. *Journal of Trauma & Dissociation, 12,* 510–525. http://dx.doi.org/10.1080/15299732.2011.593260

Costello, A. H., Roben, C. K. P., & Dozier, M. (2018). Attachment and biobehavioral catch-up. In A. S. Morris & A. C. Williamson (Eds.), *Building early social and emotional relationships with infants and toddlers* (pp. 213–236). Cham, Switzerland: Springer. http://dx.doi.org/10.1007/978-3-030-03110-7_9

Counts, J. M., Gillam, R. J., Perico, S., & Eggers, K. L. (2017). Lemonade for life—A pilot study on a hope-infused, trauma-informed approach to help families understand their past and focus on the future. *Children and Youth Services Review, 79,* 228–234. http://dx.doi.org/10.1016/j.childyouth.2017.05.036

Cramer, H., Anheyer, D., Saha, F. J., & Dobos, G. (2018). Yoga for posttraumatic stress disorder—A systematic review and meta-analysis. *BMC Psychiatry, 18,* 72. http://dx.doi.org/10.1186/s12888-018-1650-x

Criss, M. M., Henry, C. S., Harrist, A. W., & Larzelere, R. E. (2015). Interdisciplinary and innovative approaches to strengthening family and individual resilience: An introduction to the special issue. *Family Relations, 64,* 1–4. http://dx.doi.org/10.1111/fare.12109

Crnic, K. A., Gaze, C., & Hoffman, C. (2005). Cumulative parenting stress across the preschool period: Relations to maternal parenting and child behaviour at age 5. *Infant and Child Development, 14,* 117–132. http://dx.doi.org/10.1002/icd.384

Crosnoe, R., Erickson, K. G., & Dornbusch, S. M. (2002). Protective functions of family relationships and school factors on the deviant behavior of adolescent boys and girls: Reducing the impact of risky friendships. *Youth & Society, 33,* 515–544. http://dx.doi.org/10.1177/0044118X02033004002

Crowell, J. A., & Treboux, D. (1995). A review of adult attachment measures: Implications for theory and research. *Social Development, 4,* 294–327. http://dx.doi.org/10.1111/j.1467-9507.1995.tb00067.x

Dahl, R. E. (2004). Adolescent brain development: A period of vulnerabilities and opportunities. Keynote address. *Annals of the New York Academy of Sciences, 1021,* 1–22. http://dx.doi.org/10.1196/annals.1308.001

Danese, A., & Lewis, S. J. (2017). Psychoneuroimmunology of early-life stress: The hidden wounds of childhood trauma? *Neuropsychopharmacology, 42,* 99–114. http://dx.doi.org/10.1038/npp.2016.198

Danese, A., & McEwen, B. S. (2012). Adverse childhood experiences, allostasis, allostatic load, and age-related disease. *Physiology & Behavior, 106,* 29–39. http://dx.doi.org/10.1016/j.physbeh.2011.08.019

Danese, A., Moffitt, T. E., Harrington, H., Milne, B. J., Polanczyk, G., Pariante, C. M., . . . Caspi, A. (2009). Adverse childhood experiences and adult risk factors for age-related disease: Depression, inflammation, and clustering of metabolic risk markers. *Archives of Pediatrics & Adolescent Medicine, 163*, 1135–1143. http://dx.doi.org/10.1001/archpediatrics.2009.214

D'Angiulli, A., Van Roon, P. M., Weinberg, J., Oberlander, T. F., Grunau, R. E., Hertzman, C., & Maggi, S. (2012). Frontal EEG/ERP correlates of attentional processes, cortisol and motivational states in adolescents from lower and higher socioeconomic status. *Frontiers in Human Neuroscience, 6*, 306. http://dx.doi.org/10.3389/fnhum.2012.00306

Daubenmier, J., Lin, J., Blackburn, E., Hecht, F. M., Kristeller, J., Maninger, N., . . . Epel, E. (2012). Changes in stress, eating, and metabolic factors are related to changes in telomerase activity in a randomized mindfulness intervention pilot study. *Psychoneuroendocrinology, 37*, 917–928. http://dx.doi.org/10.1016/j.psyneuen.2011.10.008

Deater-Deckard, K. (2014). Family matters: Intergenerational and interpersonal processes of executive function and attentive behavior. *Current Directions in Psychological Science, 23*, 230–236. http://dx.doi.org/10.1177/0963721414531597

Deater-Deckard, K., Wang, Z., Chen, N., & Bell, M. A. (2012). Maternal executive function, harsh parenting, and child conduct problems. *Journal of Child Psychology and Psychiatry, 53*, 1084–1091. http://dx.doi.org/10.1111/j.1469-7610.2012.02582.x

De Bellis, M. D., Keshavan, M. S., Clark, D. B., Casey, B. J., Giedd, J. N., Boring, A. M., . . . Ryan, N. D. (1999). Developmental traumatology part II: Brain development. *Biological Psychiatry, 45*, 1271–1284. http://dx.doi.org/10.1016/S0006-3223(99)00045-1

DeCasper, A. J., & Fifer, W. P. (1980). Of human bonding: Newborns prefer their mothers' voices. *Science, 208*, 1174–1176. http://dx.doi.org/10.1126/science.7375928

Deighton, S., Neville, A., Pusch, D., & Dobson, K. (2018). Biomarkers of adverse childhood experiences: A scoping review. *Psychiatry Research, 269*, 719–732. http://dx.doi.org/10.1016/j.psychres.2018.08.097

de la Peña, C. M., Pineda, L., & Punsky, B. (2019). Working with parents and children separated at the border: Examining the impact of the zero tolerance policy and beyond. *Journal of Child & Adolescent Trauma, 12*, 153–164. http://dx.doi.org/10.1007/s40653-019-00262-4

Diamond, A., & Lee, K. (2011). Interventions shown to aid executive function development in children 4 to 12 years old. *Science, 333*, 959–964. http://dx.doi.org/10.1126/science.1204529

Dias, B. G., & Ressler, K. J. (2014). Parental olfactory experience influences behavior and neural structure in subsequent generations. *Nature Neuroscience, 17*, 89–96. http://dx.doi.org/10.1038/nn.3594

Dick, A. M., Niles, B. L., Street, A. E., DiMartino, D. M., & Mitchell, K. S. (2014). Examining mechanisms of change in a yoga intervention for women: The influence of mindfulness, psychological flexibility, and emotion regulation on PTSD symptoms. *Journal of Clinical Psychology, 70*, 1170–1182. http://dx.doi.org/10.1002/jclp.22104

Dietz, P. M., Spitz, A. M., Anda, R. F., Williamson, D. F., McMahon, P. M., Santelli, J. S., . . . Kendrick, J. S. (1999). Unintended pregnancy among adult women exposed to abuse or household dysfunction during their childhood. *Journal of the American Medical Association*, *282*, 1359–1364. http://dx.doi.org/10.1001/jama.282.14.1359

Dillon, D. G., Holmes, A. J., Birk, J. L., Brooks, N., Lyons-Ruth, K., & Pizzagalli, D. A. (2009). Childhood adversity is associated with left basal ganglia dysfunction during reward anticipation in adulthood. *Biological Psychiatry*, *66*, 206–213. http://dx.doi.org/10.1016/j.biopsych.2009.02.019

Doan, S. N., Dich, N., & Evans, G. W. (2014). Childhood cumulative risk and later allostatic load: Mediating role of substance use. *Health Psychology*, *33*, 1402–1409. http://dx.doi.org/10.1037/a0034790

Doherty, T. S., & Roth, T. L. (2016). Insight from animal models of environmentally driven epigenetic changes in the developing and adult brain. *Development and Psychopathology, 28*(4pt2), 1229–1243. http://dx.doi.org/10.1017/S095457941600081X

Dong, M., Anda, R. F., Felitti, V. J., Dube, S. R., Williamson, D. F., Thompson, T. J., . . . Giles, W. H. (2004). The interrelatedness of multiple forms of childhood abuse, neglect, and household dysfunction. *Child Abuse & Neglect*, *28*, 771–784. http://dx.doi.org/10.1016/j.chiabu.2004.01.008

Dong, M., Dube, S. R., Felitti, V. J., Giles, W. H., & Anda, R. F. (2003). Adverse childhood experiences and self-reported liver disease: New insights into the causal pathway. *Archives of Internal Medicine*, *163*, 1949–1956. http://dx.doi.org/10.1001/archinte.163.16.1949

Dong, M., Giles, W. H., Felitti, V. J., Dube, S. R., Williams, J. E., Chapman, D. P., & Anda, R. F. (2004). Insights into causal pathways for ischemic heart disease: Adverse childhood experiences study. *Circulation*, *110*, 1761–1766. http://dx.doi.org/10.1161/01.CIR.0000143074.54995.7F

Dorado, J. S., Martinez, M., McArthur, L. E., & Leibovitz, T. (2016). Healthy environments and response to trauma in schools (hearts): A whole-school, multi-level, prevention and intervention program for creating trauma-informed, safe and supportive schools. *School Mental Health, 8*, 163–176. http://dx.doi.org/10.1007/s12310-016-9177-0

Dornbusch, S. M., Ritter, P. L., Leiderman, P. H., Roberts, D. F., & Fraleigh, M. J. (1987). The relation of parenting style to adolescent school performance. *Child Development*, *58*, 1244–1257. http://dx.doi.org/10.2307/1130618

Dozier, M. (2000). Motivation for caregiving from an ethological perspective. *Psychological Inquiry*, *11*, 97–100.

Dozier, M., & Bernard, K. (2019). *Coaching parents of vulnerable infants: The attachment and biobehavioral catch-up approach*. New York, NY: Guilford Press.

Drevets, W. C., Videen, T. O., Price, J. L., Preskorn, S. H., Carmichael, S. T., & Raichle, M. E. (1992). A functional anatomical study of unipolar depression. *The Journal of Neuroscience*, *12*, 3628–3641. http://dx.doi.org/10.1523/JNEUROSCI.12-09-03628.1992

Dube, S. R. (2018). Continuing conversations about adverse childhood experiences (ACEs) screening: A public health perspective. *Child Abuse & Neglect*, *85*, 180–184. http://dx.doi.org/10.1016/j.chiabu.2018.03.007

Dube, S. R., Anda, R. F., Felitti, V. J., Edwards, V. J., & Croft, J. B. (2002). Adverse childhood experiences and personal alcohol abuse as an adult. *Addictive Behaviors, 27*, 713–725. http://dx.doi.org/10.1016/S0306-4603(01)00204-0

Dube, S. R., Fairweather, D., Pearson, W. S., Felitti, V. J., Anda, R. F., & Croft, J. B. (2009). Cumulative childhood stress and autoimmune diseases in adults. *Psychosomatic Medicine, 71*, 243–250. http://dx.doi.org/10.1097/PSY.0b013e3181907888

DuBois, D. L., Felner, R. D., Brand, S., Adan, A. M., & Evans, E. G. (1992). A prospective study of life stress, social support, and adaptation in early adolescence. *Child Development, 63*, 542–557. http://dx.doi.org/10.2307/1131345

Duffy, K. A., McLaughlin, K. A., & Green, P. A. (2018). Early life adversity and health-risk behaviors: Proposed psychological and neural mechanisms. *Annals of the New York Academy of Sciences, 1428*, 151–169. http://dx.doi.org/10.1111/nyas.13928

Duncan, G. J., & Brooks-Gunn, J. (2000). Family poverty, welfare reform, and child development. *Child Development, 71*, 188–196. http://dx.doi.org/10.1111/1467-8624.00133

Duncan, G. J., Brooks-Gunn, J., & Klebanov, P. K. (1994). Economic deprivation and early childhood development. *Child Development, 65*, 296–318. http://dx.doi.org/10.2307/1131385

Duncan, L. G., Coatsworth, J. D., & Greenberg, M. T. (2009). A model of mindful parenting: Implications for parent–child relationships and prevention research. *Clinical Child and Family Psychology Review, 12*, 255–270. http://dx.doi.org/10.1007/s10567-009-0046-3

Duval, E. R., Garfinkel, S. N., Swain, J. E., Evans, G. W., Blackburn, E. K., Angstadt, M., . . . Liberzon, I. (2017). Childhood poverty is associated with altered hippocampal function and visuospatial memory in adulthood. *Developmental Cognitive Neuroscience, 23*, 39–44. http://dx.doi.org/10.1016/j.dcn.2016.11.006

Dybdahl, R. (2001). Children and mothers in war: An outcome study of a psychosocial intervention program. *Child Development, 72*, 1214–1230. http://dx.doi.org/10.1111/1467-8624.00343

Earley, M. D., Chesney, M. A., Frye, J., Greene, P. A., Berman, B., & Kimbrough, E. (2014). Mindfulness intervention for child abuse survivors: A 2.5-year follow-up. *Journal of Clinical Psychology, 70*, 933–941. http://dx.doi.org/10.1002/jclp.22102

Easterlin, M. C., Chung, P. J., Leng, M., & Dudovitz, R. (2019). Association of team sports participation with long-term mental health outcomes among individuals exposed to adverse childhood experiences. *JAMA Pediatrics, 173*, 681–688. http://dx.doi.org/10.1001/jamapediatrics.2019.1212

Edenfield, T. M., & Blumenthal, J. A. (2011). Exercise and stress reduction. In R. J. Contrada & A. Baum (Eds.), *The handbook of stress science: Biology, psychology, and health* (pp. 301–319). New York, NY: Springer.

Egan, T. (2006). *The worst hard time: The untold story of those who survived the great American dust bowl.* Boston, MA: Houghton Mifflin Harcourt.

Eisenberg, M. E., Olson, R. E., Neumark-Sztainer, D., Story, M., & Bearinger, L. H. (2004). Correlations between family meals and psychosocial well-being among adolescents. *Archives of Pediatrics & Adolescent Medicine, 158*, 792–796. http://dx.doi.org/10.1001/archpedi.158.8.792

Eisenberg, N., Morris, A. S., McDaniel, B., & Spinrad, T. L. (2009). Moral cognitions and prosocial responding in adolescence. In R. M. Lerner & L. Steinberg (Eds.), *Handbook of adolescent psychology: Vol. 1. Moral cognitions and prosocial responding in adolescence* (pp. 229–265). http://dx.doi.org/10.1002/9780470479193.adlpsy001009

Elgar, F. J., Donnelly, P. D., Michaelson, V., Gariépy, G., Riehm, K. E., Walsh, S. D., & Pickett, W. (2018). Corporal punishment bans and physical fighting in adolescents: An ecological study of 88 countries. *British Medical Journal Open*, *8*, 1–8. e021616.

El-Sheikh, M., Kouros, C. D., Erath, S., Cummings, E. M., Keller, P., & Staton, L. (2009). Marital conflict and children's externalizing behavior: Interactions between parasympathetic and sympathetic nervous system activity. *Monographs of the Society for Research in Child Development*, *74*, vii–79.

Ellis, B. J., & Garber, J. (2000). Psychosocial antecedents of variation in girls' pubertal timing: Maternal depression, stepfather presence, and marital and family stress. *Child Development*, *71*, 485–501. http://dx.doi.org/10.1111/1467-8624.00159

Ellis, B. J., McFadyen-Ketchum, S., Dodge, K. A., Pettit, G. S., & Bates, J. E. (1999). Quality of early family relationships and individual differences in the timing of pubertal maturation in girls: A longitudinal test of an evolutionary model. *Journal of Personality and Social Psychology*, *77*, 387–401. http://dx.doi.org/10.1037/0022-3514.77.2.387

Ellis, W. R., & Dietz, W. H. (2017). A new framework for addressing adverse childhood and community experiences: The building community resilience model. *Academic Pediatrics*, *17*(Suppl. 7), S86–S93. http://dx.doi.org/10.1016/j.acap.2016.12.011

Ellis, W. R., & Dietz, W. H. (2018, September). *Introducing the "Pair of ACEs" tree*. Retrieved from The George Washington University, Milken Institute School of Public Health website: https://publichealth.gwu.edu/sites/default/files/downloads/Redstone-Center/BCR%20Pair%20of%20ACEs%20Webinar%20Slides.pdf

Ellison, R. (2003). *Going to the territory*. New York, NY: Modern Library Classics.

Erikson, E. H. (1993). *Childhood and society*. New York, NY: Norton.

Erikson, E. H. (1994). *Identity: Youth and crisis*. New York, NY: Norton.

Esaki, N., & Larkin, H. (2013). Prevalence of adverse childhood experiences (ACEs) among child service providers. *Families in Society*, *94*, 31–37. http://dx.doi.org/10.1606/1044-3894.4257

Essex, M. J., Boyce, W. T., Hertzman, C., Lam, L. L., Armstrong, J. M., Neumann, S. M., & Kobor, M. S. (2013). Epigenetic vestiges of early developmental adversity: Childhood stress exposure and DNA methylation in adolescence. *Child Development*, *84*, 58–75. http://dx.doi.org/10.1111/j.1467-8624.2011.01641.x

Essex, M. J., Klein, M. H., Cho, E., & Kalin, N. H. (2002). Maternal stress beginning in infancy may sensitize children to later stress exposure: Effects on cortisol and behavior. *Biological Psychiatry*, *52*, 776–784. http://dx.doi.org/10.1016/S0006-3223(02)01553-6

Essex, M. J., Shirtcliff, E. A., Burk, L. R., Ruttle, P. L., Klein, M. H., Slattery, M. J., . . . Armstrong, J. M. (2011). Influence of early life stress on later hypothalamic-pituitary-adrenal axis functioning and its covariation with mental health symptoms: A study of the allostatic process from childhood into adolescence. *Development and Psychopathology*, *23*, 1039–1058. http://dx.doi.org/10.1017/S0954579411000484

Evans, G. W. (2003). A multimethodological analysis of cumulative risk and allostatic load among rural children. *Developmental Psychology*, *39*, 924–933. http://dx.doi.org/10.1037/0012-1649.39.5.924

Evans, G. W., & English, K. (2002). The environment of poverty: Multiple stressor exposure, psychophysiological stress, and socioemotional adjustment. *Child Development, 73*, 1238–1248. http://dx.doi.org/10.1111/1467-8624.00469

Evans, G. W., & Kim, P. (2007). Childhood poverty and health: Cumulative risk exposure and stress dysregulation. *Psychological Science, 18*, 953–957. http://dx.doi.org/10.1111/j.1467-9280.2007.02008.x

Evans, G. W., Kim, P., Ting, A. H., Tesher, H. B., & Shannis, D. (2007). Cumulative risk, maternal responsiveness, and allostatic load among young adolescents. *Developmental Psychology, 43*, 341–351. http://dx.doi.org/10.1037/0012-1649.43.2.341

Evans-Campbell, T. (2008). Historical trauma in American Indian/Native Alaska communities: A multilevel framework for exploring impacts on individuals, families, and communities. *Journal of Interpersonal Violence, 23*, 316–338. http://dx.doi.org/10.1177/0886260507312290

Fancourt, D., Perkins, R., Ascenso, S., Carvalho, L. A., Steptoe, A., & Williamon, A. (2016). Effects of group drumming interventions on anxiety, depression, social resilience and inflammatory immune response among mental health service users. *PLoS ONE, 11*, e0151136. http://dx.doi.org/10.1371/journal.pone.0151136

Fareri, D. S., & Tottenham, N. (2016). Effects of early life stress on amygdala and striatal development. *Developmental Cognitive Neuroscience, 19*, 233–247. http://dx.doi.org/10.1016/j.dcn.2016.04.005

Feeding America. (2018). *Hunger deprives our kids of more than just food.* Retrieved from https://www.feedingamerica.org/hunger-in-america/child-hunger-facts

Feeney, J. A., & Noller, P. (1990). Attachment style as a predictor of adult romantic relationships. *Journal of Personality and Social Psychology, 58*, 281–291. http://dx.doi.org/10.1037/0022-3514.58.2.281

Feinstein, J., Khalsa, S., Al Zoubi, O., Yeh, H., Simmons, W. K., Stein, M., & Paulus, M. (2018). F34. Examining the short-term anxiolytic effect of floatation-REST. *Biological Psychiatry, 83*(Suppl.), S250–S251. http://dx.doi.org/10.1016/j.biopsych.2018.02.647

Feinstein, J. S., Khalsa, S. S., Yeh, H., Al Zoubi, O., Arevian, A. C., Wohlrab, C., . . . Paulus, M. P. (2018). The elicitation of relaxation and interoceptive awareness using floatation therapy in individuals with high anxiety sensitivity. *Biological Psychiatry: Cognitive Neuroscience and Neuroimaging, 3*, 555–562.

Feldman, R. (2003). Infant–mother and infant–father synchrony: The coregulation of positive arousal. *Infant Mental Health Journal, 24*, 1–23. http://dx.doi.org/10.1002/imhj.10041

Feldman, R. (2015). The adaptive human parental brain: Implications for children's social development. *Trends in Neurosciences, 38*, 387–399. http://dx.doi.org/10.1016/j.tins.2015.04.004

Feldman, R. (2017). The neurobiology of human attachments. *Trends in Cognitive Sciences, 21*, 80–99. http://dx.doi.org/10.1016/j.tics.2016.11.007

Felitti, V. J. (2018, October). *Reflections on twenty years of ACEs and toxic stress science.* Presentation at the 2018 ACEs Conference, San Francisco, CA.

Felitti, V. J. (2019). Health appraisal and the Adverse Childhood Experiences Study: National implications for health care, cost, and utilization. *The Permanente Journal, 23*, 18–026. http://dx.doi.org/10.7812/TPP/18-026

Felitti, V. J., Anda, R. F., Nordenberg, D., Williamson, D. F., Spitz, A. M., Edwards, V., . . . Marks, J. S. (1998). Relationship of childhood abuse and household dysfunction to many of the leading causes of death in adults. The Adverse Childhood Experiences (ACE) Study. *American Journal of Preventive Medicine, 14*, 245–258. http://dx.doi.org/10.1016/S0749-3797(98)00017-8

Finkelhor, D. (2018). Screening for adverse childhood experiences (ACEs): Cautions and suggestions. *Child Abuse & Neglect, 85*, 174–179. http://dx.doi.org/10.1016/j.chiabu.2017.07.016

Finkelhor, D., & Kendall-Tackett, K. (1997). A developmental perspective on the childhood impact of crime, abuse, and violent victimization. In D. Cicchetti & S. L. Toth (Eds.), *Rochester symposium on developmental psychology: Vol. 8. Developmental perspectives on trauma: Theory, research, and intervention* (pp. 1–32). Rochester, NY: University of Rochester Press.

Finkelhor, D., Ormrod, R. K., & Turner, H. A. (2007). Poly-victimization: A neglected component in child victimization. *Child Abuse & Neglect, 31*, 7–26. http://dx.doi.org/10.1016/j.chiabu.2006.06.008

Fisher, P. A., Frenkel, T. I., Noll, L. K., Berry, M., & Yockelson, M. (2016). Promoting healthy child development via a two-generation translational neuroscience framework: The Filming Interactions to Nurture Development video coaching program. *Child Development Perspectives, 10*, 251–256. http://dx.doi.org/10.1111/cdep.12195

Flanagan, T., Alabaster, A., McCaw, B., Stoller, N., Watson, C., & Young-Wolff, K. C. (2018). Feasibility and acceptability of screening for adverse childhood experiences in prenatal care. *Journal of Women's Health, 27*, 903–911. http://dx.doi.org/10.1089/jwh.2017.6649

Flook, L., Goldberg, S. B., Pinger, L., & Davidson, R. J. (2015). Promoting pro-social behavior and self-regulatory skills in preschool children through a mindfulness-based Kindness Curriculum. *Developmental Psychology, 51*, 44–51. http://dx.doi.org/10.1037/a0038256

Ford, D. E. (2017). The community and public well-being model: A new framework and graduate curriculum for addressing adverse childhood experiences. *Academic Pediatrics, 17*(Suppl. 7), S9–S11. http://dx.doi.org/10.1016/j.acap.2017.04.011

Fox, B. H., Perez, N., Cass, E., Baglivio, M. T., & Epps, N. (2015). Trauma changes everything: Examining the relationship between adverse childhood experiences and serious, violent and chronic juvenile offenders. *Child Abuse & Neglect, 46*, 163–173. http://dx.doi.org/10.1016/j.chiabu.2015.01.011

Fox, C. L., & Boulton, M. J. (2006). Friendship as a moderator of the relationship between social skills problems and peer victimisation. *Aggressive Behavior, 32*, 110–121. http://dx.doi.org/10.1002/ab.20114

Fox, K. R. (1999). The influence of physical activity on mental well-being. *Public Health Nutrition, 2*, 411–418. http://dx.doi.org/10.1017/S1368980099000567

Fraiberg, S., Adelson, E., & Shapiro, V. (1975). Ghosts in the nursery. A psychoanalytic approach to the problems of impaired infant–mother relationships. *Journal of the American Academy of Child Psychiatry, 14*, 387–421. http://dx.doi.org/10.1016/S0002-7138(09)61442-4

Fraley, R. C., & Shaver, P. R. (2000). Adult romantic attachment: Theoretical developments, emerging controversies, and unanswered questions. *Review of General Psychology, 4*, 132–154. http://dx.doi.org/10.1037/1089-2680.4.2.132

Fraley, R. C., Waller, N. G., & Brennan, K. A. (2000). An item response theory analysis of self-report measures of adult attachment. *Journal of Personality and Social Psychology, 78*, 350–365. http://dx.doi.org/10.1037/0022-3514.78.2.350

Francis, D., Diorio, J., Liu, D., & Meaney, M. J. (1999). Nongenomic transmission across generations of maternal behavior and stress responses in the rat. *Science*, *286*, 1155–1158. http://dx.doi.org/10.1126/science.286.5442.1155

Francisco, M. A., Hicks, K., Powell, J., Styles, K., Tabor, J. L., & Hulton, L. J. (2008). The effect of childhood sexual abuse on adolescent pregnancy: An integrative research review. *Journal for Specialists in Pediatric Nursing*, *13*, 237–248. http://dx.doi.org/10.1111/j.1744-6155.2008.00160.x

Frank, R. G., Strobino, D., Salkever, D. S., & Jackson, C. A. (1991). *Updated estimates of the impact of prenatal care on birthweight outcomes by race* (No. w3624). Cambridge, MA: National Bureau of Economic Research.

Frankl, V. E. (1985). *Man's search for meaning*. New York, NY: Simon & Schuster.

Franklin, T. B., Linder, N., Russig, H., Thöny, B., & Mansuy, I. M. (2011). Influence of early stress on social abilities and serotonergic functions across generations in mice. *PLoS ONE*, *6*, e21842. http://dx.doi.org/10.1371/journal.pone.0021842

Franklin, T. B., Russig, H., Weiss, I. C., Gräff, J., Linder, N., Michalon, A., . . . Mansuy, I. M. (2010). Epigenetic transmission of the impact of early stress across generations. *Biological Psychiatry*, *68*, 408–415. http://dx.doi.org/10.1016/j.biopsych.2010.05.036

Fraser-Thomas, J. L., Côté, J., & Deakin, J. (2005). Youth sport programs: An avenue to foster positive youth development. *Physical Education and Sport Pedagogy*, *10*, 19–40. http://dx.doi.org/10.1080/1740898042000334890

Fredricks, J. A., & Eccles, J. S. (2006). Is extracurricular participation associated with beneficial outcomes? Concurrent and longitudinal relations. *Developmental Psychology*, *42*, 698–713. http://dx.doi.org/10.1037/0012-1649.42.4.698

Fredricks, J. A., & Eccles, J. S. (2010). Breadth of extracurricular participation and adolescent adjustment among African-American and European-American youth. *Journal of Research on Adolescence*, *20*, 307–333. http://dx.doi.org/10.1111/j.1532-7795.2009.00627.x

Frodi, A. M., Lamb, M. E., Leavitt, L. A., & Donovan, W. L. (1978). Fathers' and mothers' responses to infant smiles and cries. *Infant Behavior and Development*, *1*, 187–198. http://dx.doi.org/10.1016/S0163-6383(78)80029-0

Frodl, T., & O'Keane, V. (2013). How does the brain deal with cumulative stress? A review with focus on developmental stress, HPA axis function and hippocampal structure in humans. *Neurobiology of Disease*, *52*, 24–37. http://dx.doi.org/10.1016/j.nbd.2012.03.012

Frodl, T., Schaub, A., Banac, S., Charypar, M., Jäger, M., Kümmler, P., . . . Meisenzahl, E. M. (2006). Reduced hippocampal volume correlates with executive dysfunctioning in major depression. *Journal of Psychiatry & Neuroscience*, *31*, 316–323.

Frydman, J. S., & Mayor, C. (2017). Trauma and early adolescent development: Case examples from a trauma-informed public health middle school program. *Children & Schools*, *39*, 238–247. http://dx.doi.org/10.1093/cs/cdx017

Fulkerson, J. A., Story, M., Mellin, A., Leffert, N., Neumark-Sztainer, D., & French, S. A. (2006). Family dinner meal frequency and adolescent development: Relationships with developmental assets and high-risk behaviors. *Journal of Adolescent Health*, *39*, 337–345. http://dx.doi.org/10.1016/j.jadohealth.2005.12.026

Gallant, S. N. (2016). Mindfulness meditation practice and executive functioning: Breaking down the benefit. *Consciousness and Cognition*, *40*, 116–130. http://dx.doi.org/10.1016/j.concog.2016.01.005

Galván, A. (2017). *The neuroscience of adolescence*. New York, NY: Cambridge University Press. http://dx.doi.org/10.1017/9781316106143

Gapen, M., van der Kolk, B. A., Hamlin, E., Hirshberg, L., Suvak, M., & Spinazzola, J. (2016). A pilot study of neurofeedback for chronic PTSD. *Applied Psychophysiology and Biofeedback, 41*, 251–261. http://dx.doi.org/10.1007/s10484-015-9326-5

Garbarino, J. (2017). ACEs in the criminal justice system. *Academic Pediatrics, 17*(Suppl. 7), S32–S33. http://dx.doi.org/10.1016/j.acap.2016.09.003

Gerber, S. B. (1996). Extracurricular activities and academic achievement. *Journal of Research & Development in Education, 30*, 42–50.

Gershoff, E. T. (2013). Spanking and child development: We know enough now to stop hitting our children. *Child Development Perspectives, 7*, 133–137. http://dx.doi.org/10.1111/cdep.12038

Gershoff, E. T., Goodman, G. S., Miller-Perrin, C. L., Holden, G. W., Jackson, Y., & Kazdin, A. E. (2018). The strength of the causal evidence against physical punishment of children and its implications for parents, psychologists, and policymakers. *American Psychologist, 73*, 626–638. http://dx.doi.org/10.1037/amp0000327

Gershon, N. B., & High, P. C. (2015). Epigenetics and child abuse: Modern-day Darwinism—The miraculous ability of the human genome to adapt, and then adapt again. *American Journal of Medical Genetics: Part C. Seminars in Medical Genetics, 169*, 353–360. http://dx.doi.org/10.1002/ajmg.c.31467

Geuze, E., Vermetten, E., & Bremner, J. D. (2005). MR-based in vivo hippocampal volumetrics: 2. Findings in neuropsychiatric disorders. *Molecular Psychiatry, 10*, 160–184. http://dx.doi.org/10.1038/sj.mp.4001579

Ginsburg, K. R., & Jablow, M. M. (2005). *Building resilience in children and teens: Giving kids roots and wings*. Elk Grove Village, IL: American Academy of Pediatrics.

Gluckman, P. D., & Hanson, M. A. (2004a). Developmental origins of disease paradigm: A mechanistic and evolutionary perspective. *Pediatric Research, 56*, 311–317. http://dx.doi.org/10.1203/01.PDR.0000135998.08025.FB

Gluckman, P. D., & Hanson, M. A. (2004b). The developmental origins of the metabolic syndrome. *Trends in Endocrinology and Metabolism, 15*, 183–187. http://dx.doi.org/10.1016/j.tem.2004.03.002

Goldstein, E., Murray-García, J., Sciolla, A. F., & Topitzes, J. (2018). Medical students' perspectives on trauma-informed care training. *The Permanente Journal, 22*, 17–126. http://dx.doi.org/10.7812/TPP/17-126

Golinkoff, R. M., Hoff, E., Rowe, M. L., Tamis-LeMonda, C. S., & Hirsh-Pasek, K. (2019). Language matters: Denying the existence of the 30-million-word gap has serious consequences. *Child Development, 90*, 985–992.

Gonzalez-Mena, J. (2004). What can an orphanage teach us? Lessons from Budapest. *Young Children, 59*, 26.

Gonzalez-Mena, J., & Briley, L. (2011, December 15). *Improving infant mental health in orphanages: A goal worth considering*. Tampere, Finland: World Association for Infant Mental Health. Retrieved from https://perspectives.waimh.org/2011/12/15/improving-infant-mental-health-orphanages-goal-worth-considering/

Gortner, E.-M., Rude, S. S., & Pennebaker, J. W. (2006). Benefits of expressive writing in lowering rumination and depressive symptoms. *Behavior Therapy, 37*, 292–303. http://dx.doi.org/10.1016/j.beth.2006.01.004

Gotink, R. A., Meijboom, R., Vernooij, M. W., Smits, M., & Hunink, M. G. (2016). 8-week Mindfulness Based Stress Reduction induces brain changes similar to traditional long-term meditation practice—a systematic review. *Brain and Cognition*, *108*, 32–41. http://dx.doi.org/10.1016/j.bandc.2016.07.001

Gottman, J. M., Katz, L. F., & Hooven, C. (1996). Parental meta-emotion philosophy and the emotional life of families: Theoretical models and preliminary data. *Journal of Family Psychology*, *10*, 243–268. http://dx.doi.org/10.1037/0893-3200.10.3.243

Graham, H., & Power, C. (2004). Childhood disadvantage and health inequalities: A framework for policy based on lifecourse research. *Child: Care, Health and Development*, *30*, 671–678. http://dx.doi.org/10.1111/j.1365-2214.2004.00457.x

Grant, K. E., Compas, B. E., Stuhlmacher, A. F., Thurm, A. E., McMahon, S. D., & Halpert, J. A. (2003). Stressors and child and adolescent psychopathology: Moving from markers to mechanisms of risk. *Psychological Bulletin*, *129*, 447–466. http://dx.doi.org/10.1037/0033-2909.129.3.447

Green, J. G., McLaughlin, K. A., Berglund, P. A., Gruber, M. J., Sampson, N. A., Zaslavsky, A. M., & Kessler, R. C. (2010). Childhood adversities and adult psychiatric disorders in the national comorbidity survey replication I: Associations with first onset of *DSM–IV* disorders. *Archives of General Psychiatry*, *67*, 113–123. http://dx.doi.org/10.1001/archgenpsychiatry.2009.186

Greenberg, J., Romero, V. L., Elkin-Frankston, S., Bezdek, M. A., Schumacher, E. H., & Lazar, S. W. (2019). Reduced interference in working memory following mindfulness training is associated with increases in hippocampal volume. *Brain Imaging and Behavior*, *13*, 366–376.

Gröger, N., Matas, E., Gos, T., Lesse, A., Poeggel, G., Braun, K., & Bock, J. (2016). The transgenerational transmission of childhood adversity: Behavioral, cellular, and epigenetic correlates. *Journal of Neural Transmission*, *123*, 1037–1052. http://dx.doi.org/10.1007/s00702-016-1570-1

Grossman, P., Niemann, L., Schmidt, S., & Walach, H. (2004). Mindfulness-based stress reduction and health benefits. A meta-analysis. *Journal of Psychosomatic Research*, *57*, 35–43. http://dx.doi.org/10.1016/S0022-3999(03)00573-7

Grossmann, K., Grossmann, K. E., Fremmer-Bombik, E., Kindler, H., Scheuerer-Englisch, H., & Zimmermann, P. (2002). The uniqueness of the child–father attachment relationship: Fathers' sensitive and challenging play as a pivotal variable in a 16-year longitudinal study. *Social Development*, *11*, 301–337. http://dx.doi.org/10.1111/1467-9507.00202

Hair, N. L., Hanson, J. L., Wolfe, B. L., & Pollak, S. D. (2015). Association of child poverty, brain development, and academic achievement. *JAMA Pediatrics*, *169*, 822–829. http://dx.doi.org/10.1001/jamapediatrics.2015.1475

Haley, D. W., & Stansbury, K. (2003). Infant stress and parent responsiveness: Regulation of physiology and behavior during still-face and reunion. *Child Development*, *74*, 1534–1546. http://dx.doi.org/10.1111/1467-8624.00621

Halfon, N., Larson, K., Lu, M., Tullis, E., & Russ, S. (2014). Lifecourse health development: Past, present and future. *Maternal and Child Health Journal*, *18*, 344–365. http://dx.doi.org/10.1007/s10995-013-1346-2

Hanson, J. L., Gillmore, A. D., Yu, T., Holmes, C. J., Hallowell, E. S., Barton, A. W., . . . Brody, G. H. (2019). A family focused intervention influences hippocampal-prefrontal connectivity through gains in self-regulation. *Child Development*, *90*, 1389–1401. http://dx.doi.org/10.1111/cdev.13154

Hargrave, A. C., & Sénéchal, M. (2000). A book reading intervention with pre-school children who have limited vocabularies: The benefits of regular reading and dialogic reading. *Early Childhood Research Quarterly, 15,* 75–90. http://dx.doi.org/10.1016/S0885-2006(99)00038-1

Hargreaves, M. B., Pecora, P. J., & Williamson, G. (2017). Aligning community capacity, networks, and solutions to address adverse childhood experiences and increase resilience. *Academic Pediatrics, 17*(Suppl. 7), S7–S8. http://dx.doi.org/10.1016/j.acap.2017.04.004

Harlow, H. F., & Zimmermann, R. R. (1959). Affectional responses in the infant monkey; orphaned baby monkeys develop a strong and persistent attachment to inanimate surrogate mothers. *Science, 130,* 421–432. http://dx.doi.org/10.1126/science.130.3373.421

Harris, M., & Fallot, R. D. (2001a). Envisioning a trauma-informed service system: A vital paradigm shift. *New Directions for Mental Health Services, 2001,* 3–22. http://dx.doi.org/10.1002/yd.23320018903

Harris, M., & Fallot, R. D. (2001b). *Using trauma theory to design service systems.* San Francisco, CA: Jossey-Bass.

Harris, N. B. (2018). *The deepest well: Healing the long-term effects of childhood adversity.* Boston, MA: Houghton Mifflin Harcourt.

Harrist, A. W., Henry, C. S., Liu, C., & Morris, A. S. (2019). Family resilience: The power of rituals and routines in family adaptive systems. In B. H. Fiese, M. Celano, K. Deater-Deckard, E. N. Jouriles, & M. A. Whisman (Eds.), *APA handbook of contemporary family psychology: Foundations, methods, and contemporary issues across the lifespan* (pp. 223–239). Washington, DC: American Psychological Association.

Harrist, A. W., & Waugh, R. M. (2002). Dyadic synchrony: Its structure and function in children's development. *Developmental Review, 22,* 555–592. http://dx.doi.org/10.1016/S0273-2297(02)00500-2

Hart, B., & Risley, T. (1995). *Meaningful differences in the everyday life of America's children.* Baltimore, MD: Paul Brookes.

Hart, B., & Risley, T. R. (2003). The early catastrophe: The 30 million word gap by age 3. *American Educator, 27,* 4–9.

Harter, S. (1998). The development of self-representations. In W. Damon & N. Eisenberg (Eds.), *Handbook of child psychology: Social, emotional, and personality development* (pp. 553–617). Hoboken, NJ: Wiley.

Hatchard, T., Mioduszewski, O., Zambrana, A., O'Farrell, E., Caluyong, M., Poulin, P. A., & Smith, A. M. (2017). Neural changes associated with mindfulness-based stress reduction (MBSR): Current knowledge, limitations, and future directions. *Psychology & Neuroscience, 10,* 41–56. http://dx.doi.org/10.1037/pne0000073

Havighurst, S. S., Kehoe, C. E., & Harley, A. E. (2015). Tuning in to teens: Improving parental responses to anger and reducing youth externalizing behavior problems. *Journal of Adolescence, 42,* 148–158. http://dx.doi.org/10.1016/j.adolescence.2015.04.005

Havighurst, S. S., Wilson, K. R., Harley, A. E., Kehoe, C., Efron, D., & Prior, M. R. (2013). "Tuning into Kids": Reducing young children's behavior problems using an emotion coaching parenting program. *Child Psychiatry and Human Development, 44,* 247–264. http://dx.doi.org/10.1007/s10578-012-0322-1

Hays-Grudo, J., & Morris, A. S. (2018). *Creating Protective and Compensatory Experiences (PACEs) to buffer the damaging effects of early life adversity.* Paper presented at the World Congress of the World Association for Infant Mental Health, Rome, Italy.

Hays-Grudo, J., Slocum, R., Root, J. D., Bosler, C., & Morris, A. S. (2019). Tulsa Children's Project: Applying evidence-based interventions in early childhood settings. In A. S. Morris & A. W. Payton (Eds.), *Building early social and emotional relationships in infants and toddlers* (pp. 207–303). Cham, Switzerland: Springer.

Hays-Grudo, L., Welch, G., & Shellhammer, L. (2018, October). *An examination of the prevalence of ACEs and PACEs in a rural parenting sample*. Workshop presented at the Zero to Three annual conference, Denver, CO.

Hazan, C., & Shaver, P. (1987). Romantic love conceptualized as an attachment process. *Journal of Personality and Social Psychology, 52*, 511–524. http://dx.doi.org/10.1037/0022-3514.52.3.511

Heckman, J. J. (2006). Skill formation and the economics of investing in disadvantaged children. *Science, 312*, 1900–1902. http://dx.doi.org/10.1126/science.1128898

Heckman, J. J. (2011). The economics of inequality: The value of early childhood education. *American Educator, 35*, 31.

Heckman, J. J. (2015). *Four big benefits of investing in early childhood development*. Retrieved from https://heckmanequation.org

Heijmans, B. T., Tobi, E. W., Stein, A. D., Putter, H., Blauw, G. J., Susser, E. S., . . . Lumey, L. H. (2008). Persistent epigenetic differences associated with prenatal exposure to famine in humans. *Proceedings of the National Academy of Sciences of the United States of America, 105*, 17046–17049. http://dx.doi.org/10.1073/pnas.0806560105

Heim, C. M., Mayberg, H. S., Mletzko, T., Nemeroff, C. B., & Pruessner, J. C. (2013). Decreased cortical representation of genital somatosensory field after childhood sexual abuse. *The American Journal of Psychiatry, 170*, 616–623. http://dx.doi.org/10.1176/appi.ajp.2013.12070950

Hembree-Kigin, T. L., & McNeil, C. B. (2013). *Parent–child interaction therapy*. New York, NY: Springer Science + Business Media.

Henry, C. S., Morris, A., & Harrist, A. W. (2015). Family resilience: Moving into the third wave. *Family Relations, 64*, 22–43. http://dx.doi.org/10.1111/fare.12106

Herrenkohl, T. I., Klika, J. B., Brown, E. C., Herrenkohl, R. C., & Leeb, R. T. (2013). Tests of the mitigating effects of caring and supportive relationships in the study of abusive disciplining over two generations. *Journal of Adolescent Health, 53*(Suppl. 4), S18–S24. http://dx.doi.org/10.1016/j.jadohealth.2013.04.009

Hertzman, C. (2012). Putting the concept of biological embedding in historical perspective. *Proceedings of the National Academy of Sciences, 109*(Suppl. 2), 17160–17167.

Hillis, S., Mercy, J., Amobi, A., & Kress, H. (2016). Global prevalence of past-year violence against children: A systematic review and minimum estimates. *Pediatrics, 137*, e20154079. http://dx.doi.org/10.1542/peds.2015-4079

Hillis, S. D., Anda, R. F., Dube, S. R., Felitti, V. J., Marchbanks, P. A., Macaluso, M., & Marks, J. S. (2010). The protective effect of family strengths in childhood against adolescent pregnancy and its long-term psychosocial consequences. *The Permanente Journal, 14*, 18–27. http://dx.doi.org/10.7812/TPP/10-028

Hillis, S. D., Anda, R. F., Dube, S. R., Felitti, V. J., Marchbanks, P. A., & Marks, J. S. (2004). The association between adverse childhood experiences and adolescent pregnancy, long-term psychosocial consequences, and fetal death. *Pediatrics, 113*, 320–327. http://dx.doi.org/10.1542/peds.113.2.320

Hillis, S. D., Anda, R. F., Felitti, V. J., & Marchbanks, P. A. (2001). Adverse childhood experiences and sexual risk behaviors in women: A retrospective cohort study. *Family Planning Perspectives, 33,* 206–211. http://dx.doi.org/10.2307/2673783

Hirshkowitz, M. Whiton, K. Albert, S. M., Alessi, C., Bruni, O., DonCarlos, L., . . . Adams Hillard, P. J. (2015). National Sleep Foundation's sleep time duration recommendations: Methodology and results summary. *Sleep Health, 1,* 40–43. http://dx.doi.org/10.1016/j.sleh.2014.12.010

Hodges, E. V., Boivin, M., Vitaro, F., & Bukowski, W. M. (1999). The power of friendship: Protection against an escalating cycle of peer victimization. *Developmental Psychology, 35,* 94–101. http://dx.doi.org/10.1037/0012-1649.35.1.94

Hoeve, M., Smeenk, W., Loeber, R., Stouthamer-Loeber, M., van der Laan, P. H., Gerris, J. R., & Dubas, J. S. (2007). Long-term effects of parenting and family characteristics on delinquency of male young adults. *European Journal of Criminology, 4,* 161–194. http://dx.doi.org/10.1177/1477370807074854

Hoff, E. (2003). The specificity of environmental influence: Socioeconomic status affects early vocabulary development via maternal speech. *Child Development, 74,* 1368–1378. http://dx.doi.org/10.1111/1467-8624.00612

Hoffman, K. T., Marvin, R. S., Cooper, G., & Powell, B. (2006). Changing toddlers' and preschoolers' attachment classifications: The Circle of Security intervention. *Journal of Consulting and Clinical Psychology, 74,* 1017–1026. http://dx.doi.org/10.1037/0022-006X.74.6.1017

Hoffman, M. L. (2001). *Empathy and moral development: Implications for caring and justice.* Cambridge, England: Cambridge University Press.

Holmes, C., Levy, M., Smith, A., Pinne, S., & Neese, P. (2015). A model for creating a supportive trauma-informed culture for children in preschool settings. *Journal of Child and Family Studies, 24,* 1650–1659. http://dx.doi.org/10.1007/s10826-014-9968-6

Holt-Lunstad, J. (2018). Why social relationships are important for physical health: A systems approach to understanding and modifying risk and protection. *Annual Review of Psychology, 69,* 437–458. http://dx.doi.org/10.1146/annurev-psych-122216-011902

Holt-Lunstad, J., Robles, T. F., & Sbarra, D. A. (2017). Advancing social connection as a public health priority in the United States. *American Psychologist, 72,* 517–530. http://dx.doi.org/10.1037/amp0000103

Holt-Lunstad, J., Smith, T. B., & Layton, J. B. (2010). Social relationships and mortality risk: A meta-analytic review. *PLoS Medicine, 7,* e1000316. http://dx.doi.org/10.1371/journal.pmed.1000316

Hölzel, B. K., Carmody, J., Evans, K. C., Hoge, E. A., Dusek, J. A., Morgan, L., . . . Lazar, S. W. (2010). Stress reduction correlates with structural changes in the amygdala. *Social Cognitive and Affective Neuroscience, 5,* 11–17. http://dx.doi.org/10.1093/scan/nsp034

Hölzel, B. K., Carmody, J., Vangel, M., Congleton, C., Yerramsetti, S. M., Gard, T., & Lazar, S. W. (2011). Mindfulness practice leads to increases in regional brain gray matter density. *Psychiatry Research: Neuroimaging, 191,* 36–43. http://dx.doi.org/10.1016/j.pscychresns.2010.08.006

Hudziak, J. J. (2018). ACEs and pregnancy: Time to support all expectant mothers. *Pediatrics, 141,* e20180232. http://dx.doi.org/10.1542/peds.2018-0232

Hughes, K., Bellis, M. A., Hardcastle, K. A., Sethi, D., Butchart, A., Mikton, C., . . . Dunne, M. P. (2017). The effect of multiple adverse childhood experiences on health: A systematic review and meta-analysis. *The Lancet. Public Health, 2,* e356–e366. http://dx.doi.org/10.1016/S2468-2667(17)30118-4

Hundeide, K. (1991). *Helping disadvantaged children: Psycho-social intervention and aid to disadvantaged children in third world countries.* London, England: Jessica Kingsley.

Hunt, T. K. A., Slack, K. S., & Berger, L. M. (2017). Adverse childhood experiences and behavioral problems in middle childhood. *Child Abuse & Neglect, 67,* 391–402. http://dx.doi.org/10.1016/j.chiabu.2016.11.005

Huston, A. C. (1991). *Children in poverty: Child development and public policy.* Cambridge, England: Cambridge University Press.

Jaffee, S. R., Hanscombe, K. B., Haworth, C. M. A., Davis, O. S. P., & Plomin, R. (2012). Chaotic homes and children's disruptive behavior: A longitudinal cross-lagged twin study. *Psychological Science, 23,* 643–650. http://dx.doi.org/10.1177/0956797611431693

Janoski, T., & Wilson, J. (1995). Pathways to voluntarism: Family socialization and status transmission models. *Social Forces, 74,* 271–292. http://dx.doi.org/10.2307/2580632

Jennings, K. D. (1993). Mastery motivation and the formation of self-concept from infancy through early childhood. In D. J. Messer (Ed.), *Mastery motivation in early childhood: Development, measurement and social processes* (pp. 36–54). London, England: Routledge. http://dx.doi.org/10.4324/9781315544250-3

Jespersen, J., Slocum, R., Hubbs-Tait, L., Love, J., Bosler, C., Hays-Grudo, J., & Morris, A. S. (2019, March). *Preliminary findings evaluating a group-based parenting program focused on responsive parenting, self-efficacy, and mindfulness.* Paper presented at the Society for Research on Child Development, Baltimore, MD.

Jimenez, M. E., Wade, R., Lin, Y., Morrow, L. M., & Reichman, N. E. (2016). Adverse experiences in early childhood and kindergarten outcomes. *Pediatrics, 137,* e20151839.

Johnson, S. B., Riis, J. L., & Noble, K. G. (2016). State of the art review: Poverty and the developing brain. *Pediatrics, 137,* e20153075. http://dx.doi.org/10.1542/peds.2015-3075

Jones, J., Reidy, M. C., Hargreaves, M., & Rog, D. (2017). Translating brain science research into community-level change. *Academic Pediatrics, 17*(Suppl. 7), S24–S25. http://dx.doi.org/10.1016/j.acap.2016.09.007

Jonsson, K., & Kjellgren, A. (2014). Curing the sick and creating supermen–how relaxation in flotation tanks is advertised on the Internet. *European Journal of Integrative Medicine, 6,* 601–609. http://dx.doi.org/10.1016/j.eujim.2014.05.005

Juonala, M., Pulkki-Råback, L., Elovainio, M., Hakulinen, C., Magnussen, C. G., Sabin, M. A., . . . Raitakari, O. T. (2016). Childhood psychosocial factors and coronary artery calcification in adulthood: The cardiovascular risk in young Finns study. *JAMA Pediatrics, 170,* 466–472. http://dx.doi.org/10.1001/jamapediatrics.2015.4121

Juster, R.-P., McEwen, B. S., & Lupien, S. J. (2010). Allostatic load biomarkers of chronic stress and impact on health and cognition. *Neuroscience & Biobehavioral Reviews, 35,* 2–16. http://dx.doi.org/10.1016/j.neubiorev.2009.10.002

Kabat-Zinn, J. (2005). *Coming to our senses: Healing ourselves and the world through mindfulness.* London, England: Hachette.

Keenan, J. T. (1992). Evaluation of a Big Brothers/Big Sisters program for children of alcoholics. *Dissertations available from ProQuest.* AAI9235161. https://repository.upenn.edu/dissertations/AAI9235161

Kehoe, C. E., Havighurst, S. S., & Harley, A. E. (2014). Tuning in to teens: Improving parent emotion socialization to reduce youth internalizing difficulties. *Social Development, 23,* 413–431. http://dx.doi.org/10.1111/sode.12060

Keller, R. T., Greenberg, N., Bobo, W. V., Roberts, P., Jones, N., & Orman, D. T. (2005). Soldier peer mentoring care and support: Bringing psychological awareness to the front. *Military Medicine, 170,* 355–361. http://dx.doi.org/10.7205/MILMED.170.5.355

Kelly-Irving, M., Lepage, B., Dedieu, D., Bartley, M., Blane, D., Grosclaude, P., . . . Delpierre, C. (2013). Adverse childhood experiences and premature all-cause mortality. *European Journal of Epidemiology, 28,* 721–734. http://dx.doi.org/10.1007/s10654-013-9832-9

Kerker, B. D., Storfer-Isser, A., Szilagyi, M., Stein, R. E., Garner, A. S., O'Connor, K. G., . . . Horwitz, S. M. (2016). Do pediatricians ask about adverse childhood experiences in pediatric primary care? *Academic Pediatrics, 16,* 154–160. http://dx.doi.org/10.1016/j.acap.2015.08.002

Kerker, B. D., Zhang, J., Nadeem, E., Stein, R. E., Hurlburt, M. S., Heneghan, A., . . . McCue Horwitz, S. (2015). Adverse childhood experiences and mental health, chronic medical conditions, and development in young children. *Academic Pediatrics, 15,* 510–517. http://dx.doi.org/10.1016/j.acap.2015.05.005

Kim, P., Leckman, J. F., Mayes, L. C., Feldman, R., Wang, X., & Swain, J. E. (2010). The plasticity of human maternal brain: Longitudinal changes in brain anatomy during the early postpartum period. *Behavioral Neuroscience, 124,* 695–700. http://dx.doi.org/10.1037/a0020884

Kimbrough, E., Magyari, T., Langenberg, P., Chesney, M., & Berman, B. (2010). Mindfulness intervention for child abuse survivors. *Journal of Clinical Psychology, 66,* 17–33.

Kinniburgh, K. J., Blaustein, M., Spinazzola, J., & van der Kolk, B. A. (2017). Attachment, self-regulation, and competency: A comprehensive intervention framework for children with complex trauma. *Psychiatric Annals, 35,* 424–430. http://dx.doi.org/10.3928/00485713-20050501-08

Kitzman, H. J., Olds, D. L., Cole, R. E., Hanks, C. A., Anson, E. A., Arcoleo, K. J., . . . Holmberg, J. R. (2010). Enduring effects of prenatal and infancy home visiting by nurses on children: Follow-up of a randomized trial among children at age 12 years. *Archives of Pediatrics & Adolescent Medicine, 164,* 412–418. http://dx.doi.org/10.1001/archpediatrics.2010.76

Kleinman, R. E., Murphy, J. M., Little, M., Pagano, M., Wehler, C. A., Regal, K., & Jellinek, M. S. (1998). Hunger in children in the United States: Potential behavioral and emotional correlates. *Pediatrics, 101,* e3. http://dx.doi.org/10.1542/peds.101.1.e3

Klengel, T., Dias, B. G., & Ressler, K. J. (2016). Models of intergenerational and transgenerational transmission of risk for psychopathology in mice. *Neuropsychopharmacology, 41,* 219–231. http://dx.doi.org/10.1038/npp.2015.249

Kluetsch, R. C., Ros, T., Théberge, J., Frewen, P. A., Calhoun, V. D., Schmahl, C., . . . Lanius, R. A. (2014). Plastic modulation of PTSD resting-state networks and subjective wellbeing by EEG neurofeedback. *Acta Psychiatrica Scandinavica, 130,* 123–136. http://dx.doi.org/10.1111/acps.12229

Ko, S. J., Ford, J. D., Kassam-Adams, N., Berkowitz, S. J., Wilson, C., Wong, M., . . . Layne, C. M. (2008). Creating trauma-informed systems: Child welfare, education, first responders, health care, juvenile justice. *Professional Psychology: Research and Practice, 39,* 396–404. http://dx.doi.org/10.1037/0735-7028.39.4.396

Korenman, S., Miller, J. E., & Sjaastad, J. E. (1995). Long-term poverty and child development in the United States: Results from the NLSY. *Children and Youth Services Review, 17,* 127–155. http://dx.doi.org/10.1016/0190-7409(95)00006-X

Korotana, L. M., Dobson, K. S., Pusch, D., & Josephson, T. (2016). A review of primary care interventions to improve health outcomes in adult survivors of adverse childhood experiences. *Clinical Psychology Review, 46,* 59–90. http://dx.doi.org/10.1016/j.cpr.2016.04.007

Koss, M. P., Yuan, N. P., Dightman, D., Prince, R. J., Polacca, M., Sanderson, B., & Goldman, D. (2003). Adverse childhood exposures and alcohol dependence among seven Native American tribes. *American Journal of Preventive Medicine, 25,* 238–244. http://dx.doi.org/10.1016/S0749-3797(03)00195-8

Krugers, H. J., Arp, J. M., Xiong, H., Kanatsou, S., Lesuis, S. L., Korosi, A., . . . Lucassen, P. J. (2017). Early life adversity: Lasting consequences for emotional learning. *Neurobiology of Stress, 6,* 14–21. http://dx.doi.org/10.1016/j.ynstr.2016.11.005

Kuh, D. (2019). A life course approach to healthy ageing. In J.-P. Michel (Ed.), *Prevention of chronic diseases and age-related disability* (pp. 1–9). Cham, Switzerland: Springer. http://dx.doi.org/10.1007/978-3-319-96529-1_1

Kuhn, T. S. (1963). *The structure of scientific revolutions* (Vol. 2). Chicago, IL: University of Chicago Press.

Lafortune, L., Martin, S., Kelly, S., Kuhn, I., Remes, O., Cowan, A., & Brayne, C. (2016). Behavioural risk factors in mid-life associated with successful ageing, disability, dementia and frailty in later life: A rapid systematic review. *PLoS ONE, 11,* e0144405. http://dx.doi.org/10.1371/journal.pone.0144405

Laird, R. D., Criss, M. M., Pettit, G. S., Dodge, K. A., & Bates, J. E. (2008). Parents' monitoring knowledge attenuates the link between antisocial friends and adolescent delinquent behavior. *Journal of Abnormal Child Psychology, 36,* 299–310. http://dx.doi.org/10.1007/s10802-007-9178-4

Lakes, K. D., & Hoyt, W. T. (2004). Promoting self-regulation through school-based martial arts training. *Journal of Applied Developmental Psychology, 25,* 283–302. http://dx.doi.org/10.1016/j.appdev.2004.04.002

Lamborn, S. D., Mounts, N. S., Steinberg, L., & Dornbusch, S. M. (1991). Patterns of competence and adjustment among adolescents from authoritative, authoritarian, indulgent, and neglectful families. *Child Development, 62,* 1049–1065. http://dx.doi.org/10.2307/1131151

Lee, G. Y., & Kisilevsky, B. S. (2014). Fetuses respond to father's voice but prefer mother's voice after birth. *Developmental Psychobiology, 56,* 1–11. http://dx.doi.org/10.1002/dev.21084

Lee, S., Aos, S., Drake, E., Pennucci, A., Miller, M., & Anderson, L. (2012). *Return on investment: Evidence-based options to improve statewide outcomes.* Olympia: Washington State Institute for Public Policy.

Lehman, B. J., Taylor, S. E., Kiefe, C. I., & Seeman, T. E. (2009). Relationship of early life stress and psychological functioning to blood pressure in the CARDIA study. *Health Psychology, 28,* 338–346. http://dx.doi.org/10.1037/a0013785

Leitch, L. (2017). Action steps using ACEs and trauma-informed care: A resilience model. *Health & Justice, 5,* Article 5. http://dx.doi.org/10.1186/s40352-017-0050-5

LeJeune, B., Beebe, D., Noll, J., Kenealy, L., Isquith, P., & Gioia, G. (2010). Psychometric support for an abbreviated version of the behavior rating inventory of executive function (brief) parent form. *Child Neuropsychology, 16,* 182–201. http://dx.doi.org/10.1080/09297040903352556

Lerner, R. M., Wang, J., Chase, P. A., Gutierrez, A. S., Harris, E. M., Rubin, R. O., & Yalin, C. (2014). Using relational developmental systems theory to link program goals, activities, and outcomes: The sample case of the 4-H Study of Positive Youth Development. *New Directions for Youth Development: Theory, Practice, Research, 2014*(144), 17–30. http://dx.doi.org/10.1002/yd.20110

Lester, B. M., Conradt, E., & Marsit, C. (2016). Introduction to the special section on epigenetics. *Child Development, 87,* 29–37. http://dx.doi.org/10.1111/cdev.12489

Lewis-Morrarty, E., Dozier, M., Bernard, K., Terracciano, S. M., & Moore, S. V. (2012). Cognitive flexibility and theory of mind outcomes among foster children: Preschool follow-up results of a randomized clinical trial. *Journal of Adolescent Health, 51*(Suppl. 2), S17–S22. http://dx.doi.org/10.1016/j.jadohealth.2012.05.005

Lieberman, A. F., Ghosh Ippen, C., & Van Horn, P. (2006). Child-parent psycho-therapy: 6-month follow-up of a randomized controlled trial. *Journal of the American Academy of Child & Adolescent Psychiatry, 45,* 913–918. http://dx.doi.org/10.1097/01.chi.0000222784.03735.92

Lieberman, A. F., Padrón, E., Van Horn, P., & Harris, W. W. (2005). Angels in the nursery: The intergenerational transmission of benevolent parental influences. *Infant Mental Health Journal, 26,* 504–520. http://dx.doi.org/10.1002/imhj.20071

Lindsey, E. W., & Caldera, Y. M. (2015). Shared affect and dyadic synchrony among secure and insecure parent–toddler dyads. *Infant and Child Development, 24,* 394–413. http://dx.doi.org/10.1002/icd.1893

Liu, D., Diorio, J., Tannenbaum, B., Caldji, C., Francis, D., Freedman, A., . . . Meaney, M. J. (1997). Maternal care, hippocampal glucocorticoid receptors, and hypothalamic-pituitary-adrenal responses to stress. *Science, 277*(5332), 1659–1662. http://dx.doi.org/10.1126/science.277.5332.1659

Lleras, C. (2008). Do skills and behaviors in high school matter? The contribution of noncognitive factors in explaining differences in educational attainment and earnings. *Social Science Research, 37,* 888–902. http://dx.doi.org/10.1016/j.ssresearch.2008.03.004

Lomanowska, A. M., Boivin, M., Hertzman, C., & Fleming, A. S. (2017). Parent-ing begets parenting: A neurobiological perspective on early adversity and the transmission of parenting styles across generations. *Neuroscience, 342,* 120–139. http://dx.doi.org/10.1016/j.neuroscience.2015.09.029

Lu, H., Song, Y., Xu, M., Wang, X., Li, X., & Liu, J. (2014). The brain structure correlates of individual differences in trait mindfulness: A voxel-based morphometry study. *Neuroscience, 272,* 21–28. http://dx.doi.org/10.1016/j.neuroscience.2014.04.051

Luby, J. L., Barch, D., Whalen, D., Tillman, R., & Belden, A. (2017). Association between early life adversity and risk for poor emotional and physical health in adolescence: A putative mechanistic neurodevelopmental pathway. *JAMA Pediatrics, 171,* 1168–1175. http://dx.doi.org/10.1001/jamapediatrics.2017.3009

Luby, J. L., Belden, A., Botteron, K., Marrus, N., Harms, M. P., Babb, C., . . . Barch, D. (2013). The effects of poverty on childhood brain development: The mediating effect of caregiving and stressful life events. *JAMA Pediatrics, 167,* 1135–1142. http://dx.doi.org/10.1001/jamapediatrics.2013.3139

Luders, E., Narr, K. L., Hamilton, L. S., Phillips, O. R., Thompson, P. M., Valle, J. S., . . . Levitt, J. G. (2009). Decreased callosal thickness in attention-deficit/hyperactivity disorder. *Biological Psychiatry, 65,* 84–88. http://dx.doi.org/10.1016/j.biopsych.2008.08.027

Luders, E., Toga, A. W., Lepore, N., & Gaser, C. (2009). The underlying anatomical correlates of long-term meditation: Larger hippocampal and frontal volumes of gray matter. *NeuroImage, 45,* 672–678. http://dx.doi.org/10.1016/j.neuroimage.2008.12.061

Lupien, S. J., King, S., Meaney, M. J., & McEwen, B. S. (2001). Can poverty get under your skin? basal cortisol levels and cognitive function in children from low and high socioeconomic status. *Development and Psychopathology, 13,* 653–676. http://dx.doi.org/10.1017/S0954579401003133

Luthar, S. S. (2015). Resilience in development: A synthesis of research across five decades. In D. Cicchetti (Ed.), *Developmental psychopathology: Vol. 3. Risk, disorder, and adaptation* (pp. 739–795). Hoboken, NJ: Wiley.

Luthar, S. S., Cicchetti, D., & Becker, B. (2000). The construct of resilience: A critical evaluation and guidelines for future work. *Child Development, 71,* 543–562. http://dx.doi.org/10.1111/1467-8624.00164

Luthar, S. S., & Ciciolla, L. (2015). Who mothers mommy? Factors that contribute to mothers' well-being. *Developmental Psychology, 51,* 1812–1823. http://dx.doi.org/10.1037/dev0000051

Luthar, S. S., Curlee, A., Tye, S. J., Engelman, J. C., & Stonnington, C. M. (2017). Fostering resilience among mothers under stress: "Authentic connections groups" for medical professionals. *Women's Health Issues, 27,* 382–390. http://dx.doi.org/10.1016/j.whi.2017.02.007

Luthar, S. S., & Eisenberg, N. (2017). Resilient adaptation among at-risk children: Harnessing science toward maximizing salutary environments. *Child Development, 88,* 337–349. http://dx.doi.org/10.1111/cdev.12737

Luthar, S. S., Sawyer, J. A., & Brown, P. J. (2006). Conceptual issues in studies of resilience: Past, present, and future research. *Annals of the New York Academy of Sciences, 1094,* 105–115. http://dx.doi.org/10.1196/annals.1376.009

Maccoby, E., & Martin, J. (1983). *Handbook of child psychology: Vol. 4. Socialization in the context of the family* (pp. 1–102). New York, NY: Wiley.

Macy, R. J., Jones, E., Graham, L. M., & Roach, L. (2018). Yoga for trauma and related mental health problems: A meta-review with clinical and service recommendations. *Trauma, Violence, & Abuse, 19,* 35–57. http://dx.doi.org/10.1177/1524838015620834

Magon, N., & Kalra, S. (2011). The orgasmic history of oxytocin: Love, lust, and labor. *Indian Journal of Endocrinology and Metabolism, 15*(Suppl. 3), S156–S161. http://dx.doi.org/10.4103/2230-8210.84851

Mahoney, J. L. (2000). School extracurricular activity participation as a moderator in the development of antisocial patterns. *Child Development, 71,* 502–516. http://dx.doi.org/10.1111/1467-8624.00160

Main, M., Kaplan, N., & Cassidy, J. (1985). Security in infancy, childhood, and adulthood: A move to the level of representation. *Monographs of the Society for Research in Child Development, 50,* 66–104. http://dx.doi.org/10.2307/3333827

Main, M., & Solomon, J. (1986). Discovery of an insecure-disorganized/disoriented attachment pattern. In T. B. Brazelton & M. W. Yogman (Eds.), *Affective development in infancy* (pp. 95–124). Westport, CT: Ablex.

Maniam, J., Antoniadis, C., & Morris, M. J. (2014). Early-life stress, HPA axis adaptation, and mechanisms contributing to later health outcomes. *Frontiers in Endocrinology, 5,* 73. http://dx.doi.org/10.3389/fendo.2014.00073

Marans, S., Berkowitz, S. J., & Cohen, D. J. (1998). Police and mental health professionals. Collaborative responses to the impact of violence on children and families. *Child and Adolescent Psychiatric Clinics of North America*, 7, 635–651. http://dx.doi.org/10.1016/S1056-4993(18)30233-5

Maras, D., Flament, M. F., Murray, M., Buchholz, A., Henderson, K. A., Obeid, N., & Goldfield, G. S. (2015). Screen time is associated with depression and anxiety in Canadian youth. *Preventive Medicine*, *73*, 133–138. http://dx.doi.org/10.1016/j.ypmed.2015.01.029

Marcia, J. E. (1966). Development and validation of ego-identity status. *Journal of Personality and Social Psychology*, *3*, 551–558. http://dx.doi.org/10.1037/h0023281

Marcia, J. E. (1980). *Handbook of adolescent psychology: Vols. 159–187. Ego identity development*. New York, NY: Wiley.

Marmot, M., & Allen, J. J. (2014). Social determinants of health equity. *American Journal of Public Health*, *104*(Suppl. 4), S517–S519. http://dx.doi.org/10.2105/AJPH.2014.302200

Marsac, M. L., Kassam-Adams, N., Hildenbrand, A. K., Nicholls, E., Winston, F. K., Leff, S. S., & Fein, J. (2016). Implementing a trauma-informed approach in pediatric health care networks. *JAMA Pediatrics*, *170*, 70–77. http://dx.doi.org/10.1001/jamapediatrics.2015.2206

Marvin, R., Cooper, G., Hoffman, K., & Powell, B. (2002). The Circle of Security project: Attachment-based intervention with caregiver-pre-school child dyads. *Attachment & Human Development*, *4*, 107–124. http://dx.doi.org/10.1080/14616730252982491

Maslow, A. H. (1943). A theory of human motivation. *Psychological Review*, *50*, 370–396. http://dx.doi.org/10.1037/h0054346

Masten, A. S. (2001). Ordinary magic. Resilience processes in development. *American Psychologist*, *56*, 227–238. http://dx.doi.org/10.1037/0003-066X.56.3.227

Masten, A. S. (2007). Resilience in developing systems: Progress and promise as the fourth wave rises. *Development and Psychopathology*, *19*, 921–930. http://dx.doi.org/10.1017/S0954579407000442

Masten, A. S. (2014). Global perspectives on resilience in children and youth. *Child Development*, *85*, 6–20. http://dx.doi.org/10.1111/cdev.12205

Masten, A. S. (2015). *Ordinary magic: Resilience in development*. New York, NY: Guilford Press.

Masten, A. S., Best, K. M., & Garmezy, N. (1990). Resilience and development: Contributions from the study of children who overcome adversity. *Development and Psychopathology*, *2*, 425–444. http://dx.doi.org/10.1017/S0954579400005812

Masten, A. S., & Cicchetti, D. (2010). Developmental cascades. *Development and Psychopathology*, *22*, 491–495. http://dx.doi.org/10.1017/S0954579410000222

Masten, A. S., & Coatsworth, J. D. (1998). The development of competence in favorable and unfavorable environments. Lessons from research on successful children. *American Psychologist*, *53*, 205–220. http://dx.doi.org/10.1037/0003-066X.53.2.205

McCall, R. B. (1981). Nature-nurture and the two realms of development: A proposed integration with respect to mental development. *Child Development*, *52*, 1–12. http://dx.doi.org/10.2307/1129210

McConnico, N., Boynton-Jarrett, R., Bailey, C., & Nandi, M. (2016). A framework for trauma-sensitive schools. *Zero to Three*, *36*, 36–44.

McEwen, B. S. (1998). Protective and damaging effects of stress mediators. *The New England Journal of Medicine*, *338*, 171–179. http://dx.doi.org/10.1056/NEJM199801153380307

McEwen, B. S. (2012). Brain on stress: How the social environment gets under the skin. *Proceedings of the National Academy of Sciences of the United States of America, 109*(Suppl. 2), 17180–17185. http://dx.doi.org/10.1073/pnas.1121254109

McGowan, P. O., Sasaki, A., D'Alessio, A. C., Dymov, S., Labonté, B., Szyf, M., . . . Meaney, M. J. (2009). Epigenetic regulation of the glucocorticoid receptor in human brain associates with childhood abuse. *Nature Neuroscience, 12*, 342–348. http://dx.doi.org/10.1038/nn.2270

McIsaac, H. K., & Eich, E. (2004). Vantage point in traumatic memory. *Psychological Science, 15*, 248–253. http://dx.doi.org/10.1111/j.0956-7976.2004.00660.x

McKelvey, L. M., Edge, N. C., Mesman, G. R., Whiteside-Mansell, L., & Bradley, R. H. (2018). Adverse experiences in infancy and toddlerhood: Relations to adaptive behavior and academic status in middle childhood. *Child Abuse & Neglect, 82*, 168–177. http://dx.doi.org/10.1016/j.chiabu.2018.05.026

McLaughlin, K. A., & Sheridan, M. A. (2016). Beyond cumulative risk: A dimensional approach to childhood adversity. *Current Directions in Psychological Science, 25*, 239–245. http://dx.doi.org/10.1177/0963721416655883

McLaughlin, K. A., Sheridan, M. A., & Lambert, H. K. (2014). Childhood adversity and neural development: Deprivation and threat as distinct dimensions of early experience. *Neuroscience and Biobehavioral Reviews, 47*, 578–591. http://dx.doi.org/10.1016/j.neubiorev.2014.10.012

McLeod, J. D., & Shanahan, M. J. (1996). Trajectories of poverty and children's mental health. *Journal of Health and Social Behavior, 37*, 207–220. http://dx.doi.org/10.2307/2137292

McLoyd, V. C. (1998). Socioeconomic disadvantage and child development. *American Psychologist, 53*, 185–204. http://dx.doi.org/10.1037/0003-066X.53.2.185

Mehta, M. A., Gore-Langton, E., Golembo, N., Colvert, E., Williams, S. C., & Sonuga-Barke, E. (2010). Hyporesponsive reward anticipation in the basal ganglia following severe institutional deprivation early in life. *Journal of Cognitive Neuroscience, 22*, 2316–2325. http://dx.doi.org/10.1162/jocn.2009.21394

Melchior, M., Moffitt, T. E., Milne, B. J., Poulton, R., & Caspi, A. (2007). Why do children from socioeconomically disadvantaged families suffer from poor health when they reach adulthood? A life-course study. *American Journal of Epidemiology, 166*, 966–974. http://dx.doi.org/10.1093/aje/kwm155

Mendelson, T., Tandon, S. D., O'Brennan, L., Leaf, P. J., & Ialongo, N. S. (2015). Brief report: Moving prevention into schools: The impact of a trauma-informed school-based intervention. *Journal of Adolescence, 43*, 142–147. http://dx.doi.org/10.1016/j.adolescence.2015.05.017

Merrick, M. T., Ford, D. C., Ports, K. A., & Guinn, A. S. (2018). Prevalence of adverse childhood experiences from the 2011–2014 Behavioral Risk Factor Surveillance System in 23 states. *JAMA Pediatrics, 172*, 1038–1044. http://dx.doi.org/10.1001/jamapediatrics.2018.2537

Mersky, J. P., Janczewski, C. E., & Topitzes, J. (2017). Rethinking the measurement of adversity. *Child Maltreatment, 22*, 58–68. http://dx.doi.org/10.1177/1077559516679513

Messer, C. M., Shriver, T. E., & Beamon, K. K. (2017). Official frames and the Tulsa race riot of 1921: The struggle for reparations. *Sociology of Race and Ethnicity, 4*, 386–399.

Milkman, H. B. (2017, December 6). Iceland succeeds at reversing teenage substance abuse: The U.S. should follow suit. *Huffington Post.* Retrieved from https://www.

huffingtonpost.com/harvey-b-milkman-phd/iceland-succeeds-at-rever_b_
9892758.html

Miller, G. E., Chen, E., & Parker, K. J. (2011). Psychological stress in childhood
and susceptibility to the chronic diseases of aging: Moving toward a model of
behavioral and biological mechanisms. *Psychological Bulletin, 137,* 959–997.
http://dx.doi.org/10.1037/a0024768

Minkler, M., & Wallerstein, N. (2011). *Community-based participatory research for
health: From process to outcomes.* New York, NY: Wiley.

Misaki, M., Phillips, R., Zotev, V., Wong, C.-K., Wurfel, B. E., Krueger, F., . . .
Bodurka, J. (2018). Real-time fMRI amygdala neurofeedback positive emotional
training normalized resting-state functional connectivity in combat veterans
with and without PTSD: A connectome-wide investigation. *NeuroImage: Clinical,
20,* 543–555. http://dx.doi.org/10.1016/j.nicl.2018.08.025

Mitchell, K. S., Dick, A. M., DiMartino, D. M., Smith, B. N., Niles, B., Koenen,
K. C., & Street, A. (2014). A pilot study of a randomized controlled trial of yoga
as an intervention for PTSD symptoms in women. *Journal of Traumatic Stress, 27,*
121–128. http://dx.doi.org/10.1002/jts.21903

Moffitt, T. E. (2013). Childhood exposure to violence and lifelong health: Clinical
intervention science and stress-biology research join forces. *Development and
Psychopathology, 25,* 1619–1634. http://dx.doi.org/10.1017/S0954579413000801

Montirosso, R., Provenzi, L., Fumagalli, M., Sirgiovanni, I., Giorda, R., Pozzoli, U., . . .
Borgatti, R. (2016). Serotonin transporter gene (SLC6A4) methylation associates with neonatal intensive care unit stay and 3-month-old temperament
in preterm infants. *Child Development, 87,* 38–48. http://dx.doi.org/10.1111/
cdev.12492

Moore, C. W., & Allen, J. P. (1996). The effects of volunteering on the young
volunteer. *The Journal of Primary Prevention, 17,* 231–258. http://dx.doi.org/
10.1007/BF02248794

Moore, K. S. (2013). A systematic review on the neural effects of music on
emotion regulation: Implications for music therapy practice. *Journal of Music
Therapy, 50,* 198–242. http://dx.doi.org/10.1093/jmt/50.3.198

Morris, A. S., Criss, M. M., Silk, J. S., & Houltberg, B. J. (2017). The impact of
parenting on emotion regulation during childhood and adolescence. *Child
Development Perspectives, 11,* 233–238. http://dx.doi.org/10.1111/cdep.12238

Morris, A. S., Cui, L., & Steinberg, L. (2013). Parenting research and themes:
What we have learned and where to go next. In R. E. Larzelere, A. S. Morris, &
A. W. Harrist (Eds.), *Authoritative parenting: Synthesizing nurturance and discipline
for optimal child development* (pp. 35–58). Washington, DC: American Psychological
Association. http://dx.doi.org/10.1037/13948-003

Morris, A. S., Hays-Grudo, J., Treat, A. E., Williamson, A. C., Huffer, A., Roblyer,
M. Z., & Staton, J. (2015, March). *Assessing resilience using the protective and compensatory experiences survey (PACEs).* Paper presented at the Society for Research
in Child Development, Philadelphia, PA.

Morris, A. S., Hays-Grudo, J., Williamson, A. C., Treat, A. E., Huffer, A., & Slocum, R.
(2016). *Aces and paces: The development of the protective and compensatory experiences
survey (paces).* Paper presented at the World Congress of the World Association
for Infant Mental Health, Prague, Czech Republic.

Morris, A. S., Robinson, L. R., Hays-Grudo, J., Claussen, A. H., Hartwig, S. A., &
Treat, A. E. (2017). Targeting parenting in early childhood: A public health

approach to improve outcomes for children living in poverty. *Child Development*, *88*, 388–397. http://dx.doi.org/10.1111/cdev.12743

Morris, A. S., Silk, J. S., Steinberg, L., Myers, S. S., & Robinson, L. R. (2007). The role of the family context in the development of emotion regulation. *Social Development, 16*, 361–388. http://dx.doi.org/10.1111/j.1467-9507.2007.00389.x

Morris, A. S., Squeglia, L. M., Jacobus, J., & Silk, J. S. (2018). Adolescent brain development: Implications for understanding risk and resilience processes through neuroimaging research. *Journal of Research on Adolescence, 28*, 4–9. http://dx.doi.org/10.1111/jora.12379

Morris, A. S., Treat, A. E., Hays-Grudo, J., Chesher, T., Williamson, A. C., & Mendez, J. (2018). Integrating research and theory on early relationships to guide intervention and prevention. In A. S. Morris & A. C. Williams (Eds.), *Building early social and emotional relationships with infants and toddlers* (pp. 1–26). Cham, Switzerland: Springer. http://dx.doi.org/10.1007/978-3-030-03110-7_1

Moulson, M. C., Fox, N. A., Zeanah, C. H., & Nelson, C. A. (2009). Early adverse experiences and the neurobiology of facial emotion processing. *Developmental Psychology, 45*, 17–30. http://dx.doi.org/10.1037/a0014035

Munson, M. R., & McMillen, J. C. (2009). Natural mentoring and psychosocial outcomes among older youth transitioning from foster care [erratum: http://dx.doi.org/10.1038/nn0510-649e]. *Children and Youth Services Review, 31*, 104–111. http://dx.doi.org/10.1016/j.childyouth.2008.06.003

Murgatroyd, C., Patchev, A. V., Wu, Y., Micale, V., Bockmühl, Y., Fischer, D., . . . Spengler, D. (2009). Dynamic DNA methylation programs persistent adverse effects of early-life stress. *Nature Neuroscience, 12*, 1559–1566. http://dx.doi.org/10.1038/nn.2436

Murphey, D., & Bartlett, J. D. (2019). Childhood adversity screenings are just one part of an effective policy response to childhood trauma. *Child Trends*. Retrieved from https://www.childtrends.org/publications/childhood-adversity-screenings-are-just-one-part-of-an-effective-policy-response-to-childhood-trauma

Nagasawa, M., Kikusui, T., Onaka, T., & Ohta, M. (2009). Dog's gaze at its owner increases owner's urinary oxytocin during social interaction. *Hormones and Behavior, 55*, 434–441. http://dx.doi.org/10.1016/j.yhbeh.2008.12.002

Nakazawa, D. J. (2015). *Childhood disrupted: How your biography becomes your biology, and how you can heal.* New York, NY: Simon & Schuster.

Narayan, A. J., Ippen, C. G., Harris, W. W., & Lieberman, A. F. (2019). Protective factors that buffer against the intergenerational transmission of trauma from mothers to young children: A replication study of angels in the nursery. *Development and Psychopathology, 31*, 173–187. http://dx.doi.org/10.1017/S0954579418001530

Narayan, A. J., Kalstabakken, A. W., Labella, M. H., Nerenberg, L. S., Monn, A. R., & Masten, A. S. (2017). Intergenerational continuity of adverse childhood experiences in homeless families: Unpacking exposure to maltreatment versus family dysfunction. *American Journal of Orthopsychiatry, 87*, 3–14. http://dx.doi.org/10.1037/ort0000133

National Academies of Sciences, Engineering, and Medicine. (2019a). *The promise of adolescence: Realizing opportunity for all youth.* Washington, DC: National Academies Press. http://dx.doi.org/10.17226/25388

National Academies of Sciences, Engineering, and Medicine. (2019b). *Vibrant and healthy kids: Aligning science, practice, and policy to advance health equity.* Washington, DC: National Academies Press. http://dx.doi.org/10.17226/25466

National Center for Children in Poverty. (2018). *Child poverty.* Retrieved from http://www.nccp.org/topics/childpoverty.html

National Center for Complementary and Integrative Health. (2018). *Yoga: What you need to know.* Retrieved from https://nccih.nih.gov/health/yoga/introduction.htm#hed1

National Child Traumatic Stress Network. (2003). *Definition of medical traumatic stress.* Paper presented at the Medical Traumatic Stress Working Group Meeting, Philadelphia, PA.

National Institute on Minority Health and Health Disparities. (2018). *Community-based participatory research guidelines* (NIH Guide No. RFA-MD-15-0101). Retrieved from https://www.nimhd.nih.gov/programs/extramural/community-based-participatory.html#goals

Naumova, O. Y., Hein, S., Suderman, M., Barbot, B., Lee, M., Raefski, A., . . . Grigorenko, E. L. (2016). Epigenetic patterns modulate the connection between developmental dynamics of parenting and offspring psychosocial adjustment. *Child Development, 87,* 98–110. http://dx.doi.org/10.1111/cdev.12485

Nelson, C. A., III. (2013). Biological embedding of early life adversity. *JAMA Pediatrics, 167,* 1098–1100. http://dx.doi.org/10.1001/jamapediatrics.2013.3768

Nelson, C. A., III. (2017). Hazards to early development: The biological embedding of early life adversity. *Neuron, 96,* 262–266. http://dx.doi.org/10.1016/j.neuron.2017.09.027

Nelson, C. A., III. (2018). Hazards to early development: The biological embedding of early life adversity. *Biological Psychiatry, 83*(Suppl.), S7–S8. http://dx.doi.org/10.1016/j.biopsych.2018.02.036

Nelson, C. A., Fox, N. A., & Zeanah, C. H. (2014). *Romania's abandoned children: Deprivation, brain development, and the struggle for recovery.* Cambridge, MA: Harvard University Press. http://dx.doi.org/10.4159/harvard.9780674726079

Nemeroff, C. B. (2016). Paradise lost: The neurobiological and clinical consequences of child abuse and neglect. *Neuron, 89,* 892–909. http://dx.doi.org/10.1016/j.neuron.2016.01.019

Nemoda, Z., Massart, R., Suderman, M., Hallett, M., Li, T., Coote, M., . . . Szyf, M. (2015). Maternal depression is associated with DNA methylation changes in cord blood T lymphocytes and adult hippocampi. *Translational Psychiatry, 5,* e545. http://dx.doi.org/10.1038/tp.2015.32

Neville, H. J., Stevens, C., Pakulak, E., Bell, T. A., Fanning, J., Klein, S., & Isbell, E. (2013). Family-based training program improves brain function, cognition, and behavior in lower socioeconomic status preschoolers. *Proceedings of the National Academy of Sciences of the United States of America, 110,* 12138–12143. http://dx.doi.org/10.1073/pnas.1304437110

Nicholson, A. A., Rabellino, D., Densmore, M., Frewen, P. A., Paret, C., Kluetsch, R., . . . Lanius, R. A. (2017). The neurobiology of emotion regulation in posttraumatic stress disorder: Amygdala downregulation via real-time fMRI neurofeedback. *Human Brain Mapping, 38,* 541–560. http://dx.doi.org/10.1002/hbm.23402

Noble, K. G., Houston, S. M., Brito, N. H., Bartsch, H., Kan, E., Kuperman, J. M., . . . Sowell, E. R. (2015). Family income, parental education and brain structure in children and adolescents. *Nature Neuroscience, 18,* 773–778. http://dx.doi.org/10.1038/nn.3983

Noble, K. G., Wolmetz, M. E., Ochs, L. G., Farah, M. J., & McCandliss, B. D. (2006). Brain–behavior relationships in reading acquisition are modulated by socioeconomic factors. *Developmental Science, 9*, 642–654. http://dx.doi.org/10.1111/j.1467-7687.2006.00542.x

Nusslock, R., & Miller, G. E. (2016). Early-life adversity and physical and emotional health across the lifespan: A neuroimmune network hypothesis. *Biological Psychiatry, 80*, 23–32. http://dx.doi.org/10.1016/j.biopsych.2015.05.017

Oberlander, T. F., Weinberg, J., Papsdorf, M., Grunau, R., Misri, S., & Devlin, A. M. (2008). Prenatal exposure to maternal depression, neonatal methylation of human glucocorticoid receptor gene (NR3C1) and infant cortisol stress responses. *Epigenetics, 3*, 97–106. http://dx.doi.org/10.4161/epi.3.2.6034

Olds, D. L. (2006). The nurse–family partnership: An evidence-based preventive intervention. *Infant Mental Health Journal, 27*, 5–25. http://dx.doi.org/10.1002/imhj.20077

Olds, D. L., Kitzman, H., Cole, R., Robinson, J., Sidora, K., Luckey, D. W., . . . Holmberg, J. (2004). Effects of nurse home-visiting on maternal life course and child development: Age 6 follow-up results of a randomized trial. *Pediatrics, 114*, 1550–1559. http://dx.doi.org/10.1542/peds.2004-0962

Olds, D. L., Kitzman, H., Knudtson, M. D., Anson, E., Smith, J. A., & Cole, R. (2014). Effect of home visiting by nurses on maternal and child mortality: Results of a 2-decade follow-up of a randomized clinical trial. *JAMA Pediatrics, 168*, 800–806. http://dx.doi.org/10.1001/jamapediatrics.2014.472

Oral, R., Ramirez, M., Coohey, C., Nakada, S., Walz, A., Kuntz, A., . . . Peek-Asa, C. (2016). Adverse childhood experiences and trauma informed care: The future of health care. *Pediatric Research, 79*, 227–233. http://dx.doi.org/10.1038/pr.2015.197

Origua Rios, S., Marks, J., Estevan, I., & Barnett, L. M. (2018). Health benefits of hard martial arts in adults: A systematic review. *Journal of Sports Sciences, 36*, 1614–1622. http://dx.doi.org/10.1080/02640414.2017.1406297

Oshri, A., Lucier-Greer, M., O'Neal, C. W., Arnold, A. L., Mancini, J. A., & Ford, J. L. (2015). Adverse childhood experiences, family functioning, and resilience in military families: A pattern-based approach. *Family Relations, 64*, 44–63. http://dx.doi.org/10.1111/fare.12108

Overstreet, S., & Chafouleas, S. M. (2016). Trauma-informed schools: Introduction to the special issue. *School Mental Health, 8*, 1–6.

Painter, R. C., Osmond, C., Gluckman, P., Hanson, M., Phillips, D. I., & Roseboom, T. J. (2008). Transgenerational effects of prenatal exposure to the Dutch famine on neonatal adiposity and health in later life. *BJOG, 115*, 1243–1249. http://dx.doi.org/10.1111/j.1471-0528.2008.01822.x

Papale, L. A., Seltzer, L. J., Madrid, A., Pollak, S. D., & Alisch, R. S. (2018). Differentially methylated genes in saliva are linked to childhood stress. *Scientific Reports, 8*, 10785. http://dx.doi.org/10.1038/s41598-018-29107-0

Parker, S. W., Nelson, C. A., & the Bucharest Early Intervention Project Core Group. (2005a). An event-related potential study of the impact of institutional rearing on face recognition. *Development and Psychopathology, 17*, 621–639. http://dx.doi.org/10.1017/S0954579405050303

Parker, S. W., Nelson, C. A., & the Bucharest Early Intervention Project Core Group. (2005b). The impact of early institutional rearing on the ability to discriminate facial expressions of emotion: An event-related potential study. *Child Development, 76*, 54–72. http://dx.doi.org/10.1111/j.1467-8624.2005.00829.x

Patel, P. D., Katz, M., Karssen, A. M., & Lyons, D. M. (2008). Stress-induced changes in corticosteroid receptor expression in primate hippocampus and prefrontal cortex. *Psychoneuroendocrinology, 33,* 360–367. http://dx.doi.org/10.1016/j.psyneuen.2007.12.003

Paulus, M. P. (2016). Neural basis of mindfulness interventions that moderate the impact of stress on the brain. *Neuropsychopharmacology, 41,* 373. http://dx.doi.org/10.1038/npp.2015.239

Pechtel, P., & Pizzagalli, D. A. (2011). Effects of early life stress on cognitive and affective function: An integrated review of human literature. *Psychopharmacology, 214,* 55–70. http://dx.doi.org/10.1007/s00213-010-2009-2

Pecora, P., Whittaker, J., Barth, R., Maluccio, A. N., DePanfilis, D., & Plotnick, R. D. (2017). *The child welfare challenge: Policy, practice, and research.* New York, NY: Routledge. http://dx.doi.org/10.4324/9781315131238

Penedo, F. J., & Dahn, J. R. (2005). Exercise and well-being: A review of mental and physical health benefits associated with physical activity. *Current Opinion in Psychiatry, 18,* 189–193. http://dx.doi.org/10.1097/00001504-200503000-00013

Pennebaker, J. W. (1989). Confession, inhibition, and disease. *Advances in Experimental Social Psychology, 22,* 211–244. http://dx.doi.org/10.1016/S0065-2601(08)60309-3

Pennebaker, J. W. (1997). Writing about emotional experiences as a therapeutic process. *Psychological Science, 8,* 162–166. http://dx.doi.org/10.1111/j.1467-9280.1997.tb00403.x

Pennebaker, J. W. (2018). Expressive writing in psychological science. *Perspectives on Psychological Science, 13,* 226–229. http://dx.doi.org/10.1177/1745691617707315

Perez, N. M., Jennings, W. G., & Baglivio, M. T. (2018). A path to serious, violent, chronic delinquency: The harmful aftermath of adverse childhood experiences. *Crime & Delinquency, 64,* 3–25. http://dx.doi.org/10.1177/0011128716684806

Perou, R., Elliott, M. N., Visser, S. N., Claussen, A. H., Scott, K. G., Beckwith, L. H., . . . Smith, D. C. (2012). Legacy for Children™: A pair of randomized controlled trials of a public health model to improve developmental outcomes among children in poverty. *BMC Public Health, 12,* 691. http://dx.doi.org/10.1186/1471-2458-12-691

Perroud, N., Paoloni-Giacobino, A., Prada, P., Olié, E., Salzmann, A., Nicastro, R., . . . Malafosse, A. (2011). Increased methylation of glucocorticoid receptor gene (NR3C1) in adults with a history of childhood maltreatment: A link with the severity and type of trauma. *Translational Psychiatry, 1,* e59. http://dx.doi.org/10.1038/tp.2011.60

Perry, B. D. (2002). Childhood experience and the expression of genetic potential: What childhood neglect tells us about nature and nurture. *Brain & Mind, 1,* 79–100. http://dx.doi.org/10.1023/A:1016557824657

Perry, B. D. (2006). Applying principles of neurodevelopment to clinical work with maltreated and traumatized children: The neurosequential model of therapeutics. In N. B. Webb (Ed.), *Social work practice with children and families: Working with traumatized youth in child welfare* (pp. 27–52). New York, NY: Guilford Press.

Perry, B. D. (2009). Examining child maltreatment through a neurodevelopmental lens: Clinical applications of the neurosequential model of therapeutics. *Journal of Loss and Trauma, 14,* 240–255. http://dx.doi.org/10.1080/15325020903004350

Pettit, G. S., Laird, R. D., Dodge, K. A., Bates, J. E., & Criss, M. M. (2001). Antecedents and behavior-problem outcomes of parental monitoring and psychological control in early adolescence. *Child Development, 72,* 583–598. http://dx.doi.org/10.1111/1467-8624.00298

Phillips, D. A., & Shonkoff, J. P. (2000). *From neurons to neighborhoods: The science of early childhood development.* Washington, DC: National Academies Press.

Pohlack, S. T., Meyer, P., Cacciaglia, R., Liebscher, C., Ridder, S., & Flor, H. (2014). Bigger is better! Hippocampal volume and declarative memory performance in healthy young men. *Brain Structure & Function, 219,* 255–267. http://dx.doi.org/10.1007/s00429-012-0497-z

Pollak, S. D., Cicchetti, D., Klorman, R., & Brumaghim, J. T. (1997). Cognitive brain event-related potentials and emotion processing in maltreated children. *Child Development, 68,* 773–787. http://dx.doi.org/10.2307/1132032

Pollak, S. D., Messner, M., Kistler, D. J., & Cohn, J. F. (2009). Development of perceptual expertise in emotion recognition. *Cognition, 110,* 242–247. http://dx.doi.org/10.1016/j.cognition.2008.10.010

Pollak, S. D., & Tolley-Schell, S. A. (2003). Selective attention to facial emotion in physically abused children. *Journal of Abnormal Psychology, 112,* 323–338. http://dx.doi.org/10.1037/0021-843X.112.3.323

Poole, J. C., Dobson, K. S., & Pusch, D. (2018). Do adverse childhood experiences predict adult interpersonal difficulties? The role of emotion dysregulation. *Child Abuse & Neglect, 80,* 123–133. http://dx.doi.org/10.1016/j.chiabu.2018.03.006

Popkin, M. (2014). *Active parenting: A parent's guide to raising happy and successful children* (4th ed.). Atlanta, GA: Active Parenting.

Popkin, M. (2017). *Active parenting: First five years.* Marietta, GA: Active Parenting.

Porter, L., Martin, K., & Anda, R. (2017). Culture matters: Direct service programs cannot solve widespread, complex, intergenerational social problems. Culture change can. *Academic Pediatrics, 17*(Suppl. 7), S22–S23. http://dx.doi.org/10.1016/j.acap.2016.11.006

Powell, B., Cooper, G., Hoffman, K., & Marvin, B. (2013). *The circle of security intervention: Enhancing attachment in early parent-child relationships.* New York, NY: Guilford Press.

Prado, E. L., & Dewey, K. G. (2014). Nutrition and brain development in early life. *Nutrition Reviews, 72,* 267–284. http://dx.doi.org/10.1111/nure.12102

Prakash, R. S., Hussain, M. A., & Schirda, B. (2015). The role of emotion regulation and cognitive control in the association between mindfulness disposition and stress. *Psychology and Aging, 30,* 160–171. http://dx.doi.org/10.1037/a0038544

Price, M., Spinazzola, J., Musicaro, R., Turner, J., Suvak, M., Emerson, D., & van der Kolk, B. (2017). Effectiveness of an extended yoga treatment for women with chronic posttraumatic stress disorder [erratum: http://dx.doi.org/10.1007/s11121-014-0538-3]. *Journal of Alternative and Complementary Medicine, 23,* 300–309. http://dx.doi.org/10.1089/acm.2015.0266

Prinz, R. J., Sanders, M. R., Shapiro, C. J., Whitaker, D. J., & Lutzker, J. R. (2009). Population-based prevention of child maltreatment: The U.S. Triple P system population trial. *Prevention Science, 10,* 1–12. http://dx.doi.org/10.1007/s11121-009-0123-3

Pritzker, K. (Producer), & Redford, J. (Producer & Director). (2016). *Resilience: The biology of stress and the science of hope.* United States: KPJR Films.

Purtle, J., & Lewis, M. (2017). Mapping "trauma-informed" legislative proposals in U.S. Congress. *Administration and Policy in Mental Health and Mental Health Services Research, 44,* 867–876. http://dx.doi.org/10.1007/s10488-017-0799-9

Raby, K. L., Lawler, J. M., Shlafer, R. J., Hesemeyer, P. S., Collins, W. A., & Sroufe, L. A. (2015). The interpersonal antecedents of supportive parenting: A prospective, longitudinal study from infancy to adulthood. *Developmental Psychology, 51*, 115–123. http://dx.doi.org/10.1037/a0038336

Racine, N., Madigan, S., Plamondon, A., Hetherington, E., McDonald, S., & Tough, S. (2018). Maternal adverse childhood experiences and antepartum risks: The moderating role of social support. *Archives of Women's Mental Health, 21*, 663–670. http://dx.doi.org/10.1007/s00737-018-0826-1

Rai, A. A., Stanton, B., Wu, Y., Li, X., Galbraith, J., Cottrell, L., . . . Burns, J. (2003). Relative influences of perceived parental monitoring and perceived peer involvement on adolescent risk behaviors: An analysis of six cross-sectional data sets. *Journal of Adolescent Health, 33*, 108–118. http://dx.doi.org/10.1016/S1054-139X(03)00179-4

Raikes, H. H., Brooks-Gunn, J., & Love, J. M. (2013). I. Background literature review pertaining to the early head start study. *Monographs of the Society for Research in Child Development, 78*, 1–19. http://dx.doi.org/10.1111/j.1540-5834.2012.00700.x

Ramiro, L. S., Madrid, B. J., & Brown, D. W. (2010). Adverse childhood experiences (ACE) and health-risk behaviors among adults in a developing country setting. *Child Abuse & Neglect, 34*, 842–855. http://dx.doi.org/10.1016/j.chiabu.2010.02.012

Ratliff, E. L., Morris, A. S., Beasley, L. O., Hays-Grudo, J., Jespersen, J., Kerr, K., & Ciciolla, L. (2019, March). *Threat and deprivation: Investigating outcomes associated with two different dimensions of adverse childhood experiences.* Paper presented at the Society for Research in Child Development, Baltimore, MD.

Razza, R. A., Bergen-Cico, D., & Raymond, K. (2015). Enhancing preschoolers' self-regulation via mindful yoga. *Journal of Child and Family Studies, 24*, 372–385. http://dx.doi.org/10.1007/s10826-013-9847-6

Reck, C., Hunt, A., Fuchs, T., Weiss, R., Noon, A., Moehler, E., . . . Mundt, C. (2004). Interactive regulation of affect in postpartum depressed mothers and their infants: An overview. *Psychopathology, 37*, 272–280. http://dx.doi.org/10.1159/000081983

Reichman, N. E., Teitler, J. O., Garfinkel, I., & McLanahan, S. S. (2001). Fragile families: Sample and design. *Children and Youth Services Review, 23*, 303–326. http://dx.doi.org/10.1016/S0190-7409(01)00141-4

Reiter, K., Andersen, S. B., & Carlsson, J. (2016). Neurofeedback treatment and posttraumatic stress disorder: Effectiveness of neurofeedback on posttraumatic stress disorder and the optimal choice of protocol. *Journal of Nervous and Mental Disease, 204*, 69–77. http://dx.doi.org/10.1097/NMD.0000000000000418

Repetti, R. L., Taylor, S. E., & Seeman, T. E. (2002). Risky families: Family social environments and the mental and physical health of offspring. *Psychological Bulletin, 128*, 330–366. http://dx.doi.org/10.1037/0033-2909.128.2.330

Resnick, M. D., Harris, L. J., & Blum, R. W. (1993). The impact of caring and connectedness on adolescent health and well-being. *Journal of Paediatrics and Child Health, 29*(Suppl. 1), S3–S9. http://dx.doi.org/10.1111/j.1440-1754.1993.tb02257.x

Reynolds, A. J., Temple, J. A., Ou, S.-R., Arteaga, I. A., & White, B. A. B. (2011). School-based early childhood education and age-28 well-being: Effects by timing, dosage, and subgroups. *Science, 333*(6040), 360–364. http://dx.doi.org/10.1126/science.1203618

Reynolds, A. J., Temple, J. A., Ou, S.-R., Robertson, D. L., Mersky, J. P., Topitzes, J. W., & Niles, M. D. (2007). Effects of a school-based, early childhood intervention on adult health and well-being: A 19-year follow-up of low-income families. *Archives of Pediatrics & Adolescent Medicine, 161*, 730–739. http://dx.doi.org/10.1001/archpedi.161.8.730

Rilling, J. K., Glasser, M. F., Preuss, T. M., Ma, X., Zhao, T., Hu, X., & Behrens, T. E. (2008). The evolution of the arcuate fasciculus revealed with comparative DTI. *Nature Neuroscience, 11*, 426–428. http://dx.doi.org/10.1038/nn2072

Roberts, G. A., Daer, J. L., Espeleta, H. C., Ridings, L. E., Morris, A. S., & Beasley, L. O. (2015). *Childhood protective factors and adult optimism as a possible mediator in the relation between adverse childhood experiences and anxiety symptoms.* Paper presented at the Oklahoma State University Research Symposium, Stillwater, OK.

Robinson, L. R., Hartwig, S. A., Smith, C., Lee, A. H., Forbes, L. W., Perou, R., & Fitzmorris, D. (2018). Supporting early social and emotional relationships through a public health parenting program: The legacy for children intervention. In A. S. Morris & A. C. Williamson (Eds.), *Building early social and emotional relationships with infants and toddlers* (pp. 183–212). Cham, Switzerland: Springer. http://dx.doi.org/10.1007/978-3-030-03110-7_8

Romens, S. E., McDonald, J., Svaren, J., & Pollak, S. D. (2015). Associations between early life stress and gene methylation in children. *Child Development, 86*, 303–309. http://dx.doi.org/10.1111/cdev.12270

Rose-Jacobs, R., Black, M. M., Casey, P. H., Cook, J. T., Cutts, D. B., Chilton, M., . . . Frank, D. A. (2008). Household food insecurity: Associations with at-risk infant and toddler development. *Pediatrics, 121*, 65–72. http://dx.doi.org/10.1542/peds.2006-3717

Rosenkranz, M. A., Davidson, R. J., Maccoon, D. G., Sheridan, J. F., Kalin, N. H., & Lutz, A. (2013). A comparison of mindfulness-based stress reduction and an active control in modulation of neurogenic inflammation. *Brain, Behavior, and Immunity, 27*, 174–184. http://dx.doi.org/10.1016/j.bbi.2012.10.013

Rosenman, S., & Rodgers, B. (2004). Childhood adversity in an Australian population. *Social Psychiatry and Psychiatric Epidemiology, 39*, 695–702. http://dx.doi.org/10.1007/s00127-004-0802-0

Roth, T. L., Lubin, F. D., Funk, A. J., & Sweatt, J. D. (2009). Lasting epigenetic influence of early-life adversity on the BDNF gene. *Biological Psychiatry, 65*, 760–769. http://dx.doi.org/10.1016/j.biopsych.2008.11.028

Roth, T. L., & Sweatt, J. D. (2011). Epigenetic marking of the *BDNF* gene by early-life adverse experiences. *Hormones and Behavior, 59*, 315–320. http://dx.doi.org/10.1016/j.yhbeh.2010.05.005

Rutter, M. (1987). Psychosocial resilience and protective mechanisms. *American Journal of Orthopsychiatry, 57*, 316–331. http://dx.doi.org/10.1111/j.1939-0025.1987.tb03541.x

Sameroff, A. (1975). Transactional models in early social relations. *Human Development, 18*, 65–79.

Sameroff, A. J., & Fiese, B. H. (2000). Transactional regulation: The developmental ecology of early intervention. In J. P. Schonkoff & S. J. Meisels (Eds.), *Handbook of early childhood intervention* (Vol. 2, pp. 135–159). New York, NY: Cambridge University Press. http://dx.doi.org/10.1017/CBO9780511529320.009

Sanders, J., Munford, R., Thimasarn-Anwar, T., Liebenberg, L., & Ungar, M. (2015). The role of positive youth development practices in building resilience and enhancing wellbeing for at-risk youth. *Child Abuse & Neglect, 42*, 40–53. http://dx.doi.org/10.1016/j.chiabu.2015.02.006

Sanders, M. R. (2008). Triple P-Positive Parenting Program as a public health approach to strengthening parenting. *Journal of Family Psychology, 22*, 506–517. http://dx.doi.org/10.1037/0893-3200.22.3.506

Sanders, M. R., & Hall, S. L. (2018). Trauma-informed care in the newborn intensive care unit: Promoting safety, security and connectedness. *Journal of Perinatology, 38*, 3–10. http://dx.doi.org/10.1038/jp.2017.124

Sanders, M. R., Kirby, J. N., Tellegen, C. L., & Day, J. J. (2014). The Triple P-Positive Parenting Program: A systematic review and meta-analysis of a multi-level system of parenting support [erratum: http://dx.doi.org/10.1016/j.cpr.2014.09.001]. *Clinical Psychology Review, 34*, 337–357. http://dx.doi.org/10.1016/j.cpr.2014.04.003

Sapolsky, R. M. (1992). *Stress, the aging brain, and the mechanisms of neuron death.* Cambridge, MA: MIT Press.

Sapolsky, R. M. (1996). Why stress is bad for your brain. *Science, 273*, 749–750. http://dx.doi.org/10.1126/science.273.5276.749

Sapolsky, R. M. (2017). *Behave: The biology of humans at our best and at our worst.* New York, NY: Penguin.

Sapolsky, R. M., Krey, L. C., & McEwen, B. S. (1985). Prolonged glucocorticoid exposure reduces hippocampal neuron number: Implications for aging. *The Journal of Neuroscience, 5*, 1222–1227. http://dx.doi.org/10.1523/JNEUROSCI.05-05-01222.1985

Sapolsky, R. M., Krey, L. C., & McEwen, B. S. (1986). The neuroendocrinology of stress and aging: The glucocorticoid cascade hypothesis. *Endocrine Reviews, 7*, 284–301. http://dx.doi.org/10.1210/edrv-7-3-284

Sarrieau, A., Dussaillant, M., Agid, F., Philibert, D., Agid, Y., & Rostene, W. (1986). Autoradiographic localization of glucocorticosteroid and progesterone binding sites in the human post-mortem brain. *Journal of Steroid Biochemistry, 25*, 717–721. http://dx.doi.org/10.1016/0022-4731(86)90300-6

Saunders, B. E., & Adams, Z. W. (2014). Epidemiology of traumatic experiences in childhood. *Child and Adolescent Psychiatric Clinics of North America, 23*, 167–184, vii. http://dx.doi.org/10.1016/j.chc.2013.12.003

Sayer, N. A., Noorbaloochi, S., Frazier, P. A., Pennebaker, J. W., Orazem, R. J., Schnurr, P. P., . . . Litz, B. T. (2015). Randomized controlled trial of online expressive writing to address readjustment difficulties among U.S. Afghanistan and Iraq war veterans. *Journal of Traumatic Stress, 28*, 381–390. http://dx.doi.org/10.1002/jts.22047

Schwartz, D., Lansford, J. E., Dodge, K. A., Pettit, G. S., & Bates, J. E. (2013). The link between harsh home environments and negative academic trajectories is exacerbated by victimization in the elementary school peer group. *Developmental Psychology, 49*, 305–316. http://dx.doi.org/10.1037/a0028249

Sciaraffa, M. A., Zeanah, P. D., & Zeanah, C. H. (2018). Understanding and promoting resilience in the context of adverse childhood experiences. *Early Childhood Education Journal, 46*, 343–353. http://dx.doi.org/10.1007/s10643-017-0869-3

Sedlmeier, P., Eberth, J., Schwarz, M., Zimmermann, D., Haarig, F., Jaeger, S., & Kunze, S. (2012). The psychological effects of meditation: A meta-analysis. *Psychological Bulletin, 138*, 1139–1171. http://dx.doi.org/10.1037/a0028168

Segal, Z. V., Gemar, M., & Williams, S. (1999). Differential cognitive response to a mood challenge following successful cognitive therapy or pharmacotherapy for unipolar depression. *Journal of Abnormal Psychology, 108*, 3–10. http://dx.doi.org/10.1037/0021-843X.108.1.3

Seih, Y.-T., Chung, C. K., & Pennebaker, J. W. (2011). Experimental manipulations of perspective taking and perspective switching in expressive writing. *Cognition and Emotion, 25*, 926–938. http://dx.doi.org/10.1080/02699931.2010.512123

Selye, H. (1956). *The stress of life*. New York, NY: McGraw Hill.

Serpeloni, F., Radtke, K., de Assis, S. G., Henning, F., Nätt, D., & Elbert, T. (2017). Grandmaternal stress during pregnancy and DNA methylation of the third generation: An epigenome-wide association study. *Translational Psychiatry, 7*, e1202. http://dx.doi.org/10.1038/tp.2017.153

Sheridan, M. A., McLaughlin, K. A., Winter, W., Fox, N., Zeanah, C., & Nelson, C. A. (2018). Early deprivation disruption of associative learning is a developmental pathway to depression and social problems. *Nature Communications, 9*, 2216. http://dx.doi.org/10.1038/s41467-018-04381-8

Sherr, L., Skar, A.-M. S., Clucas, C., von Tetzchner, S., & Hundeide, K. (2014). Evaluation of the International Child Development Programme (ICDP) as a community-wide parenting programme. *European Journal of Developmental Psychology, 11*, 1–17.

Shochat, T., Cohen-Zion, M., & Tzischinsky, O. (2014). Functional consequences of inadequate sleep in adolescents: A systematic review. *Sleep Medicine Reviews, 18*, 75–87. http://dx.doi.org/10.1016/j.smrv.2013.03.005

Shonkoff, J. P. (2010). Building a new biodevelopmental framework to guide the future of early childhood policy. *Child Development, 81*, 357–367. http://dx.doi.org/10.1111/j.1467-8624.2009.01399.x

Shonkoff, J. P. (2012). Leveraging the biology of adversity to address the roots of disparities in health and development. *Proceedings of the National Academy of Sciences of the United States of America, 109*(Suppl. 2), 17302–17307. http://dx.doi.org/10.1073/pnas.1121259109

Shonkoff, J. P., Garner, A. S., Siegel, B. S., Dobbins, M. I., Earls, M. F., McGuinn, L., . . . Wegner, L. W. (2012). The lifelong effects of early childhood adversity and toxic stress. *Pediatrics, 129*, e232–e246. http://dx.doi.org/10.1542/peds.2011-2663

Short, M. M., Mazmanian, D., Oinonen, K., & Mushquash, C. J. (2016). Executive function and self-regulation mediate dispositional mindfulness and well-being. *Personality and Individual Differences, 93*, 97–103. http://dx.doi.org/10.1016/j.paid.2015.08.007

Silverman, W. K., Ortiz, C. D., Viswesvaran, C., Burns, B. J., Kolko, D. J., Putnam, F. W., & Amaya-Jackson, L. (2008). Evidence-based psychosocial treatments for children and adolescents exposed to traumatic events. *Journal of Clinical Child and Adolescent Psychology, 37*, 156–183. http://dx.doi.org/10.1080/15374410701818293

Simpkins, S. D., Eccles, J. S., & Becnel, J. N. (2008). The mediational role of adolescents' friends in relations between activity breadth and adjustment. *Developmental Psychology, 44*, 1081–1094. http://dx.doi.org/10.1037/0012-1649.44.4.1081

Sinclair, D., Webster, M. J., Wong, J., & Weickert, C. S. (2011). Dynamic molecular and anatomical changes in the glucocorticoid receptor in human cortical development. *Molecular Psychiatry, 16*, 504–515. http://dx.doi.org/10.1038/mp.2010.28

Singh, R., Zapata, M., & Morris, A. S. (2018, May). *Talk, read, sing campaign: Attitudes and behavior towards talking, reading, and signing to babies*. Paper presented at the World Congress of the World Association for Infant Mental Health, Rome, Italy.

Skodol, A. E., Bender, D. S., Pagano, M. E., Shea, M. T., Yen, S., Sanislow, C. A., . . . Gunderson, J. G. (2007). Positive childhood experiences: Resilience and recovery from personality disorder in early adulthood. *The Journal of Clinical Psychiatry*, *68*, 1102–1108. http://dx.doi.org/10.4088/JCP.v68n0719

Slocum, R., Hays-Grudo, J., Morris, A. S., & Bosler, C. (2016). *Super parents: A research-based parenting program targeting the parent–child relationship.* Paper presented at the World Congress of the World Association for Infant Mental Health, Prague, Czech Republic.

Slopen, N., Fitzmaurice, G., Williams, D. R., & Gilman, S. E. (2010). Poverty, food insecurity, and the behavior for childhood internalizing and externalizing disorders. *Journal of the American Academy of Child & Adolescent Psychiatry*, *49*, 444–452. http://dx.doi.org/10.1097/00004583-201005000-00005

Slopen, N., Kubzansky, L. D., McLaughlin, K. A., & Koenen, K. C. (2013). Childhood adversity and inflammatory processes in youth: A prospective study. *Psychoneuroendocrinology*, *38*, 188–200. http://dx.doi.org/10.1016/j.psyneuen.2012.05.013

Slopen, N., McLaughlin, K. A., Dunn, E. C., & Koenen, K. C. (2013). Childhood adversity and cell-mediated immunity in young adulthood: Does type and timing matter? *Brain, Behavior, and Immunity*, *28*, 63–71. http://dx.doi.org/10.1016/j.bbi.2012.10.018

Smaldone, A., Honig, J. C., & Byrne, M. W. (2007). Sleepless in America: Inadequate sleep and relationships to health and well-being of our nation's children. *Pediatrics*, *119*(Suppl. 1), S29–S37. http://dx.doi.org/10.1542/peds.2006-2089F

Smearman, E. L., Almli, L. M., Conneely, K. N., Brody, G. H., Sales, J. M., Bradley, B., . . . Smith, A. K. (2016). Oxytocin receptor genetic and epigenetic variations: Association with child abuse and adult psychiatric symptoms. *Child Development*, *87*, 122–134. http://dx.doi.org/10.1111/cdev.12493

Smith, P. K. (1989). The role of rough-and-tumble play in the development of social competence: Theoretical perspectives and empirical evidence. In B. Schneider, G. Attili, J. Nadel, & R. P. Weissberg (Eds.), *Social competence in developmental perspective* (pp. 239–255). New York, NY: Kluwer Academic/Plenum. http://dx.doi.org/10.1007/978-94-009-2442-0_15

Smyth, J., & Helm, R. (2003). Focused expressive writing as self-help for stress and trauma. *Journal of Clinical Psychology*, *59*, 227–235. http://dx.doi.org/10.1002/jclp.10144

Snyder, R., Shapiro, S., & Treleaven, D. (2012). Attachment theory and mindfulness. *Journal of Child and Family Studies*, *21*, 709–717. http://dx.doi.org/10.1007/s10826-011-9522-8

Sobal, J., & Stunkard, A. J. (1989). Socioeconomic status and obesity: A review of the literature. *Psychological Bulletin*, *105*, 260–275. http://dx.doi.org/10.1037/0033-2909.105.2.260

Solomon, J., & George, C. (2008). The measurement of attachment security and related constructs in infancy and early childhood. *Handbook of attachment: Theory, research, and clinical applications*, *2*, 383–416.

Somaini, L., Donnini, C., Manfredini, M., Raggi, M. A., Saracino, M. A., Gerra, M. L., . . . Gerra, G. (2011). Adverse childhood experiences (ACEs), genetic polymorphisms and neurochemical correlates in experimentation with psychotropic drugs among adolescents. *Neuroscience and Biobehavioral Reviews*, *35*, 1771–1778. http://dx.doi.org/10.1016/j.neubiorev.2010.11.008

Sowa, A., Tobiasz-Adamczyk, B., Topór-Madry, R., Poscia, A., & la Milia, D. I. (2016). Predictors of healthy ageing: Public health policy targets. *BMC Health Services Research*, *16*(Suppl. 5), 289. http://dx.doi.org/10.1186/s12913-016-1520-5

Spagnola, M., & Fiese, B. H. (2007). Family routines and rituals: A context for development in the lives of young children. *Infants & Young Children*, *20*, 284–299. http://dx.doi.org/10.1097/01.IYC.0000290352.32170.5a

Sprang, G. (2009). The efficacy of a relational treatment for maltreated children and their families. *Child and Adolescent Mental Health*, *14*, 81–88. http://dx.doi.org/10.1111/j.1475-3588.2008.00499.x

Sroufe, L. A. (2000). Early relationships and the development of children. *Infant Mental Health Journal*, *21*(1-2), 67–74. http://dx.doi.org/10.1002/(SICI)1097-0355(200001/04)21:1/2<67::AID-IMHJ8>3.0.CO;2-2

Sroufe, L. A. (2005). Attachment and development: A prospective, longitudinal study from birth to adulthood. *Attachment & Human Development*, *7*, 349–367. http://dx.doi.org/10.1080/14616730500365928

Sroufe, L. A., Carlson, E. A., Levy, A. K., & Egeland, B. (1999). Implications of attachment theory for developmental psychopathology. *Development and Psychopathology*, *11*, 1–13. http://dx.doi.org/10.1017/S0954579499001923

Steele, H., Bate, J., Steele, M., Dube, S. R., Danskin, K., Knafo, H., . . . Murphy, A. (2016). Adverse childhood experiences, poverty, and parenting stress. *Canadian Journal of Behavioural Science*, *48*, 32–38. http://dx.doi.org/10.1037/cbs0000034

Stein, M. B., Simmons, A. N., Feinstein, J. S., & Paulus, M. P. (2007). Increased amygdala and insula activation during emotion processing in anxiety-prone subjects. *The American Journal of Psychiatry*, *164*, 318–327. http://dx.doi.org/10.1176/ajp.2007.164.2.318

Steinberg, L. (1990). Autonomy, conflict, and harmony in the family relationship. In S. S. Feldman & G. R. Elliott (Eds.), *At the threshold: The developing adolescent* (pp. 255–276). Cambridge, MA: Harvard University Press.

Steinberg, L. (2001). We know some things: Parent–adolescent relationships in retrospect and prospect. *Journal of Research on Adolescence*, *11*, 1–19. http://dx.doi.org/10.1111/1532-7795.00001

Steinberg, L. (2014). *Age of opportunity: Lessons from the new science of adolescence*. New York, NY: Houghton Mifflin Harcourt.

Steinberg, L., Dornbusch, S. M., & Brown, B. B. (1992). Ethnic differences in adolescent achievement. An ecological perspective. *American Psychologist*, *47*, 723–729. http://dx.doi.org/10.1037/0003-066X.47.6.723

Steinberg, L., Lamborn, S. D., Darling, N., Mounts, N. S., & Dornbusch, S. M. (1994). Over-time changes in adjustment and competence among adolescents from authoritative, authoritarian, indulgent, and neglectful families. *Child Development*, *65*, 754–770. http://dx.doi.org/10.2307/1131416

Stevens, J. (2017). How social journalism accelerates the ACEs movement. *Academic Pediatrics*, *17*(Suppl. 7), S26–S27. http://dx.doi.org/10.1016/j.acap.2016.12.015

Stoppler, M. C. (2018). *Puberty*. Retrieved from https://www.medicinenet.com/puberty/article.htm#what_are_the_physical_stages_of_puberty_in_girls_and_boys

Stout, M. D. (2015). Using public sociology to increase citizen participation in a medium-sized midwestern city. In K. O. Korgen, J. M. White, & S. K. White

(Eds.), *Sociologists in action: Sociology, social change, and social justice* (2nd ed., pp. 156–160). Thousand Oaks, CA: Sage.

Stovall-McClough, K. C., & Dozier, M. (2004). Forming attachments in foster care: Infant attachment behaviors during the first 2 months of placement. *Development and Psychopathology*, *16*, 253–271. http://dx.doi.org/10.1017/S0954579404044505

Straus, M., & Gelles, R. J. (1990). *Physical violence in American families: Risk factors and adaptations to violence in 8,145 families*. New Brunswick, NJ: Transaction Press.

Substance Abuse and Mental Health Services Administration. (2014). *SAMHSA's concept of trauma and guidance for a trauma-informed approach* (HHA Publication No. [SMA] 14-4884). Rockville, MD: Author.

Swain, J. E., Kim, P., & Ho, S. S. (2011). Neuroendocrinology of parental response to baby-cry. *Journal of Neuroendocrinology*, *23*, 1036–1041. http://dx.doi.org/10.1111/j.1365-2826.2011.02212.x

Swain, J. E., Lorberbaum, J. P., Kose, S., & Strathearn, L. (2007). Brain basis of early parent–infant interactions: Psychology, physiology, and in vivo functional neuroimaging studies. *Journal of Child Psychology and Psychiatry*, *48*, 262–287. http://dx.doi.org/10.1111/j.1469-7610.2007.01731.x

Sweeney, A., Filson, B., Kennedy, A., Collinson, L., & Gillard, S. (2018). A paradigm shift: Relationships in trauma-informed mental health services. *BJPsych Advances*, *24*, 319–333. http://dx.doi.org/10.1192/bja.2018.29

Szilagyi, M., Kerker, B. D., Storfer-Isser, A., Stein, R. E., Garner, A., O'Connor, K. G., . . . McCue Horwitz, S. (2016). Factors associated with whether pediatricians inquire about parents' adverse childhood experiences. *Academic Pediatrics*, *16*, 668–675. http://dx.doi.org/10.1016/j.acap.2016.04.013

Szyf, M., McGowan, P., & Meaney, M. J. (2008). The social environment and the epigenome. *Environmental and Molecular Mutagenesis*, *49*, 46–60. http://dx.doi.org/10.1002/em.20357

Talmi, A., Muther, E. F., Margolis, K., Buchholz, M., Asherin, R., & Bunik, M. (2016). The scope of behavioral health integration in a pediatric primary care setting. *Journal of Pediatric Psychology*, *41*, 1120–1132. http://dx.doi.org/10.1093/jpepsy/jsw065

Tang, Y. Y., Hölzel, B. K., & Posner, M. I. (2015). The neuroscience of mindfulness meditation. *Nature Reviews Neuroscience*, *16*, 213–225. http://dx.doi.org/10.1038/nrn3916

Tardos, A. (2011). Being with babies. *Exchange*, *33*, 87–89.

Taylor, S. E., Lehman, B. J., Kiefe, C. I., & Seeman, T. E. (2006). Relationship of early life stress and psychological functioning to adult C-reactive protein in the coronary artery risk development in young adults study. *Biological Psychiatry*, *60*, 819–824. http://dx.doi.org/10.1016/j.biopsych.2006.03.016

Taylor, S. E., Repetti, R. L., & Seeman, T. (1997). Health psychology: What is an unhealthy environment and how does it get under the skin? *Annual Review of Psychology*, *48*, 411–447. http://dx.doi.org/10.1146/annurev.psych.48.1.411

Tedeschi, R. G., & Calhoun, L. G. (2004). Posttraumatic growth: Conceptual foundations and empirical evidence. *Psychological Inquiry*, *15*, 1–18. http://dx.doi.org/10.1207/s15327965pli1501_01

Teicher, M. H., Andersen, S. L., Polcari, A., Anderson, C. M., Navalta, C. P., & Kim, D. M. (2003). The neurobiological consequences of early stress and childhood maltreatment. *Neuroscience and Biobehavioral Reviews*, *27*(1–2), 33–44. http://dx.doi.org/10.1016/S0149-7634(03)00007-1

Teicher, M. H., & Parigger, A. (2015). The "Maltreatment and Abuse Chronology of Exposure" (MACE) scale for the retrospective assessment of abuse and neglect during development. *PLoS ONE*, *10*, e0117423. http://dx.doi.org/10.1371/journal.pone.0117423

Teicher, M. H., & Samson, J. A. (2016). Annual Research Review: Enduring neurobiological effects of childhood abuse and neglect. *Journal of Child Psychology and Psychiatry*, *57*, 241–266. http://dx.doi.org/10.1111/jcpp.12507

Thierry, K. L., Bryant, H. L., Nobles, S. S., & Norris, K. S. (2016). Two-year impact of a mindfulness-based program on preschoolers' self-regulation and academic performance. *Early Education and Development*, *27*, 805–821. http://dx.doi.org/10.1080/10409289.2016.1141616

Thurston, H., Bell, J. F., & Induni, M. (2018). Community-level adverse experiences and emotional regulation in children and adolescents. *Journal of Pediatric Nursing*, *42*, 25–33. http://dx.doi.org/10.1016/j.pedn.2018.06.008

Toda, H., Boku, S., Nakagawa, S., Inoue, T., Kato, A., Takamura, N., . . . Kusumi, I. (2014). Maternal separation enhances conditioned fear and decreases the mRNA levels of the neurotensin receptor 1 gene with hypermethylation of this gene in the rat amygdala. *PLoS ONE*, *9*, e97421. http://dx.doi.org/10.1371/journal.pone.0097421

Toepfer, P., Heim, C., Entringer, S., Binder, E., Wadhwa, P., & Buss, C. (2017). Oxytocin pathways in the intergenerational transmission of maternal early life stress. *Neuroscience and Biobehavioral Reviews*, *73*, 293–308. http://dx.doi.org/10.1016/j.neubiorev.2016.12.026

Tomoda, A., Sheu, Y.-S., Rabi, K., Suzuki, H., Navalta, C. P., Polcari, A., & Teicher, M. H. (2011). Exposure to parental verbal abuse is associated with increased gray matter volume in superior temporal gyrus. *NeuroImage*, *54*(Suppl. 1), S280–S286. http://dx.doi.org/10.1016/j.neuroimage.2010.05.027

Tomoda, A., Suzuki, H., Rabi, K., Sheu, Y.-S., Polcari, A., & Teicher, M. H. (2009). Reduced prefrontal cortical gray matter volume in young adults exposed to harsh corporal punishment. *NeuroImage*, *47*(Suppl. 2), T66–T71. http://dx.doi.org/10.1016/j.neuroimage.2009.03.005

Topham, G. L. (2018). The Circle of Security intervention: Building early attachment security. In A. S. Morris & A. C. Williamson (Eds.), *Building early social and emotional relationships in infants and toddlers: Integrating research and practice* (pp. 237–258). Cham, Switzerland: Springer. http://dx.doi.org/10.1007/978-3-030-03110-7_10

Tottenham, N., & Sheridan, M. A. (2010). A review of adversity, the amygdala and the hippocampus: A consideration of developmental timing. *Frontiers in Human Neuroscience*, *3*, 68.

Tronick, E., Brazelton, T., & Als, H. (1978). The structure of face-to-face interaction and its developmental functions. *Sign Language Studies*, *18*, 1–16. http://dx.doi.org/10.1353/sls.1978.0011

Tudge, J. (1992). Vygotsky, the zone of proximal development, and peer collaboration: Implications for classroom practice. In L. C. Moll (Ed.), *Vygotsky and education: Instructional implications and applications of sociohistorical psychology* (pp. 155–172). New York, NY: Cambridge University Press.

Turner, H. A., Shattuck, A., Finkelhor, D., & Hamby, S. (2016). Polyvictimization and youth violence exposure across contexts. *Journal of Adolescent Health*, *58*, 208–214. http://dx.doi.org/10.1016/j.jadohealth.2015.09.021

Tyrka, A. R., Parade, S. H., Eslinger, N. M., Marsit, C. J., Lesseur, C., Armstrong, D. A., . . . Seifer, R. (2015). Methylation of exons 1D, 1F, and 1H of the glucocorticoid receptor gene promoter and exposure to adversity in preschool-aged children. *Development and Psychopathology*, *27*, 577–585. http://dx.doi.org/10.1017/S0954579415000176

Ungar, M. (2004). *Nurturing hidden resilience in troubled youth*. Toronto, Ontario, Canada: University of Toronto Press. http://dx.doi.org/10.3138/9781442677975

Ungar, M. (2013). Resilience, trauma, context, and culture. *Trauma, Violence, & Abuse*, *14*, 255–266. http://dx.doi.org/10.1177/1524838013487805

Ungar, M. (2018). Systemic resilience: Principles and processes for a science of change in contexts of adversity. *Ecology and Society*, *23*(4). http://dx.doi.org/10.5751/ES-10385-230434

UNICEF. (2017). *A world free from child poverty: A guide to the tasks to achieve the vision*. Retrieved from https://www.unicef.org/reports/world-free-child-poverty

U.S. Department of Health and Human Services. (2019). *Physical activity guidelines for Americans*. Retrieved from https://www.hhs.gov/fitness/be-active/physical-activity-guidelines-for-americans/index.html

U.S. Health Resources and Services Administration. (2019). *Home visiting*. Retrieved from https://mchb.hrsa.gov/maternal-child-health-initiatives/home-visiting-overview

Valiente, C., Lemery-Chalfant, K., & Reiser, M. (2007). Pathways to problem behaviors: Chaotic homes, parent and child effortful control, and parenting. *Social Development*, *16*, 249–267. http://dx.doi.org/10.1111/j.1467-9507.2007.00383.x

van der Kolk, B. A. (2015). *The body keeps the score: Brain, mind, and body in the healing of trauma*. New York, NY: Penguin Books.

van der Kolk, B. (2016). Commentary: The devastating effects of ignoring child maltreatment in psychiatry—A commentary on Teicher and Samson 2016. *Journal of Child Psychology and Psychiatry*, *57*, 267–270. http://dx.doi.org/10.1111/jcpp.12540

van der Kolk, B. A., Pelcovitz, D., Roth, S., Mandel, F. S., McFarlane, A., & Herman, J. L. (1996). Dissociation, somatization, and affect dysregulation: The complexity of adaptation of trauma. *The American Journal of Psychiatry*, *153*(Suppl. 7), 83–93. http://dx.doi.org/10.1176/ajp.153.7.83

van der Kolk, B. A., Perry, J. C., & Herman, J. L. (1991). Childhood origins of self-destructive behavior. *The American Journal of Psychiatry*, *148*, 1665–1671. http://dx.doi.org/10.1176/ajp.148.12.1665

van der Kolk, B. A., Stone, L., West, J., Rhodes, A., Emerson, D., Suvak, M., & Spinazzola, J. (2014). Yoga as an adjunctive treatment for posttraumatic stress disorder: A randomized controlled trial. *The Journal of Clinical Psychiatry*, *75*, e559–e565. http://dx.doi.org/10.4088/JCP.13m08561

van IJzendoorn, M. H., & De Wolff, M. S. (1997). In search of the absent father—meta-analyses of infant-father attachment: A rejoinder to our discussants. *Child Development*, *68*, 604–609. http://dx.doi.org/10.1111/j.1467-8624.1997.tb04223.x

van IJzendoorn, M. H., Juffer, F., & Duyvesteyn, M. G. (1995). Breaking the intergenerational cycle of insecure attachment: A review of the effects of attachment-based interventions on maternal sensitivity and infant security. *Journal of Child Psychology and Psychiatry*, *36*, 225–248. http://dx.doi.org/10.1111/j.1469-7610.1995.tb01822.x

van IJzendoorn, M. H., Schuengel, C., & Bakermans-Kranenburg, M. J. (1999). Disorganized attachment in early childhood: Meta-analysis of precursors, concomitants, and sequelae. *Development and Psychopathology*, *11*, 225–249. http://dx.doi.org/10.1017/S0954579499002035

Vernon-Feagans, L., Willoughby, M., Garrett-Peters, P., & The Family Life Project Key Investigators. (2016). Predictors of behavioral regulation in kindergarten: Household chaos, parenting, and early executive functions. *Developmental Psychology*, *52*, 430–441. http://dx.doi.org/10.1037/dev0000087

Videon, T. M., & Manning, C. K. (2003). Influences on adolescent eating patterns: The importance of family meals. *Journal of Adolescent Health*, *32*, 365–373. http://dx.doi.org/10.1016/S1054-139X(02)00711-5

Vygotsky, L. S. (1967). Play and its role in the mental development of the child. *Soviet Psychology*, *5*, 6–18.

Vygotsky, L. S. (1978). *Mind in society*. Cambridge, MA: Harvard University Press.

Waddington, C. (1942). Canalization of development and the inheritance of acquired characters. *Nature*, *150*, 3.

Wade, R., Jr., Shea, J. A., Rubin, D., & Wood, J. (2014). Adverse childhood experiences of low-income urban youth. *Pediatrics*, *134*, e13–e20. http://dx.doi.org/10.1542/peds.2013-2475

Wadsworth, M. E., & Kuh, D. J. (1997). Childhood influences on adult health: A review of recent work from the British 1946 national birth cohort study, the MRC National Survey of Health and Development. *Paediatric and Perinatal Epidemiology*, *11*, 2–20. http://dx.doi.org/10.1046/j.1365-3016.1997.d01-7.x

Waechter, R. L., & Wekerle, C. (2015). Promoting resilience among maltreated youth using meditation, yoga, tai chi and qigong: A scoping review of the literature. *Child & Adolescent Social Work Journal*, *32*, 17–31. http://dx.doi.org/10.1007/s10560-014-0356-2

Walker, D., Greenwood, C., Hart, B., & Carta, J. (1994). Prediction of school outcomes based on early language production and socioeconomic factors. *Child Development*, *65*, 606–621. http://dx.doi.org/10.2307/1131404

Wang, L., Dai, Z., Peng, H., Tan, L., Ding, Y., He, Z., . . . Li, L. (2014). Overlapping and segregated resting-state functional connectivity in patients with major depressive disorder with and without childhood neglect. *Human Brain Mapping*, *35*, 1154–1166. http://dx.doi.org/10.1002/hbm.22241

Wang, M.-T., Brinkworth, M., & Eccles, J. (2013). Moderating effects of teacher–student relationship in adolescent trajectories of emotional and behavioral adjustment. *Developmental Psychology, 49*, 690–705. http://dx.doi.org/10.1037/a0027916

Weatherston, D. J. (2001). Infant mental health: A review of relevant literature. *Psychoanalytical Social Work, 8*, 43–71. http://dx.doi.org/10.1300/J032v08n01_04

Weaver, I. C., Cervoni, N., Champagne, F. A., D'Alessio, A. C., Sharma, S., Seckl, J. R., . . . Meaney, M. J. (2004). Epigenetic programming by maternal behavior. *Nature Neuroscience*, *7*, 847–854. http://dx.doi.org/10.1038/nn1276

Webster-Stratton, C., & Reid, M. (2010). Adapting the Incredible Years, an evidence-based parenting programme, for families involved in the child welfare system. *Journal of Children's Services*, *5*, 25–42. http://dx.doi.org/10.5042/jcs.2010.0115

Weiser, M., Kutz, I., Kutz, S. J., & Weiser, D. (1995). Psychotherapeutic aspects of the martial arts. *American Journal of Psychotherapy, 49*, 118–127. http://dx.doi.org/10.1176/appi.psychotherapy.1995.49.1.118

Wentzel, K. R., & Caldwell, K. (1997). Friendships, peer acceptance, and group membership: Relations to academic achievement in middle school. *Child Development, 68*, 1198–1209. http://dx.doi.org/10.2307/1132301

Werner, E. E. (1995). Resilience in development. *Current Directions in Psychological Science, 4*, 81–84.

Werner, E. E., & Smith, R. S. (1992). *Overcoming the odds: High risk children from birth to adulthood*. Ithaca, NY: Cornell University Press.

Whitaker, R. C., Dearth-Wesley, T., Gooze, R. A., Becker, B. D., Gallagher, K. C., & McEwen, B. S. (2014). Adverse childhood experiences, dispositional mindfulness, and adult health. *Preventive Medicine, 67*, 147–153. http://dx.doi.org/10.1016/j.ypmed.2014.07.029

Whitehurst, G. J., Arnold, D. S., Epstein, J. N., Angell, A. L., Smith, M., & Fischel, J. E. (1994). A picture book reading intervention in day care and home for children from low-income families. *Developmental Psychology, 30*, 679–689. http://dx.doi.org/10.1037/0012-1649.30.5.679

Whitfield, C. L., Anda, R. F., Dube, S. R., & Felitti, V. J. (2003). Violent childhood experiences and the risk of intimate partner violence in adults: Assessment in a large health maintenance organization. *Journal of Interpersonal Violence, 18*, 166–185. http://dx.doi.org/10.1177/0886260502238733

Wisconsin Department of Children and Families. (n.d.). *Wisconsin Trauma Project*. Retrieved from https://dcf.wisconsin.gov/cwportal/prevention/trauma

Woods, N. F., Rillamas-Sun, E., Cochrane, B. B., La Croix, A. Z., Seeman, T. E., Tindle, H. A., . . . Manson, J. E. (2016). Aging well: Observations from the women's health initiative study. *Journals of Gerontology: Series A. Biomedical Sciences and Medical Sciences, 71*(Suppl. 1), S3–S12.

Woods-Jaeger, B. A., Cho, B., Sexton, C. C., Slagel, L., & Goggin, K. (2018). Promoting resilience: Breaking the intergenerational cycle of adverse childhood experiences. *Health Education & Behavior, 45*, 772–780. http://dx.doi.org/10.1177/1090198117752785

Woolley, M. E., & Bowen, G. L. (2007). In the context of risk: Supportive adults and the school engagement of middle school students. *Family Relations, 56*, 92–104. http://dx.doi.org/10.1111/j.1741-3729.2007.00442.x

World Health Organization. (2012). *Adverse Childhood Experiences International Questionnaire (ACE–IQ)—Rationale for ACE–IQ*. Geneva, Switzerland: Author.

Wurster, H. E., Sarche, M., Trucksess, C., Morse, B., & Biringen, Z. (2019). Parents' adverse childhood experiences and parent–child emotional availability in an American Indian community: Relations with young children's social-emotional development. *Development and Psychopathology, 31*, 1–12. http://dx.doi.org/10.1017/S095457941900018X

Wyatt, G. E. (1985). The sexual abuse of Afro-American and White-American women in childhood. *Child Abuse & Neglect, 9*, 507–519. http://dx.doi.org/10.1016/0145-2134(85)90060-2

Yamaoka, Y., & Bard, D. E. (2019). Positive parenting matters in the face of early adversity. *American Journal of Preventive Medicine, 56*, 530–539. http://dx.doi.org/10.1016/j.amepre.2018.11.018

Yates, M., & Youniss, J. (1996). A developmental perspective on community service in adolescence. *Social Development*, 5, 85–111. http://dx.doi.org/10.1111/j.1467-9507.1996.tb00073.x

Yehuda, R., Daskalakis, N. P., Bierer, L. M., Bader, H. N., Klengel, T., Holsboer, F., & Binder, E. B. (2016). Holocaust exposure induced intergenerational effects on fkbp5 methylation. *Biological Psychiatry*, 80, 372–380. http://dx.doi.org/10.1016/j.biopsych.2015.08.005

Yehuda, R., & Lehrner, A. (2018). Intergenerational transmission of trauma effects: Putative role of epigenetic mechanisms. *World Psychiatry*, 17, 243–257. http://dx.doi.org/10.1002/wps.20568

Yoshikawa, H., Aber, J. L., & Beardslee, W. R. (2012). The effects of poverty on the mental, emotional, and behavioral health of children and youth: Implications for prevention. *American Psychologist*, 67, 272–284. http://dx.doi.org/10.1037/a0028015

Young, E. (2017, January 19). How Iceland got teens to say no to drugs. *The Atlantic*, pp. 1–15.

Young, J. C., & Widom, C. S. (2014). Long-term effects of child abuse and neglect on emotion processing in adulthood. *Child Abuse & Neglect*, 38, 1369–1381. http://dx.doi.org/10.1016/j.chiabu.2014.03.008

Young, K. D., Siegle, G. J., Zotev, V., Phillips, R., Misaki, M., Yuan, H., . . . Bodurka, J. (2017). Randomized clinical trial of real-time fMRI amygdala neurofeedback for major depressive disorder: Effects on symptoms and autobiographical memory recall. *The American Journal of Psychiatry*, 174, 748–755. http://dx.doi.org/10.1176/appi.ajp.2017.16060637

Zanetti, C. A., Powell, B., Cooper, G., & Hoffman, K. (2011). The Circle of Security intervention: Using the therapeutic relationship to ameliorate attachment security in disorganized dyads. In J. Solomon & C. George (Eds.), *Disorganized attachment and caregiving* (pp. 318–342). New York, NY: Guilford Press.

Zarobe, L., & Bungay, H. (2017). The role of arts activities in developing resilience and mental wellbeing in children and young people a rapid review of the literature. *Perspectives in Public Health*, 137, 337–347. http://dx.doi.org/10.1177/1757913917712283

Zaslavsky, O., Cochrane, B. B., Woods, N. F., LaCroix, A. Z., Liu, J., Herting, J. R., . . . Tinker, L. F. (2014). Trajectories of positive aging: Observations from the women's health initiative study. *International Psychogeriatrics*, 26, 1351–1362. http://dx.doi.org/10.1017/S1041610214000593

Zeanah, C. H. (2009). *Handbook of infant mental health*. New York, NY: Guilford Press.

Zeanah, C. H., Nelson, C. A., Fox, N. A., Smyke, A. T., Marshall, P., Parker, S. W., & Koga, S. (2003). Designing research to study the effects of institutionalization on brain and behavioral development: The Bucharest Early Intervention Project. *Development and Psychopathology*, 15, 885–907. http://dx.doi.org/10.1017/S0954579403000452

Zero to Three. (2019). *Safe Babies Court Team*™. Retrieved from https://www.zerotothree.org/our-work/safe-babies-court-team

Zotev, V., Phillips, R., Misaki, M., Wong, C. K., Wurfel, B. E., Krueger, F., . . . Bodurka, J. (2018). Real-time fMRI neurofeedback training of the amygdala activity with simultaneous EEG in veterans with combat-related PTSD. *NeuroImage Clinical*, 19, 106–121. http://dx.doi.org/10.1016/j.nicl.2018.04.010

INDEX

ABOUT THE AUTHORS

Jennifer Hays-Grudo, PhD, is a Regents Professor of Psychiatry and Behavioral Sciences at the Center for Health Sciences and the past department head of Human Development and Family Science at Oklahoma State University (OU). She is the director of the Center for Integrative Research on Childhood Adversity, an NIH-funded research program focused on understanding the effects of early life experience on health and development and is cochair of the Oklahoma Legislative Task Force on Trauma-Informed Practices. Previously, she was a George Kaiser Family Foundation Chair in Community Medicine at OU-Tulsa, where she led the Tulsa Children's Project, a highly integrated set of interventions to reduce the effects of intergenerational poverty and adversity. Prior to that, she was an associate professor and director of Health Promotion at Baylor College of Medicine in Houston, Texas, where she was principal investigator of the Baylor Clinical Center for the Women's Health Initiative. Dr. Hays-Grudo is a developmental psychologist who has published numerous scientific articles on the effects of adversity on children and families, on risk-taking in adolescents, and on the effects of nutrition and hormone therapy on women's health, quality of life, and cognition function. She is the founding editor-in-chief of *Adversity and Resilience Science: Journal of Research and Practice*.

Amanda Sheffield Morris, PhD, is a Regents Professor and the George Kaiser Family Foundation Chair in Child Development and an extension specialist at Oklahoma State University in the Department of Human Development and Family Science. She is also an adjunct professor at the Laureate Institute for Brain Research. Previously, Dr. Morris was on faculty at the University of New Orleans in the Applied Developmental Psychology Department.

235

She is an associate editor and incoming editor-in-chief of the *Journal of Research on Adolescence*. She is a co-investigator on the multi-site NIH-funded Adolescent Brain Cognitive Development study, and a principal investigator on a similar study of infant development, the Healthy Brain and Child Development study. Dr. Morris is a developmental scientist with research interests in parenting, socio-emotional development, and infant and early childhood mental health. She is endorsed as an infant mental health research mentor, Level IV, and is a certified trainer of Trainers for Active Parenting programs as well as a contributing author to the new edition of *Active Parenting: First Five Years*. Dr. Morris has authored numerous articles and chapters on child and adolescent development and the neuroscience of emotion regulation and parenting, and is co-editor of the book: *Authoritative Parenting: Synthesizing Nurturance and Discipline for Optimal Child Development*, published by the American Psychological Association.